Cambridge Studies in Ethnomusicology

General Editor: John Blacking

Music of Afghanistan

This is a unique study of musicians in the city of Herat, in western Afghanistan, a celebrated centre for Islamic culture. Drawing on fieldwork undertaken during the 1970s, the author focuses on male hereditary professional musicians, while making revealing comparisons with amateurs, women and rural performers. Various aspects of the professional musicians' world are examined in turn: their 'science of music', derived from Indian music theory; the genres of art and popular music they performed; the social organisation of the music profession; the contexts of musical performance, notably wedding parties; and ideas about the place of music within Islam.

The book opens with an outline of the history of urban Herati music from the illustrious fifteenth-century Timurid period, and concludes with a discussion of the process of Afghan musical change in relation to modernism and modernisation since the late nineteenth century. The musical discussion centres on original field recordings which are available on audio cassette.

Baily offers an invaluable and detailed portrait of Herati musical life before the Marxist *coup d'état*: soon after his research was completed Herat was devastated by warfare.

Cambridge Studies in Ethnomusicology

General Editor: John Blacking

Ethnomusicological research has shown that there are many different ingredients in musical systems. The core of this series will therefore be studies of the logics of different musics, analysed in the contexts of the societies in which they were composed and performed. The books will address specific problems related to potential musical ability and practice, such as how music is integrated with dance, theatre and the visual arts, how children develop musical perception and skills in different cultures and how musical activities affect the acquisition of other skills. Musical transcriptions will be included, sometimes introducing indigenous systems of notation. Cassettes will accompany most books.

Already published:
Bonnie C. Wade, *Khyāl: creativity within North India's classical music tradition*
Regula Burckhardt Qureshi, *Sufi Music of India and Pakistan: sound, context and meaning in Qawwali*
Peter Cooke, *The Fiddle Tradition of the Shetland Isles*
Anthony Seeger, *Why Suyá Sing: a musical anthropology of an Amazonian people*
James Kippen, *The Tabla of Lucknow: a cultural analysis of a musical tradition*

Music of Afghanistan

Professional musicians in the city of Herat

John Baily
University of Sussex

Cambridge University Press

Cambridge
New York   New Rochelle
Melbourne   Sydney

Published by the Press Syndicate of the University of Cambridge
The Pitt Building, Trumpington Street, Cambridge CB2 1RP
32 East 57th Street, New York, NY 10022, USA
10 Stamford Road, Oakleigh, Melbourne 3166, Australia

© Cambridge University Press 1988

First published 1988

Printed in Great Britain at the University Press, Cambridge

British Library cataloguing in publication data

Baily, John
Music of Afghanistan: professional musicians
in the city of Herat – (Cambridge Studies in Ethnomusicology).
1. Music – Afghanistan – Herat –
History
I. Title
780′.958′1   ML345.A3

Library of Congress cataloguing in publication data

Baily, John, 1943–
Music of Afghanistan.
(Cambridge studies in ethnomusicology)
Bibliography: p.
Includes index.
1. Music – Afghanistan – Herat – History and criticism.
2. Musicians – Afghanistan – Herat – Social life and
customs. 3. Herat (Afghanistan) – Social life and
customs. I. Title. II. Series.
ML3758.A3B3   1988   780′.958′1   87-35525

ISBN 0 521 25000 5

Contents

List of illustrations	page vii
Preface	ix
Acknowledgements	xii
Note on transliteration	xiv

	Prelude	1
1	Herat, city and province	3
	Herat in the 1970s	5
	Ethnic and religious affiliations	9
	The arts	10
2	A brief history of music in Herat	12
	The Timurid court	12
	After the Timurids	16
	Music in the nineteenth century	17
	The early twentieth century	19
3	Afghan urban music in the twentieth century	24
	Music in Kabul	24
	The Indian court musicians	25
	Kabuli art music is brought to Herat	28
	Radio broadcasting and the emergence of Afghan popular music	30
	Changes in the *dutār* of Herat	31
	Women musicians	33
	The diversity of musical phenomena in Herat	35
4	The science of music	37
	Sor (pitch)	37
	Lai (rhythm)	50
	The significance of the ʿilm-e musiqi	55
	Women's knowledge of the ʿilm-e musiqi	58
5	Kabuli art music	60
	Ghazal singing	60
	Naghmeh-ye kashāl	66

	Klāsik (khyāl)	74
	Naghmeh-ye klāsik	76
	The origins of the art music genres	78
6	Popular and Herati music	81
	The Pashtun basis of Afghan popular music	81
	Genres of popular music in Herat	83
	Herati music	94
7	The social organisation of musicians	101
	Sāzandeh and their associates in the city of Herat	103
	Musical ideology of the *sāzandeh*	110
	Musical training amongst the *sāzandeh*	113
	Social ranking amongst professional musicians	114
	Ranking behaviour	120
	The string tying ceremony	121
8	Social contexts of musical performance	124
	Wedding festivities	125
	Ramazān concerts	131
	The theatre	134
	Country fairs (*meleh*s)	136
	Private parties	140
9	Music in the Herati value system	146
	The condemnation of music	146
	The condemnation of musicians	149
	The positive values of music	152
	Music and Sufism	153
10	Interpreting musical change in Herat	156
	Modernism and modernisation	157
	Contrasts with Mashhad	160
	The high ranking hereditary musician	161
	Playing the *ustād*	163

Glossary 1: Musical instruments — 165
Glossary 2: Musical and other terms — 168
Items on the cassette — 173
Bibliography — 175
Index — 179

Illustrations

Plates

1	Ustad Amir Jan Khushnawaz of Herat, 1977	*page* xvi
2	Herat's Friday Mosque, 1974	8
3	Mohammad Karim Khan demonstrates the *chahārtār*, 1974	21
4	Amir Jan, Ghulam Nebi, and Naim playing '*Piram o ārezu* . . .', 1974	63
5	Amir Jan and Rahim playing *rubāb*, 1974	63
6	Karim Dutari and Karim Khushnawaz recording the *naghmeh-ye kashāl*, 1974	69
7	Ghulam Nebi Zendeh Del and Gada Mohammad recording '*Hai Rebābeh*', 1974	100
8	The author, Amir Jan, Rahim, his bride, and Mohammad Ali at Rahim's *shirinikhori*, 1974	126
9	Golpasand women musicians at a women's wedding party, 1977	130
10	Golpasand band at a *Ramazān* concert, 1974	133
11	Amir Mohammad and his band play at a *Ramazān* concert, 1973	133
12	Outdoor teahouse at a Takht-e Safar *meleh*, 1974	138
13	Bacheh Haji, Amin Bacheh Matari, Hakim Khushnawaz, and Gada Mohammad seated on a bandstand of wooden beds, 1974	139
14	Jalil Golpasand, Bismillah, Ghani Landai, Seid Gol, and Ghulam Haidar at a *meleh*, 1974	139
15	A dancing boy demonstrates a pose, 1974	143
16	Safar dances at a *meleh bāgh*, 1974	145

Photographs 1, 3, 10, 11, 13, and 14: the author; photographs 2, 4–9, 12, 15, and 16: Veronica Doubleday.

Maps

1	Relation of Khurasan to surrounding areas	2
2	The Herat valley	5
3	The city of Herat	7

Preface

Afghanistan is a country of considerable cultural diversity, including as it does a number of ethnic groups and distinct languages, and ranging from the urban culture of cities with long histories, to that of pastoral nomads. There are a number of distinct musics, varying with language, region, instruments, and the uses for which music is designed. In comparison to India and Iran the music of Afghanistan has attracted rather little ethnomusicological research, and this is no doubt connected to the fact that Afghanistan is not generally considered to have an 'indigenous' system of art music equivalent to the *dastgāh*s of Iran or the *rāg*s of North India. Part of the purpose of this study is to show that Afghanistan does have a distinct indigenous art music.

Two monographs on Afghan music stand out: Mark Slobin's *Music in the Culture of Northern Afghanistan* and Lorraine Sakata's *Music in the Mind*. Slobin worked mainly in the northern provinces; his work covers a large geographical area and includes discussion of a number of ethnic groups: Pashtuns, Kazakhs, Turkmens, Uzbeks, Tajiks, Pamir peoples and Mountain Tajiks. The price one pays for such a wide sweep is a certain lack of depth and detail. Nevertheless, Slobin has provided a wealth of invaluable information and many important insights into the role and status of music in Afghan society. Lorraine Sakata also worked across a wide area, in three separate Persian-speaking regions of the country: the central Hazarajat mountains, Badakhshan, and Herat. Her work is particularly orientated towards musical ethnosemantics. Both scholars have also published valuable collections of music recorded in Afghanistan.

The scope of the present work is quite different. I have provided a detailed study of music making in a single place, the city of Herat, and, within that environment, I concentrate on a distinct type of music maker, the urban male hereditary professional musician (*sāzandeh*). This social category constitutes the 'unit of analysis' of the present study. The *sāzandeh* and their originally amateur associates constituted a social group of musicians, organised around the performance of the art music of Kabul, the capital of Afghanistan. We shall consider their music theory, the genres of music in which they specialised, their social organisation, the social contexts for their performance, and their perception of the relationship between music and religion. I have also found it necessary to discuss the wider historical context in which these *sāzandeh* musicians were placed, which throws further light on the dynamics of the situation I observed.

Sakata's work also touched on this social category, but she was in contact with only some of the musicians discussed here, and did not have the opportunity to pursue them into their distinct social world. Her work is largely corroborated by my own research, and the data presented in her book have made it unnecessary for me to discuss matters such as the Herati definition of music and the distinction made between music (*musiqi*, *sāz*) and song (*āwāz*, *khāndan*). The reader will often find her or himself referred to Sakata's work, which is indispensable for a full understanding of the data that I present (Baily 1986).

Fieldwork in Herat

My fieldwork was carried out in Herat over a period of twenty-six months between 1973 and 1977, and fell into three periods: one year in 1973–4, a visit of six weeks in 1975, and another year in 1976–7. My first year's research in Herat was devoted principally to the Herati *dutār*, examining the process by which a small two stringed long-necked lute became transformed into a much larger instrument with fourteen strings, and how the changes in the design of the *dutār* were related to changes in its performance technique and repertory. This work included research with a sample of fifteen *dutār* players representing varying levels of proficiency. Ten of them were also filmed playing a standard repertory of five tunes. My focus in this first year was primarily on *traditional* Herati music as played on the *dutār*. Such a repertory certainly existed and was widely known but was not very commonly performed. *Dutār* players usually performed quite different repertories, such as popular music and, in some cases, instrumental art music. This showed there to be a considerable difference between 'Herati music' and 'the music played in Herat'. There was an emphasis on organising recording sessions in this first year, whereas later on I became more interested in recording music in its normal social context.

Besides the detailed work on the *dutār*, the first year's research served as a general introduction to the music played in Herat. A short follow-up visit allowed me to fill some of the gaps in the data, and it was during this visit that I started my study of the *rubāb* with Amir Jan, the source of much of the information given in this study. My wife and I returned again in 1976 for another year to undertake a much more ambitious and diffuse research project, 'the anthropology of music in Herat', intended to examine all varieties of music making and singing in both city and countryside. The work already carried out on the *dutār* had shown that a general study of music in Herat was bound to be in part a study of musical change, and I was interested in examining the wider social and cultural correlates of that change.

Areas of inquiry covered in this second year included, if only rather superficially: rural music, such as rural folk song and music for the *sornā* and *dohol* and the associated dances for men; Koranic recitation; Sufi ritual and *naʿt* singing; and Shiah ritual singing. But most of my attention was concentrated on male musicians in the city, both amateurs turned professional and hereditary professionals. There were at that time two rival families of hereditary male musicians (*sāzandeh*), the Khushnawazha, who were Shiah, and the Golpasandha, who were Sunni. They performed art and popular music, singing and playing the harmonium, *rubāb* and tabla, and since about 1965 had added the fourteen-stringed *dutār* to their bands, invariably played by an amateur turned professional musician. Their main source of income as musicians came from playing at wedding festivities. In particular I worked with Amir Jan, the senior member of the Khushnawazha. In my lessons with him I concentrated on collecting a repertory of instrumental compositions which constitute the Afghan instrumental art music repertory played on the *rubāb*. My work with Amir Jan gave me privileged access to the world of the urban male *sāzandeh*. At the same time, my wife Veronica was working on women's music, and with bands of hereditary women musicians, learning to sing and play the *dāireh* (frame drum). She attended many women's wedding parties as a member of one of these bands (Doubleday 1988), providing important information about music making in a social sphere that was inaccessible to me.

Preface

The aftermath

We left Herat in October 1977; Taraki's coup occurred in April 1978 and in March 1979 Herat was the scene of a large scale popular uprising against the new Marxist regime, and the city was bombed and strafed. The increasing unrest in Afghanistan led to the Soviet invasion of December 1979 and to the disastrous war which has devastated the country, killed one million of its inhabitants, and caused another four and a half million to become refugees, mainly in Pakistan and Iran. It seemed inadvisable to communicate further with our friends in Herat or Kabul for fear of arousing official interest in those who received letters from abroad. For a long time our only contact with Herat came in the form of letters from Abdul Wahed Saljuki, after he became a refugee in Iran. Other reports filtered through.

At the time of writing (1987) most of the old city of Herat has been razed: bombed, shelled and bulldozed by tanks driven through buildings mainly constructed of dried mud and timber. The ruins of the city serve as a regular battleground between government forces and the *mujāhedin* of the *Jamiat Islami* party. The villages of the Herat valley have been systematically levelled by artillery rockets fired from Mir Daud, once a favourite beauty spot with the Heratis, located in the foothills of the mountains to the south of the valley. Much of the population has sought refuge in neighbouring Iran. Historians have recorded previous times when the city of Herat was virtually destroyed – by Genghis Khan, by Tamerlane, and again in the wars with the Persians in the middle of the nineteenth century. The city will undoubtedly be rebuilt – the importance of the region as 'the granary and garden of Central Asia' guarantees that – but it remains to see when and how it will be reconstructed, and what sort of life will be lived in it.

In 1985 I visited Peshawar to make a film about Afghan musicians who were now refugees, expecting that some of the people I had known from Kabul might be there. The only musician I found from Herat was a peripheral member of the Golpasand family of hereditary musicians, Amir, and he became the subject of a portrait film. From Amir and other sources I discovered that some of the musicians I knew were dead, including Amir Jan, some were refugees, and others were still in Afghanistan. That the pattern of life and the way of music making described here have been so abruptly interrupted gives this study a special poignancy and immediate historical value. It is my earnest wish that the valuable cultural data I was able to collect in Herat in the 1970s will one day serve in the recovery of Afghanistan from the depredations of war, a process that will require a cultural reconstruction as much as a material one.

Acknowledgements

My thanks are due in the first instance to the Social Science Research Council for funding my field research, with a Post-Doctoral Fellowship 1973–5 and a Conversion Fellowship 1975–8. During this period I was a Research Fellow at The Queen's University of Belfast, where John Blacking, Professor of Social Anthropology, made possible my change of academic field from experimental psychology to ethnomusicology, and gave every encouragement to my research in Afghanistan. Lorraine Sakata and Mark Slobin, two American experts on the music of Afghanistan, gave me a lot of help in the early stages and generously shared their knowledge of Herat with me. I owe a great deal to them and to their work.

In carrying out the fieldwork I have been indebted to many people. First of all to the musicians, who took me into their lives and generously shared their music with me. In particular my thanks are due to Gada Mohammad, Karim Dutari, and Amir Jan, my three Herati music teachers for *dutār* and *rubāb*; to Ustad Mohammad Omar, of Kabul, who gave me an initial training in *rubāb* playing in 1973; and to Amir Mohammad, also of Kabul, who allowed me to record so many of his performances at wedding parties and concerts in Herat. I am deeply indebted to Safar Surmed and Abdul Wahed Saljuki, two highly educated Heratis who contributed enormously to the research, Safar in my first year, and Abdul Wahed in the second. Safar was a civil engineer who later emigrated to Australia, while Abdul Wahed taught English in one of Herat's theological colleges. His knowledge of the religious life of the city was invaluable for my research on religious singing and Sufi ritual. Ghani Niksear of the local Ministry for Information and Culture office, and editor of the Herat Literary Magazine, was a great support. My thanks also to Ustad Mohammad Ali, the calligrapher, and to Ustad Mashal, the miniature painter, for their friendship, and to Fata Baburi, my Persian teacher and transcriber/translator of many song texts and recorded interviews. I also gratefully acknowledge the help of The British Council, The British Institute for Afghan Studies, ERCON, and the Herat Livestock Development Corporation.

In the ten years since I left Herat many other people have helped me in various ways: in the analysis of the music, with transcribing and translating song texts and other documents written in Persian (and Arabic), with reading drafts of various chapters, and in a few cases with reading the whole work. I thank the following: Abbas and Fereshteh Amanat, Osman and Latifeh Lodin, Nabi and Arian Misdaq, Bahoudin Majrouh, Hormoz Farhat, Narendra Bataju, Iraj Vakili, Jean During, Hastings Donnan, Mark Slobin, Lorraine Sakata, Anthony Hyman, Bo Utas, Alan Williams, Richard and Nancy Tapper, Bruce Wannell, Keith MacLachlan, Gerd Baumann, Jim Kippen, Alastair Dick, Owen Wright, Karl Signell, Derek Hopwood, and Slavomira Kominek-Zeranska. In the final stages of preparing the manuscript I made contact with S.Q. Reshtia, a former Director of Radio Kabul and a leading Afghan historian. He provided much additional information about radio broadcasting and the recent history of music in Kabul, only some of which I have been able to incorporate at this late stage.

Acknowledgements

Without the knowledge and expertise of my wife Veronica Doubleday this book could not have been written. She has carried out much of the work on transcribing and translating song texts, and provided all the data concerning women's music making. She has criticised drafts, corrected and improved my English, and read proofs. She also took most of the photographs reproduced here.

And many, many thanks to John Blacking, who fuelled my enthusiasm, guided my fieldwork and, in the course of innumerable conversations, seminars and conferences, taught me most of what I know about 'humanly organised sound'.

Much of this book was written when I was a Visiting Research Fellow at the University of Sussex in 1983-4 and 1986-7. My thanks to the Laboratory of Experimental Psychology and the School of African and Asian Studies for the facilities provided.

And finally I must acknowledge the wonderful help and support of Rosemary Dooley and Penny Souster, past and present Music Editors of Cambridge University Press; and express my gratitude to Susan Whimster for carrying out the subediting.

Note on transliteration and pronunciation

A number of problems arise with the transcription of non-English words in this text. Firstly, Herati Persian differs in various respects from the written language. Secondly, some musical terms have been adopted by Heratis from the Hindi or Urdu of North India. I have attempted to reproduce the sounds of spoken Persian following the system adopted by Sakata (1983). For Indian musical terms I have followed the transliterations from Hindi used by Jairazbhoy (1971) but in a simplified form, using *ā* as the only diacritical, and *ch* instead of *c* to represent the ch sound in order to maintain consistency with the system used for Persian.

Pronunciation

a: Short, as in 'm*a*nner'.

ā: Long, as in 'f*a*ther'.

i: In a final syllable is long, e.g. in the names Rahim and Amir, it sounds as in 'est*ee*m' and 'adh*ere*'.

u: In a final syllable is long, e.g. in Pasht*u*n, it sounds as in 'typh*oon*'.

kh: A velar uvular with scrape as in 'Ba*ch*'.

gh and *q*: Sound similar and are uvular plosives, like a *k* produced far back in the throat.

ʿ (Arabic ʿ*Ain*): This is a glottal plosive, as a Cockney would pronounce 't' in 'What a lot of little bottles'.

Note: Herat has a long 'ā' as in 'p*a*rt'.

In Persian the possessive and descriptive may be connected to a noun with *ezāfeh*, *-e* or *-ye*, e.g. ʿ*ilm-e musiqi* ('the science of music') – but this may be omitted in many situations. In Persian the plural is *hā* and I have sometimes used this.

Plate 1 Ustad Amir Jan Khushnawaz of Herat, 1977

Prelude

We were sitting and playing really well, really good music and singing. At about two in the morning they started to get sleepy. The nights were short, two hours later it would be dawn, at about four o'clock. In springtime it gets light that early. I didn't feel sleepy. I quietly took my *rubāb* and went to sit by a big tub with flowers growing in it. I took a carpet with me and sat down quietly there. I was waiting for the first glow of dawn. Very gently I took up my *rubāb* and started to get it in tune. That gave me exquisite pleasure. I tuned it to *Āsā*, *Mānd Āsā*. I kept on tuning it until every string was completely to my satisfaction, and then I reached for my plectrum. I played the *shakl*. As I played the *shakl*, phrase by phrase, I saw the first rays of light. I saw the nightingales and other birds, singing from every direction. And from every direction the perfumes of morning came to me. It made me feel wonderfully refreshed to smell those flowers. But the others were all asleep, snoring. 'What's this! Get up!' I cried. 'That's not pleasure, this is pleasure!' They were sprawled all over the place. Some had eaten too much and their eyes were all puffed up. 'Get up!' Nothing, dead to the world. 'Get up!' One of them groaned. I took my *rubāb* again and played some more, and I saw them begin to awaken, and to listen from where they lay. 'God bless you,' one said, because when one is asleep and hears music it gives great pleasure. One by one they got up and came to sit with me. 'May God shame you, is this the time for sleep?' I said. 'Come, look: this is pleasure, this is enjoyment, taste this.' And they were saying, 'Yes, by God.' 'Observe,' I said, 'the breeze now it's light, the song-birds, the green, the scent of flowers. *Wha Wha*! And you want to sleep. What's going on?' 'Yes', they said, 'by God, you have transported us with delight.'

Amir Jan

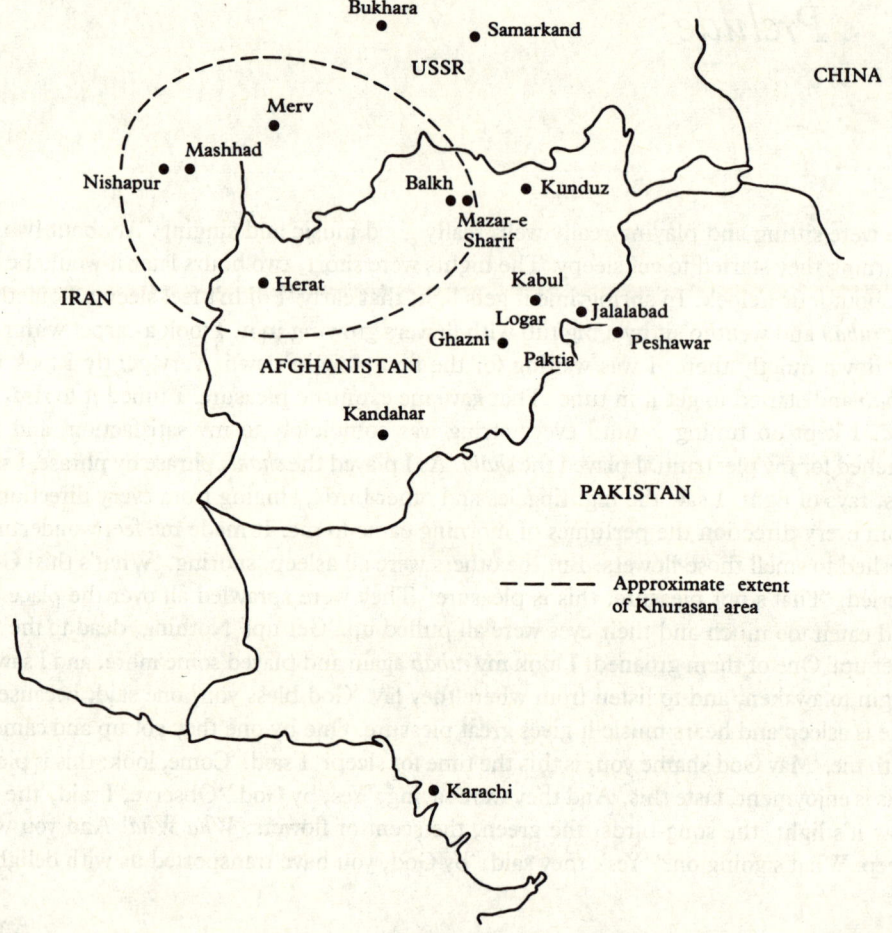

Map 1 Relation of Khurasan to surrounding areas

1 Herat, city and province

The Herat valley is a riverine oasis, some eighty-five miles long (from Ghurian to Marwa) and about fourteen miles across at its widest extent, situated in Khurasan, a region of Central Asia now divided politically between Afghanistan, Iran, and the Soviet Socialist Republic of Turkmenistan (see map 1).

Khurasan, with its four great cities of Herat, Balkh, Nishapur and Merv, was once an important centre of urban civilisation. It had many historical links with Iran and was part of the pre-Muslim Persian Empire of the Sassanians; the language of the people was Persian and the cities were like Iranian cities. Khurasan enjoyed its peak of urban civilisation in the period of the Abbasids, before the Mongol conquests of the thirteenth century, and was one of the most significant areas in the Arab–Persian world, a great centre of learning out of which came some of the most famous Islamic scholars writing in Arabic. It was also an important centre of Sufi thought, and many eminent Sufi writers lived there.

As one of the principal trading cities on the Silk Route connecting China and the Middle East, Herat has been a local centre of political power, commerce, religion, and the arts for centuries. It has shared in the rise and fall of many dynasties in the regions of the Middle East, Central Asia and the Indian Subcontinent, and was part of the Ghaznavid and Ghorid empires, which extended from Khurasan to Delhi. The city attained its peak of fame and splendour in the fifteenth century under the patronage of the Timurid rulers Shah Rukh (1405–1447) and Sultan Husein Baiqara (1468–1506), when, for the first time in its history, Herat became the capital of a large empire. During the 'Timurid Renaissance' Herat was the cultural centre of the Persian world: amongst the achievements of Timurid patronage were the arts of the book, the building of sumptuously decorated religious buildings, and the development of Turki as a literary language. Music under the patronage of the Timurid court was also a highly cultivated art. (See Wolfe 1966 and Byron 1937 for an account of these monuments.)

The Timurid era in Herat came to an end in 1507, although the dynasty continued with fresh vigour in Moghul India under Babur and his descendants. From the early sixteenth to the mid-eighteenth century, much of the territory that today constitutes Afghanistan was divided between the Safavid Empire to the west and the Moghul Empire to the east. The Safavids held Herat, the Moghuls Kabul and Ghazni, while the ancient city of Kandahar, being on the border between the two empires, changed hands a number of times (see map in L. Dupree 1973:320). Herat declined under Safavid rule. This was partly the result of Shah Abbas's decision to patronise the city of Mashhad, 225 miles north-west of Herat, as a religious centre, to be beautified like his capital Isfahan, and developed as a centre of trade and commerce at the expense of Herat.

The Pashtun tribes, the 'true Afghans', who were to establish Afghanistan as their own state, were at this time divided between the Safavid and Moghul empires, and represented a problem for both. The Pashtuns were beginning to acquire a sense of their own nationhood. The first expressions of the concept of Pashtun nationality occurred with the *Roshania* movements of the sixteenth and seventeenth centuries (Gregorian 1969:43). The Pashtun poet and tribal chieftain Kushal Khan Khattak (1613–1689) was an important figure in encouraging the emergence of a sense of national identity and advocating the need for Pashtun political unity. After several attempts to establish an autonomous Pashtun state in the eighteenth century, success was finally achieved in 1747 after the assassination of the Iranian ruler Nadir Shah Afshar. A group of Pashtun Durrani chiefs, who formed the *corps d'élite* of the Persian army, under the leadership of Ahmad Khan Abdali, seized some of the assassinated monarch's treasure and returned to Kandahar with about thirty thousand men, where Ahmad, at the age of twenty-five, was elected paramount chief of a confederacy of Pashtun tribes (L. Dupree 1973:322). This is regarded as the date of the founding of Afghanistan. In 1747 Ahmad Khan Abdali assumed the title of *Durr-e Durrān*, 'Pearl of Pearls', and was known afterwards as Ahmad Shah Durrani, and his tribe as the Durranis. His empire endured for over fifty years; the Pashtuns lost most of the Punjab in 1801, Kashmir in 1819, and Peshawar in 1832, all to the Sikh ruler Ranjit Singh.

Herat was captured by Ahmad Shah Durrani from the Persians in 1749 and united with Kandahar and Kabul in the new Afghanistan, 'the land of the Afghans'. In 1800 a long feud started between the two ruling clans of the Durranis, and in 1819 Herat became a virtually autonomous amirate under one of these factions, and remained so, with brief interruptions, for the next sixty years. The nineteenth century represents a particularly bleak period in the history of Herat, which was the subject of territorial claims by the Persians. In 1833 a Persian army invested Herat and in 1837–8 besieged it for ten months; though unsuccessful in these attempts the Persians were able to take and occupy the city in 1852 and again in 1856. The wars with the Persians led, amongst other things, to the destruction of large parts of the city, and to the depletion of its population, estimated at 45,000 in 1833 (Conolly 1838:1) and reduced to half that number in Ferrier's estimate of 1845 (Ferrier 1857:172). The economic and social condition of Herat at this time was described by a succession of European visitors (Conolly 1838; Ferrier 1857; Vámbéry 1864). Their fascinating reports are well known (see, for example, Kaye 1874; Malleson 1880; Byron 1937). They reveal the plight of the Herati people under Pashtun domination. The impression gained, even allowing for the prejudices and preconceptions of European observers, is certainly of 'a reign of terror' (Kaye 1874:214) when the predominantly Persianised population of the city, with its large number of merchants and shopkeepers, was severely oppressed by the ruling Pashtun minority. Many were sold to Turkmen as slaves. Cultural and linguistic differences between the two groups were compounded by the fact that while the merchants of the city were mostly Shiah, the rulers and their soldiery were Sunni, and there was much scope for sectarian conflict.

The dilapidated condition of Herat in this period was by no means unique: there was a decline in urban life all over Afghanistan in the first half of the nineteenth century. Herat's was just an extreme form of a common experience, exacerbated by the city's isolation and the long struggle with the Persians. Many factors were involved in this decline: one of its principal causes was the collapse of effective control from Kabul, and a resultant political fragmentation, bringing about a sharp decline in overland trade, especially on the Indo-Persian route that passed through Kabul, Kandahar, and Herat. Kandahar, which had a population of 100,000 in 1809, was reduced to between 25,000 and 30,000 in the decade between 1826 and 1836 (Gregorian 1969:60). Ghazni and Jalalabad were also much reduced in size. Only the city of Kabul remained in a healthy economic state: the population was 10,000 when Timur Shah made it the capital of Afghanistan in 1776; by the early nineteenth century the population was in the region of 60,000 (*ibid.*).

This troubled period came to an end in the reign of Abdur Rahman (1880-1901), the 'Iron Amir', who succeeded in reunifying his country in a process that Louis Dupree (1973:417) has called 'internal imperialism'. With Abdur Rahman began a new era in Afghan history and a period of relative political stability and freedom from armed conflict that lasted for almost one hundred years and was only seriously disturbed by the Bacheh Saqao insurrection of 1929.

Herat in the 1970s

The population of Herat Province in the 1970s was estimated at around 1,000,000, distributed over a large number of villages, a few small towns, which were local centres of government administration, and a single large city, with a population estimated at about 100,000 (see map 2).

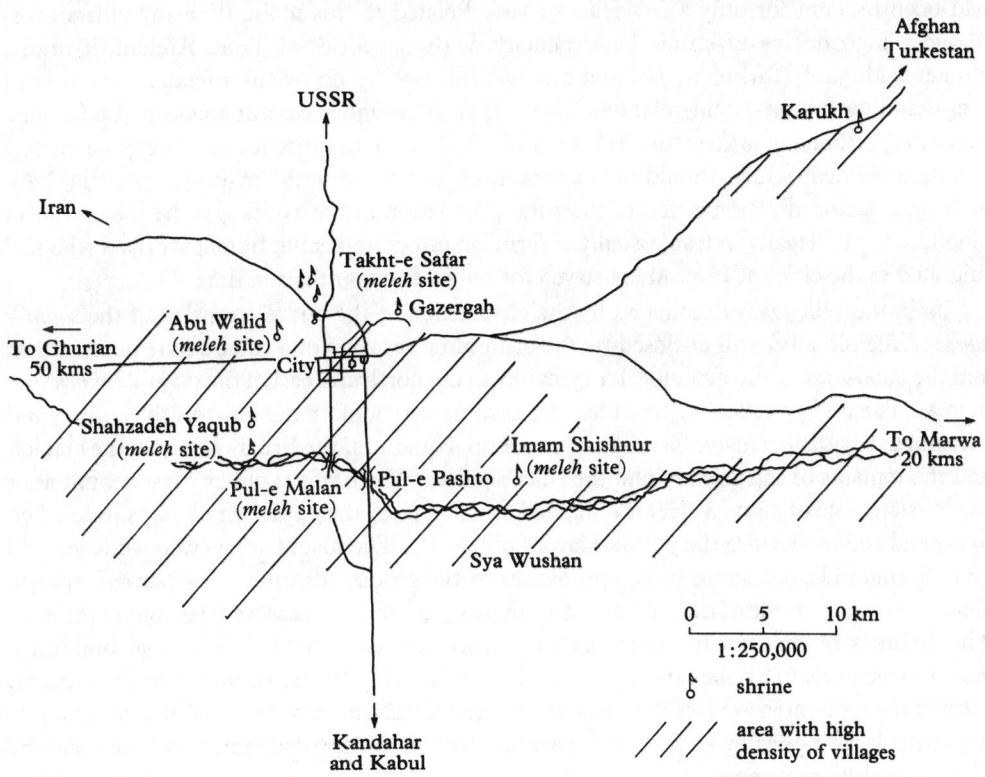

Map 2 The Herat valley

The valley was irrigated by a network of canals; the availability of water was the primary factor limiting agricultural development. The main crops were wheat, rice, cotton, cucurbits, fruit, and fodder for the estimated 5,000,000 sheep in the valley. There was very little use of artificial fertiliser, agricultural machinery or of modern farming methods. There was a complicated pattern of land ownership, with fragmented holdings, two thirds of them less than 0.5 hectare in size (two and a half *jerib*s). A hydrological survey of 1973 showed, 'Of a total area of 66,856 hectares under consideration at the Land Registration office in Herat, 64 per cent of it is in dispute.' Much of the land was owned by absentee landlords (living in the city of Herat, or even in Kabul) and farmed by tenants on a share-cropping basis. Land was a commodity in which wealthier city dwellers invested, and since urban society was relatively mobile in terms of wealth, land frequently changed hands between absentee landlords. Agreements with tenants were renewed annually.

The anthropologist Reider Grönhaug worked in a group of villages near the city in 1971–2, a period of severe drought, when the condition of the people was certainly worse than usual. He paints a bleak picture of the hardships of peasant life, the 'brutal effects' of landowner-sharecropper relations, the rural poor 'many of whom display a terrible syndrome of debt, hunger and tuberculosis' (Grönhaug 1978:83). Above all, the peasants were mobile, especially the poor. In the villages studied by Grönhaug, only a third of residents had lived there for two generations or more, a third had resided there for a decade or two, while a third had been resident for only a few years or less. Related to this mobility, many villages displayed a high degree of ethnic heterogeneity, with categories of Tajik, Afghan, Taimuri, Taimeni, Moghol, Turkmen, Jat, and others. This was by no means a feudal society, with long-standing patron–client relations (*ibid.*: 117). Through a careful analysis of economic processes, Grönhaug argues that 'relations of production and distribution contain a critical capitalist element which should not, however, be associated with "mature capitalism"'. An additional factor affecting much of the rural population in the 1970s was the movement of labour to work illegally in Iran, usually as farm labourers, replacing Iranian workers who had migrated to the cities of Iran. Many stayed for only a few months at a time.

Life in the valley was dominated by the city, which in the 1970s consisted of the *shahr-e kohneh*, 'the old city', still enclosed by the crumbling remains of a square mile of ramparts, and the *shahr-e now*, 'the new city', lying mainly to the north and east of the *shahr-e kohneh* (see map 3). The *shahr-e kohneh* represented the form the city took in the nineteenth century, and contained, besides extensive bazaars and residential quarters, the Friday Mosque, the citadel, and the remains of the granary and the ruler's palace. Much of the old city was rebuilt after the Persian siege of 1837–8. Herat remained fortified until the 1930s, when steps were taken to expand and modernise the physical layout of the city. The main bazaars were widened and great avenues cleared along three approaches to the Friday Mosque. New bazaars opened along the northern side of the old city, and extensive residential areas were laid out to the east. The facilities of modern life were placed in this new area: banks, municipal buildings, government bureaux, police headquarters, hospitals, schools, the theatre, and the cinema. Most of the residential areas of the new city were modelled on a novel pattern of modern housing, with large bungalows set in extensive gardens and inhabited, reluctantly at first, by Herat's wealthier citizens.

English (1973) gives an account of Herat in terms of the social organisation of urban space. He strongly emphasises the city's 'traditional' aspect, concluding:

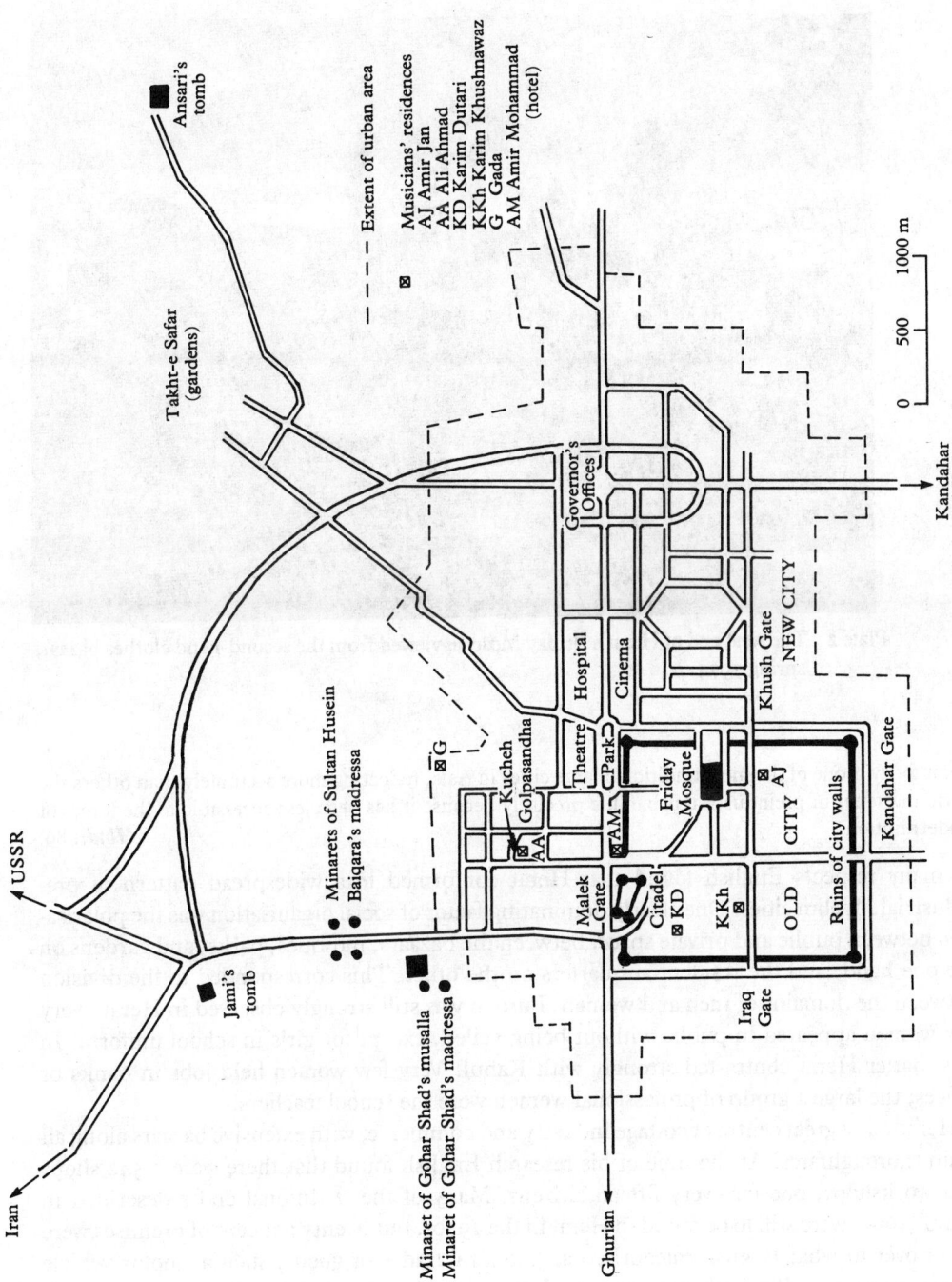

Map 3 The city of Herat c. 1977

Plate 2 The west end of Herat's Friday Mosque viewed from the second-hand clothes bazaar, spring 1974

> Herat today is one of the most traditional large cities in Asia, reflecting more accurately than others the spirit and tenor of preindustrial urban life precisely because it has been less accessible to the forces of modernisation.
>
> (*Ibid.*: 89)

In many respects English found that Herat conformed to a widespread pattern of pre-industrial Muslim cities. One clearly dominating factor of social organisation was the polarisation between public and private space, between the bazaars, mosques, parks, and gardens on the one hand, and the residential quarters on the other. This corresponded to the division between the domains of men and women. Purdah was still strongly observed in Herat. Very few women appeared in public without being veiled, except for girls in school uniform. In this matter Herat contrasted strongly with Kabul. Very few women held jobs in banks or offices; the largest group of professional women were the school teachers.

Herat was a great centre of cottage industry and commerce, with extensive bazaars along all main thoroughfares. At the time of his research English found that there were 5,542 shops and workshops, one for every fifteen citizens. Many of the traditional crafts described in Wulff (1966) were still to be found in Herat in the 1970s, but twenty per cent of premises were given over to what English categorised as 'modern' trades or goods, such as motor vehicle repair, kerosene selling, photography, or denture making. English lists twenty-seven traditional shops and crafts and fourteen modern ones.

The premises of many trades were concentrated in specific areas of the bazaar; others, such as bakers, were more evenly distributed. In the old city, central location was the most highly valued, but this pattern had been disrupted by the construction of bazaars in the new city, where modern goods and trades were concentrated. English notes the mobility of the business community, with premises undergoing frequent changes of proprietorship. Shopkeepers and artisans moved the locations of their premises according to fluctuations in their fortunes. This is reminiscent of Grönhaug's (1978) findings in the villages.

The people of the city of Herat constituted a highly differentiated and stratified society, with a considerable degree of social mobility. The members of the various occupational groups belonged to guilds (*senf*), each with its own leader (*wakil*), who acted as the channel of communication between the authorities and members of the guild. English (1973:86) stresses the weakness of guild structure and points out that the *wakil* had very little power to regulate the affairs of the guild. Most crafts were still hereditary. English cites the case of the jewellers (with 88 out of the total of 5,542 shops). Seventy per cent had followed their fathers, working in their shops since childhood. The remaining thirty per cent were apprenticed to an uncle, cousin, or other relative. Jewellers were perhaps a special case, being one of the wealthiest occupational groups (and almost exclusively Shiah). My overall impression was that the inheritance of the paternal profession was becoming less important, especially in view of the many new professions that had become available in Herat in the twentieth century.

Although English emphasises the role of Herat as a traditional city, his own findings challenge this categorisation. Herat in the 1970s had many of the facilities of a modern city: a rudimentary electrical system; a new system of standpipes in the bazaars and residential areas (but no sewerage system); municipal administration; a postal and telephone system; a newspaper and literary magazine; an airport, and a traffic problem in the old city. Although Herat gave the *appearance* of being very traditional, what was on view was a surface of poverty. Beneath it there were clearcut cultural changes, in that the Heratis saw themselves as living in a quite different world to that inhabited by their forefathers. They had become part of the modern world, however limited its impact might be in material terms.

Ethnic and religious affiliations

The population of Herat included peoples who variously identified themselves as Afghan, Pashtun, Tajik, Taimuri, Taimeni, Turkmen, Baluch, Gharibzadeh, and by the names of other very small groups. In the city the main division was between the old population of townspeople, and the Pashtuns, who had dominated them since the eighteenth century. The latter described themselves as 'Afghan', but this term must be used with some care. It refers specifically to members of those tribes called Pashtun or Pakhtun, particularly to those who adopted sedentary rural or urban life, in contrast to nomadism. The Pashtuns in Herat called themselves Afghan, or Aughan, to contrast themselves to the Tajik population, which they termed Parsi, 'Persian'. Pashtuns made up about ten per cent of the population of the valley, living in the city, in certain villages, and constituting part of the pastoral nomad population. Urban Pashtuns had become largely Persianised, and spoke Dari (Afghan Persian) rather than Pashto. But the term Afghan also refers to any citizen of Afghanistan regardless of ethnic affiliation, as stated in the Constitution. The term 'Afghan' is used in the present study in this second sense. I shall use the term 'Herati' for any native of Herat. Another term that requires clarification in this context is *qaum*, employed to indicate consanguineal social groups of varying size. *Qaum-e Afghān* referred to the people of Afghanistan, and was almost a slogan of government propaganda. *Qaum* could refer to an ethnic group, such as Pashtuns, Tajiks or

Hazaras, or it could refer to a tribe, lineage, or clan. It also referred to families with whom inter-marriage could reasonably be contemplated.

One of the major cleavages in Herati society was affiliation to Sunni and Shiah persuasions within Islam. The official form of Islam was Sunnism according to the *Hanifi* legal school and the official, government supported, theological colleges taught this system. The Friday Mosque of Herat was a Sunni institution. Shiahs accounted for perhaps ten per cent of the population of the valley as a whole, but in the city the proportion of Shiahs was much higher, perhaps forty per cent (according to an official in the Herat office of the Ministry of Information and Culture, himself a Shiah). Since the time of the Safavids, Shiism has been the form of Islam most closely associated with Iran, where it has been the state religion. The 'Afghan-Parsi' divide was couched partly in religious terms – thus non-Pashtun Sunnis might call themselves Afghan to distinguish themselves from the Parsis, whom they identified as Shiah. It seems that in other Afghan cities, particularly Kabul, there was considerable prejudice against Heratis, who were believed to be mainly Shiahs and suspected of greater allegiance to Iran than to Afghanistan.

After the incorporation of Herat into Afghanistan in 1749 there was much conflict between Sunnis and Shiahs, the latter at that time representing the majority of the urban population. The oppression of Herati merchants by their Pashtun rulers in the nineteenth century was construed as justifiable action against heretics. Up till the 1950s the Shiahs kept many of their religious activities discreetly away from public gaze. The ceremonies held during the months of mourning (*Muharram* and *Safar*) took place in secret *tekieh*s. In the 1970s there was much greater freedom of religious expression. Although there had been little open sectarian strife for many years, it was clear that religious affiliation remained important and a basis on which many social transactions were conducted. The relatively wealthy merchant and shopkeeper class were mainly Shiah.

Another important strand in the religious life of Herat was Sufism, the form of mystical Islam once so strong in Khurasan. The Herat valley is famous within Afghanistan for its many tombs of saints, some of them important places of pilgrimage. It was for this reason that Heratis sometimes spoke of Herat as *khāk-e auliyā*, 'dust of the saints'. A number of Sufi *pir*s were active in the valley in the 1970s (see Utas 1980), representing *Qādiri* and *Naqshbandi* Orders. *Zikr* was commonly practised in their *khānaqāh*s, and the measure of the acceptance of Sufism by orthodox Islam in Herat was shown by the fact that the local *Qādiriya* held a *zikr* in the Friday Mosque immediately after Friday midday prayers every week. Sufism also merged into the widely diffused folk religion of the Heratis that placed great stress on the role of holy men and on the power of their shrines.

The arts

As well as being an important centre of manufacture and commerce, Herat was a centre for the arts, not only for this region but for the whole of Afghanistan. Heratis were aware of the former greatness of their city, to which the many crumbling monuments testified. Herat enjoyed a reputation for Persian literature and claimed two great writers amongst its illustrious sons, Khwaja Abdullah Ansari (twelfth century) and Abdur Rahman Jami (fifteenth century). The Timurid miniaturist Behzad was also remembered. Herat maintained a reputation

The arts

for excellence in literature, both for literary scholarship, and as a place where poets were still active. The city had published its own literary magazine for the last forty years. The people of Herat were regarded as well educated by Afghan standards and in the city there were a number of high schools, an agricultural college, and a teacher training college, to which was attached a school for gifted children. Herat had its own antiquarians, such as Ustad Fekri Saljuki, and had revived the art of mosaic tile-making to redecorate the Friday Mosque in the 1940s, with many designs executed by Ustad Mashal Ghori, the miniaturist, and Ustad Mohammad Ali, the calligrapher. The music culture of Herat conformed to this general pattern of sophistication. It is to the history of music in Herat that we now turn.

2 A brief history of music in Herat

A rather detailed account of music at the Timurid court of Herat in the fifteenth century is available, but the preceding epochs are very unclear. It is reasonable to suppose that since Herat was part of the Arab–Persian world of the Middle East, and Persian was the language of the people, it shared in the music culture of that region. By the thirteenth century a joint Arab–Persian system of music was used through much of the Middle East and Central Asia. The system found its principal theorist in Safi al-Din Abd al-Mumin al-Urmawi of Baghdad, who established the so-called Systematist School (Wright 1978:1–19).

The Timurid court

A clear picture of music at the later Timurid court of Sultan Husein Baiqara (late fifteenth century) is given by Babur, founder of the Moghul Empire, in his celebrated memoirs, the *Bābur-Nāmeh*.* At that time Herat was the cultural capital of a vast area, and no doubt some of the best musical talents were concentrated there. At the end of a long passage recounting the nobles and men of influence at the court, Babur gives detailed descriptions of the artists and musicians (remarks in square brackets are taken from the footnotes of King's 1921 edition of Leyden and Erskine's translation):

Another was Kūl Muhammed Ūdi (the lutanist). He also performed well on the guitar [*ghichek*]. He added three strings to it. No vocal or instrumental performer ever composed so many and such excellent overtures [*pishrau*].

Another was Sheikhi Nāyi (the flute-player). He also played well on the lute [*ūd*] and guitar [*ghichek*]. From the age of twelve or thirteen, he played well on the flute [*nai*]. On one occasion he played an air beautifully before Badia-ez-zemān Mirza on the flute [*nai*]. Kūl Muhammed attempted, but was unable to play it on the guitar. He said, 'The guitar is an imperfect instrument.' Sheikhi immediately took the guitar out of Kūl Muhammed's hand, and played the same air completely and delightfully upon it. They tell of Sheikhi, that he was so accomplished in music, that on hearing any air whatever, he said, 'Such a tune of such a person resembles this.' He did not compose much. They preserve two or three of his airs [*naksh*].

Another was Shah Kuli Ghicheki (the performer on the *ghichek* or guitar). He was a native of Irāk, who came into Khorasān, and rose to fame by his excellence as a composer [*mashk-sāz*]. He composed many tunes, preludes and airs [*naksh va pīshrū va kārhā*].

Another was Hussain Udi (the lutanist), who played with great taste on the lute, and composed elegantly. He could play, using only one string of his lute at a time. He had the fault of giving himself many airs when desired to play...

---

* I use the English translation of Leyden and Erskine (1921), annotated and revised by King, which was made from a Persian version of the original Turki. Another translation, direct from the Turki, has been made (Beveridge 1922). I prefer Leyden and Erskine's prose style.

The Timurid court

Ghulām Shādi was also a musical composer. He was the son of Shādi the singer. Though a performer, yet he did not play so as to deserve to be ranked with the performers who have been mentioned. He composed sweet airs, and some finished pieces; there were few compositions of that day that could be compared to his.

Another was Mīr Azū. He was not a performer, but composed. Though his productions are few, yet they are exquisite of their kind. (Leyden and Erskine: 322-3)

It is clear from Babur's complete account that the musicians mentioned above were servants of the court, not men of noble birth. Ustad Kuli Mohammad, the celebrated Sheikhi and Husein Udi, who were so distinguished for their skill in instrumental music, attained their eminence and celebrity through the encouragement and patronage of Ali Sher Nawai, for many years the principal minister of the Sultan, a great 'patron and protector of men of ingenuity and talent' (*ibid.*: 301), and a writer and composer himself, he 'also left excellent pieces of music; they are excellent both as to the airs themselves and as to the preludes' (*ibid.*). It is also clear that others amongst the nobles were celebrated as composers and musicians. Khwaja Abdullah Marwarid, one of the Sultan's *beg*s (nobles) was famed as a player of the *qānun*, 'No person could match his playing on the *kānūn* (or dulcimer). The mode of shaking on this instrument is his invention' (*ibid.*: 308). He was a man full of accomplishments, a fine calligrapher, well versed in the epistolary style of composition, a poet, and a very pleasant companion. Another celebrated poet at the court of Sultan Husein Baiqara was Banai.

At first he was unacquainted with the science of music, and Ali Sher Beg had taunted him with his ignorance; but, one year, the Mirza having spent a winter at Merv, whither he was accompanied by Ali Sher Beg, Banāi remained behind at Heri, applied himself to the study of music, and made such rapid progress, that, before the summer, he was even able to compose some pieces. In the summer when the Mirza returned to Heri, he sang in his presence, and that to music of his own composition, to the great astonishment of Ali Sher Beg, who complimented him on the occasion. He composed several pieces of music, one of which is denominated the *Nuh-rang* (or nine measure). The parts of this *Nuh-rang*, and of the *Yaldai Naksh* (or Midwinter-Night's Air), have their modulations in tenor [*rāst*]. (*Ibid.*: 317)

He left many excellent *naksh*es and *sūt*s ['themes and airs']. (*Ibid.*: 323)

These delightful sketches afford an insight into the high value bestowed upon music at the Timurid court. Babur's account also raises certain technical issues. Several types of piece are mentioned: *pishrau*, *naksh*, *kār* and *sut*. King, who revised Erskine and Leyden's translation of Babur, states 'I have not been able to translate, with any degree of certainty, the musical terms used in the preceding pages' (*ibid.*: 323). *Pishrau* is presumably the same word as *peshrev*, used in the terminology of Turkish music for a type of 'instrumental prelude' played in the classical *fasil*, 'modal suite' (Signell 1977: 17). *Kār* was one of the main vocal forms in Turkish music of the Ottoman period, a severely classical vocal form rarely performed today, being too heavy for contemporary taste. *Sut* is probably derived from Arabic *saut* ('sound, voice'), variously used as the label for an individual song, or later as the middle section in a three-part vocal form in Arab–Persian music. *Naksh*, or *naqsh* (Arabic for 'embellishment') was a rather free instrumental form consisting of a string of first sections from a number of separate pieces. In Ottoman music it referred to a song with shortened verses and an embellished refrain.*

The four instruments mentioned by Babur, the *'ud, gheichak, ney* and *qānun*, are also of

---
* I am indebted to Dr Owen Wright and Dr Karl Signell for their comments on the meanings of these terms.

interest. Their identity is fairly clear. The ʿud is presumably a form of the instrument we know today as the Arab lute, al-ʿud, the pre-eminent instrument in Arabic musical treatises of the medieval Islamic period. Similarly the *ney*, the rim blown oblique flute, and the *qānun*, the plucked board zither, are instruments of the Arab–Persian Middle Eastern tradition. These three instruments may be seen depicted in Persian miniature paintings executed during the Timurid period. The identity of the *qheichak* is slightly less certain, for at least two kinds of bowed lute are known by this name, the spike-fiddle of the *rabāb* type (like the *kemāncheh* of contemporary Iran), and instruments of the *sarinda* type. In twentieth century northern Afghanistan, *qheichak* denoted a fiddle, usually with a gallon petrol can as resonator (Slobin 1976:243–8). In the miniatures it is the *rabāb* type of fiddle which is depicted, never the *sarinda* type, and we may identify Babur's *qheichak* as a spike-fiddle.

Another point to emerge from Babur's description concerns the seemingly dynamic state of musical creativity at that time. A clear distinction was drawn between the activities of performer and composer, and men were remembered by the excellence of their musical compositions. The Timurids obviously had a well articulated concept of composition as a distinct activity and new work was presumably regarded as the product of individual talent and genius, like a new poem or a new painting. We are clearly dealing with an art music having all the properties of the aesthetic as defined by Merriam (1964: chapter 13). Farmer comments:

The whole of this period, from the coming of the Mongols to the fall of the Tīmūrids, is a glorious one for Persian art in general. Together with painting and the industrial arts, as well as poetry and *belles lettres*, music made great strides. (Farmer 1939: 2,799–800)

What was the music like? As we have seen, the instruments mentioned by Babur connect the music of the Timurid court with the music of Persia and the Middle East. Farmer implies that Timurid court music belonged to one period in the history of Persian music, when the political and cultural centre of the Persian world shifted for over a hundred years north-east to Samarkand and Herat, then shifted back to Iran under the Safavids. Further support for this interpretation might be forthcoming from a short treatise on music written in Persian at this time by Jami, a prolific author of prose and poetry (see Browne 1928:507–48). A translation has been published in Russian (Beliaev 1960).* In a preface, Jami explains that when he was young he studied the *ʿilm-e musiqi*, the 'science of music', but had not spoken about it for many years. Recently some exalted personages had asked him to write on this subject. Jami asks the reader not to form a bigoted opinion of the author (for writing about music) and not to think of music as incompatible with Islam.

Jami's treatise is essentially a summary of earlier works, very much in the Systematist tradition of Safi al-Din of Baghdad, and little more than a paraphrase of Abd al-Qadir's work (Wright, personal communication). Jami describes the twelve *maqām*s of this theoretical school (*Ushāq, Navā, Busaliq, Rāst, Huseini, Hijāz, Rahawi, Zanguleh, Irāq, Isfahān, Zirafkand*, and *Bozorg*) and indicates their scales with reference to positions on diagrams of the finger-board of the *ʿud*. Besides the twelve *maqām*s he describes five *āwāzeh* and twenty-four *shobeh*, 'secondary' and 'tertiary' scales. Beliaev, in his commentary, interprets the intervals of these scales in terms of a seventeen-tone scale constructed of limas and commas (intervals of ninety and twenty-four cents in the Ellis system, see Kunst 1959:2–9). In addition to numer-

---

* I am grateful to Dr Slawomira Kominek-Zeranska for her comments on this work.

The Timurid court

ous short chapters on the nature of intervals, scales, modes, and musical metres, Jami also considers the definition of music, the emotional connotations of the various *maqām*s, and the origins of music.

Jami's treatise is important because it was written in Herat, but what does it tell us about performance practice in the Timurid court? Possibly not very much; the interpretation of such treatises depends on one's view of the relationship between theory and practice. Farmer (1939) evidently believes that in general Arab–Persian theory described the practice, and points out that some of the great theorists were competent musicians. Another view of the Middle Eastern tradition of theorising about music is that it came to have rather little to do with practice. Theoretical scales were constructed according to mathematical and geometrical proportions, modes were classified to give primacy to the number twelve, to match the signs of the zodiac and the months of the year. This speculative science dealt with music and cosmology, and with ideas about music's spiritual essence and effect on the human soul. Jami was writing in this tradition of Arab and Persian scholarship, and the system he described could have been radically different from that actually used by the musicians at the Timurid court.

A rather different assessment of Timurid court music is given by Slobin, who takes the view that this was 'a joint Turco-Iranian classical music culture' (Slobin 1976:73). The Timurids were a Turkic people and their native language was Turki. As rulers of the Timurid Empire they embraced many aspects of Persian culture, including the Persian language, but at the same time they promoted their mother tongue, which Nawai established as a 'Turco-Persian' literary language. Nawai was also a composer of music and Slobin speculates that his compositions 'reflected a joint Turco-Persian classical music culture of the sophisticated Timurid courts' (*ibid*.). Slobin suggests that this fusion of Turkic and Persian musical elements was further crystallised in the sixteenth and seventeenth centuries in Bukhara and Samarkand to become that form of Central Asian art music called *Shashmaqām*. This occurred after the rise of the Shiah Safavid dynasty in Iran in the sixteenth century isolated Sunni Central Asia from the rest of the Sunni Middle East. Slobin's hypothesis seems reasonable, especially when viewed in relation to a much larger pattern of Persian–Turkic cultural interaction that has been going on in Central Asia for many centuries (*ibid*.: 66–81). In this view, Timurid art music was in a sense the precursor of contemporary Uzbek and Tajik court music, and *Shashmaqām* represents the closest living relative to the music of the Timurids.

After the demise of the Timurid court at Herat, musicians from Khurasan received patronage at the Moghul court. The following imperial musicians were at the court of Akbar in Delhi:

Ustā Dost, of Mashhad, plays on the flute (*nay*).
Mir Sayyid ʿAli, of Mashhad, plays on the *ghichak*.
Ustā Yūsuf, of Hirāt, plays on the *tamburā*.
Bahram Quli, of Hirāt, plays on the *ghichak*.
Sultān Hāshim, of Mashhad, plays on the *tamburā*.
Hāfiz Khwājah ʿAlī, of Mashhad, chants.
Pīrzada, nephew of Mir Dawam, of Khurasan, sings and chants. (Abu'l-Fazl 1927:681–2)

Two other players of 'Middle Eastern' instruments at Akbar's court mentioned in the *Ā'īn-i Akbarī* are Mir Abdullah, the *qānun* player, and Usta Mohammad Husein, the *tamburā* player, but the origins of these men are not given. The *tamburā* is the type of long-necked lute which eventually gave rise to the Indian sitar in the eighteenth century.

Although it is sometimes asserted that these musicians performed 'Persian music' (see, for example, Zonis 1973:37-8) at the Moghul courts, there can be no certainty in this respect; it seems likely that they played in the style of the former Timurid court, whatever that was. In any case, it seems to have been a music in decline. At the court of Akbar's grandson, Shah Jahan, there were only two musicians representing the 'Persian school'; Mohammad Baqi Mughal, a composer, and Mir Imad, also a musician-composer, a Sayyid of Herat whose father had migrated from Central Asia (Halim 1945:359). The complex question of the 'Muslim contribution' to the music of North India has been discussed by many authors, for example, Ahmed (1954), Bhanu (1955), Halim (1956), Kaumudi (1950), and Rizvi (1941).

After the Timurids

Very little seems to be known about the state of music in Herat during the period of the Safavids, who ruled Herat after the Timurids till 1749. We can assume, perhaps, that Herat shared the music culture of other Persian cities, but that does not help us greatly because this is a rather obscure era of Iranian music history.

Notwithstanding Farmer's conviction of the healthy state of music in Safavid Iran – 'The people were very fond of music, and it could be heard all day long' (Farmer 1939:2,801) – the general view of modern commentators is that music in the time of the Safavids was under strenuous attack from the religious establishment. This was part of the general intolerance of literature, poetry, Sufism, and mysticism (Browne 1930:26-7). The repercussions of this form of puritanism were several. Very few treatises on music were written in Iran in the Safavid period, as though music had ceased to be a respectable topic for learning and scholarship, and writings on this subject were no longer patronised. Farhat (1980) argues that this neglect ultimately led to the formation of the *dastgāh* principle, which is unique to contemporary Persian music.

In medieval times, *maqām*s were rendered individually, by way of extensive improvisation and the addition of composed material in the same *maqām*, combining to make a performance of desired length. . . As musical scholarship suffered and performance ability, based on theoretic know-how, was eroded, it became increasingly difficult to present a performance of a respectable length with the use of a single *maqām*. . . Consequently, performers resorted to the device of progressing, or modulating, from one *maqām* to another, usually not too remote in its modal structure. In some cases, eventually, this stringing of *maqām*s, led to more distant modes. The musicians were sensitive enough to recognise a certain arbitrariness in this process, and realized that an element of unification would be essential. Such an element is the *forud* which ties the various *maqām*s in the group to one another, and acts as a melodic cadential pattern constantly referring back to the initial *maqām*. (Farhat 1980:5-6)

According to Farhat's theory, the *dastgāh* system came into existence in nineteenth-century Iran when music was patronised at the Qajar court and the need to create extended performances was again apparent.

Music in the nineteenth century

After the Pashtuns took control of Herat in 1749 we can assume that they patronised their own Pashtun music. Elphinstone (1815) provides important information about Pashtun music and dance in the early nineteenth century. On the subject of domestic entertainments he says:

After dinner, they sit and smoke, or form a circle to tell tales and sing. The old men are great story tellers. Their tales are of Kings and Viziers, of genii and fairies; but, principally of love and war. They are often mixed with songs and verses and always end in a moral. They delight in these tales and songs. All sit in silence while a tale is telling; and, when it is done, there is a general cry of 'Ai Shawash!' their usual expression of admiration. Their songs are mostly about love; but they have numerous ballads, celebrating the wars of their tribe, and the exploits of individual chiefs. As soon as a chief of any name dies, songs are made in honour of his memory. Besides these songs, some men recite odes, or other passages from the poets; and others play the flute, the rubaub, (a sort of lute or guitar), the camauncheh and sarindeh, (two kinds of fiddles), or the soornaun, which is a species of hautboy. The singers usually accompany their voice with the rubaub or the fiddle. Their songs are often made by the husbandmen and shepherds; oftener by professed Shauyers, (a sort of minstrel, between a poet and a ballad-singer); and, sometimes by authors of reputation, of past or present times. (Elphinstone 1815:236-7)

He also describes a royal entertainment held in Peshawar, the winter capital of the early Afghan rulers, given by three dancing girls:

Their dancing had a great deal of action. The girl scarcely ever stands while she sings, (as those in India do); but rushes forward, clasps her hands, sometimes sinks on her knees, and throws herself into other attitudes expressive of the passions, which are the subject of her song; and all this action, though violent, is perfectly graceful. Behind, stand a number of well-dressed fiddlers, drummers, and beaters of cymbals, with long beards, and an air of gravity little suited to their profession. All these disturb the concert, by shouting out their applauses of the dancers, or joining in the song with all the powers of their voice. (*Ibid*.: 279)

A rather similar description of music and dance is given by the French soldier of fortune, Ferrier, who visited Herat in 1845. Suspecting him to be a British agent, the authorities did their best to induce him to reveal his true identity and he was kept under virtual house arrest. The Sertip Lal Mohammad superintended his residence in Herat:

Sometimes the Sertip passed the evening with me, and brought with him some *bayadères*, whose dances were frequently prolonged into the night – these ladies were accompanied by a band of musicians, and the wine-cup circled with rapidity amongst them. . .The Sertip wished to include me in the libations, and seemed surprised when I showed so little inclination for them. . .[he] was the more chagrined at my abstemious habits, as he no doubt expected that I should in my cups let him into all my secrets. . . Failing to accomplish his purpose with the assistance of Bacchus, he endeavoured to do so through the seductive influence of the bayadères [*sic*]. . . The music to which they danced was not inharmonious or devoid of a certain merit; but the principal instrument, a small viol, being monotonous in the literal sense of that word, and the tone wiry, it was far from agreeable – the other instruments were much more pleasing to the ear. The tunes were varied and the execution good; and I should have listened with more attention to this part of the performance had it not served as an accompaniment to the voices of twelve herculean Afghans, who made themselves hoarse in their attempts to produce the most distressing sounds that can be conceived, he who howled the loudest being evidently considered the best singer. (Ferrier 1857:151-2)

Ferrier's description is disappointingly brief, as well as being typically prejudiced against 'native music', but provides a few useful clues. Putting his account together with that of Elphinstone, one might conclude that the kind of music and dance found at the Afghan court in Kabul (the summer capital) and Peshawar (the winter capital) was also patronised by the Pashtun elite in Herat. The question then arises whether the musicians were local, or brought from outside. In any case, the 'twelve herculean Afghans' are unlikely to have been Pashtuns, for they traditionally employed small, low ranking endogamous groups as their musicians, such as the Dom. A notable feature of these descriptions is the performance by a *group* of singers, hardly a characteristic of Afghan music one hundred years later. It is possible that the music of Kashmir retains certain aspects of Afghan music from this period (and Kashmir was part of the Afghan empire from 1752 to 1819). Some of the instruments are common to the two regions: the *rubāb*, *kemāncheh*, *sehtār*, *santur*, and *sornā*. Group singing is again found in Kashmir, for example, in *Sufyāna Kalam*, and in the past *Sufyāna Kalam* was associated with the *Hāfiza* dance (Pacholczyk 1978:13).

A kind of instrumental ensemble that certainly existed in Herat in the nineteenth century was the *naqqārakhāneh*. This was an archaic type of ensemble for the performance of what has been variously described as royal, ceremonial, civic, or military music. In its most complete form it consisted of a variety of instruments, notably oboes, trumpets, and drums, especially the *naqqāra* (kettle drum), from which the ensemble derived its name. During my fieldwork I came across one informant who remembered about the former *naqqārakhāneh* of Herat, situated in the citadel, and intended to be heard by both military personnel and the townspeople. This description probably reaches back to the nineteenth century. A fuller account is given in Baily (1980). The *naqqārakhāneh* ensemble in Herat consisted of *sornā*, *dohol*, *naqqāra*, and *karnā* (long trumpet).

The *sornā* players in this *naqqārakhāneh* apparently had recourse to 'seventy two *maqāms*', a mixed system of Persian and Indian modes. The former (*maqām-e Pārsi*, 'Persian mode') had names such as *Now Ruz Sabā*, *Now Ruz ʿArab*, *Shur*, *Chahārgāh*, *Zaoul*, *Dugāh Olang*, and *Shāhnāz-e Jamʿ* and the latter (*maqām-e Hindi*, 'Indian mode') names such as *Suni*, *Bairami*, *Āsā*, *Āsāwari*, *Shām Kelyān*, *Nat Kelyān*, and *Pāri*. There was also a timetable for the performance of the different modes during the day and night. Seventy-two is an auspicious number in Persian culture and it is unlikely that there were exactly seventy-two modes in this system, probably many less. I have suggested (*ibid.*) that the seventy-two *maqāms* were not unique to the *naqqārakhāneh* of Herat but were probably shared with similar ensembles known to have existed in Kandahar and Kabul. This modal system may ultimately have derived from Moghul India, where the *naqqārakhāneh* ensemble was especially prominent.

This mixed system of Persian and Indian modes is reminiscent of the modal system of *Sufyāna Kalam* music of Kashmir (Pacholczyk 1978), used for the group singing of mystical poetry in Persian and Kashmiri to the accompaniment of *santur*, *sehtār*, *sāz-e Kashmiri* and tabla. The same modes are also used for the Kashmiri *surnay* ensemble (*ibid.*). This raises the possibility that a mixed system of modes might have been used for vocal music in Herat in the nineteenth century, as well as for the *naqqārakhāneh*. And at the very least, these data suggest that Heratis were familiar with both Persian and Indian modes in the period in question. This 'bimusicality' forms an essential background to the musical changes that occurred in the twentieth century.

The early twentieth century

In the early part of the twentieth century 'Persian music' was very much in vogue in the city of Herat. It is difficult to date this precisely but the heyday was probably in the 1920s, during the reign of the progressive monarch Amanullah Khan. Many informants described the old music of the city as Persian (*Pārsi, Irāni*), and its identification as such is corroborated when we compare what remains of this kind of music in Herat with the contemporary art music of Iran. Interest was centred on the art of *ghazal* singing, with texts drawn from classical Persian poetry. As far as can be established, the manner of singing was often slow and in free rhythm, unmetred in the musical sense, like the *āvāz* style of Iran, with Iranian vocal technique and ornamentation. The musicians performed in a variety of what they identified as 'Persian' modes, with names such as *Shur*, *Chahārgāh*, and *Homāyun*, and they evidently understood and used the Iranian *dastgāh* principle.

One of the most obvious Persian features of this music was the use of the Iranian *tār*, called *chahārtār* in Herat. *Chahārtār* literally means 'four strings', though the *tār* as played in Iran today, and as I have observed the instrument in Afghanistan, has six strings arranged in three double courses. The Iranian *tār* is not a very old instrument; Jean During (personal communication) believes it to have originated in the Caucasus in the eighteenth century, although there is also an interesting early association with Shiraz. It became the pre-eminent instrument of court music under the patronage of the Qajars in nineteenth-century Tehran, and it may be that the instrument was not known in Herat until near the end of the century. Instruments were both imported from Iran and also made in Herat.

A typical urban music group of the 1920s consisted of several singers and *chahārtār* players, accompanied by tabla drums and two types of idiophone: the *sekh*, a rifle barrel suspended by a string and struck with a metal beater, and the *tāl*, a pair of small brass cymbals. The *santur*, another Persian instrument, seems sometimes to have been incorporated into this kind of group. The use of the tabla in this ensemble is certainly remarkable, unheard of in Iran, where the *dombak* is the normal drum for accompanying urban music. The tabla players of the 1920s did not play according to the Indian system of strokes, *bol* patterns, and *tāl*s, which were adopted later. Tablas were imported directly from India by tea merchants on their camel caravans and were never manufactured in Herat.

Other instruments used in Herat at the time were the Persian *kemāncheh* (called *gheichak* in Herat), the *sarinda* (called *sārang* in Herat), and the *rubāb*. The two-stringed *dutār* was an instrument of rural music. A pair of instruments often played together was the *tulak*, a brass transverse flute, and the *dāireh*, the frame drum. The *dāireh* was also the main instrument played by women. The *sornā* (oboe) and *dohol* (drum) were no doubt important, especially for village wedding festivities. The *zirbaghali* does not seem to have been common in Herat at this time; one report indicates that there was an institution of the *zurkhāneh* type in Herat, where a large *dombak* was played in connection with gymnastic exercises, as in Iran. The various instruments were probably associated with different musical genres. It seems, for example, that the *rubāb* was not played in the urban music ensemble along with the *chahārtār*, and I was told that this was because the fretting of the two instruments was different (i.e. they were fretted according to different tonal systems). One might doubt that as the 'real' explanation, for Heratis were ready to combine different systems of tuning in the 1970s. Whatever the reason, it seems that the *rubāb* was used for some other kind of music, and one suspects that it was principally associated with the Pashtun population of Herat and was used to play Pashtun music.

Some of the musicians from this period were still remembered by Heratis in the 1970s. The earliest to be recalled were:

> Haidar Namadmal, *chahārtār* player and singer. Lived in the city.
>
> Haidar Pineh, *chahārtār* player and singer. City dweller. By profession he was a *pinehduz*, a shoe-mender. He was the pupil of Haidar Namadmal. He was a fine singer and sometimes known as Haidar Khushkhan ('good singer'). He evidently played a crucial role on the Herati music scene, and is known to have visited Iran on several occasions to learn new material which he introduced into Herat. Later he brought the first harmonium to Herat.
>
> Seid Qoresh, a tabla player.

These three men were said to have been summoned to Kabul in the time of Habibullah Khan (1901–1919) to play for the King. This perhaps amounted to representing Herat at some grand public festivities in Kabul, possibly National Unity Day, which was inaugurated by Habibullah to celebrate the final conquest of Nuristan. Other musicians were included in this party from Herat but their names were not recalled. The singing of the group apparently earned special royal praise.

In the 1920s the most famous singer in Herat was Rahim Khushkhan, also a player of the *sekh*. He came from the village of Talaw and had a butcher's shop in the city. He sang in a group (*dasteh*) with Haidar Pineh, the above-mentioned *chahārtār* player, and Mohammad Hasan, a tabla player. They played together for many years and some of their descendants were musicians in Herat in the 1970s. For example, Rahim Khushkhan's son, Mohammad Karim Khan, learned to play the *chahārtār* from Haidar Pineh; he was my principal informant about the Persian style of the 1920s, both from statements and from his performances on the *chahārtār*. Rahim Khushkhan's grandson (through his daughter) was Nawak, one of the best known singers of Iranian popular music in Herat in the 1970s, and, like his grandfather, a butcher. Mohammad Hasan, the group's tabla player, founded the family of hereditary professional musicians calling themselves Khushnawazha; his sons established themselves as the leading Herati musicians in the late 1930s.

Some of the other musicians from this period were:

> Abdur Rahman Shadijani, *chahārtār* player and singer from the village of Shadijan, near Imam Shishnur, the site of an important Shiah shrine. He was a farmer.
>
> Ghulam Mydin, known as Bacheh Ghulam Resul Irat (son of Ghulam Resul the gunpowder maker), *chahārtār* player. He had a shop in the city selling guns and ammunition. He had three sons who played music. One was Haji Ghulam Sadiq, also known as Golsaz Sadiq-e Santuri: he played the *santur*, an instrument he made himself, and also performed *lobotak* (a kind of puppet show with small wooden figures animated by strings beneath the board on which they stood). Later in life he renounced his musical and puppeteering activities, went on the pilgrimage to Mecca, and became famous as a maker of paper flowers (*golsāz*) used at wedding festivities. He played in the Iranian style on his *santur*. Another son was Shir Mohammad, a player of the *rubāb*, who spent much of his time around the *ziyārat*s of Herat, being himself a kind of *malang* or *darwish*. The third son was Mohammad Rahim, who had a shop selling rice and seeds. He played tabla, *zirbaghali* and *dāireh*. He was the father of Karim Dutari, who perfected the fourteen-stringed *dutār*, and was an important figure amongst the musicians of Herat in the 1970s.
>
> Seid Usman, *chahārtār* player and singer. Kept a coal shop in the city.

The early twentieth century

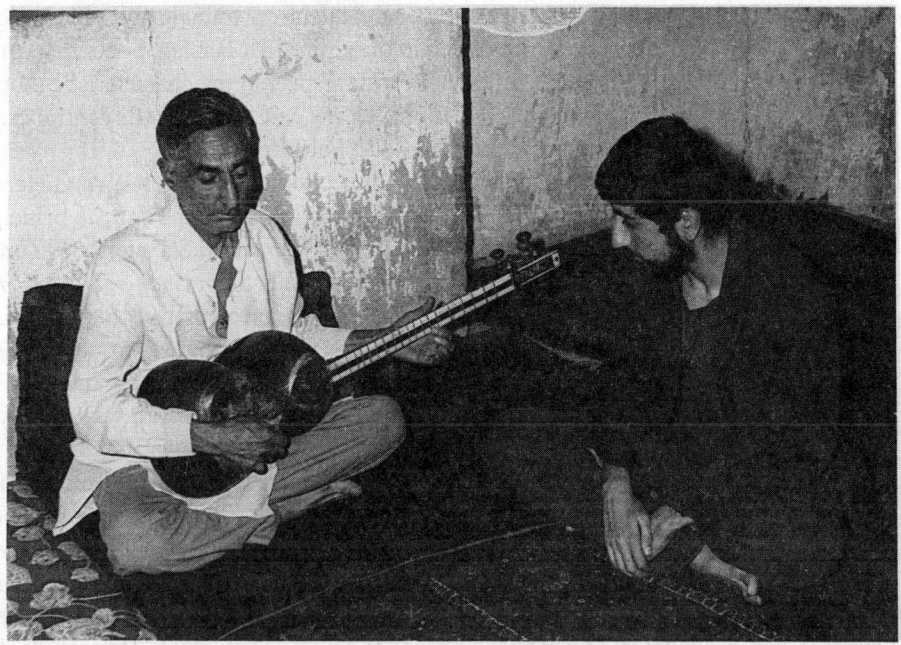

Plate 3 Mohammad Karim Khan demonstrates the *chahārtār* to his friend Ismail, 1974

Abdul Ahat, *chahārtār* player, from the village of Deh Wancheh.
Usman, *chahārtār* player and farmer, from the village of Boland Au.
Mohammad Reza Tekreh, *chahārtār* player in the city. His son Faizullah was known as a singer of Kashmiri songs in the 1930s and also played *rubāb* and *sārang*. Faizullah's son, Habibullah, was a *rubāb* player in the 1940s.
Haji Ghulam Nebi Hakak, player of the *santur*. He was by profession a metal engraver (*hakāki*), with a shop in the city; he later gave up music and continued with his metal engraving business.
Mohsen Rodeh, described as a *rubāb* player of 'the first order'.
Several tabla players were mentioned from this period, who came from low ranking barber-musician families in the old city more commonly associated with the *sornā* and *dohol*.

Several points of interest arise when we consider the recruitment of these musicians. The majority of them were described as amateur (*shauqi*), but some of them became professional, and depended on music making as their primary source of income. Some of their original professions are indicated by their *takhalos*, nickname, like Haidar Pineh (Haidar the Shoe-Mender) and Rahim Qasab (Rahim the Butcher). Some later gave up playing music and returned to their original professions or adopted others. And there were families which maintained a strong interest in performing music but retained a semi-professional status.

Information about the melodic modes used for the urban music of this time was gathered from Mohammad Karim, the son of Rahim Khushkhan, mentioned above. From Mohammad Karim I recorded performances in the following modes: *Chahārgāh*, *Shur*, *Homāyun*, *Bayāt-e Turk*, *Gereyli*, *Abu-'Atā*, *Māhur*, *Segāh*, *Dashti*, *Nawā*, *Maqām-e Rāst*, *Bayāt-e Shirāz*, *Now Ruz Sabā*, and *Hijāz*. These are all the names of modes in the Persian art music system. The Herati versions, as far as can be established from a single but well placed informant, in most cases more or less corresponded to the equivalent Persian modes in terms of scale type, but there were much greater differences with respect to the characteristic motifs of the modes (Jean During, personal communication). In any case, defining the central characteristics of a Persian mode is no easy matter (Nettl and Foltin 1972).

Correspondences of individual modes is one connection between Persian and Herati music of this period. It is also clear that the Heratis played according to the *dastgāh* principle, with modulations from the original mode (see Farhat 1965, Caron and Safvate 1966, Zonis 1973). Thus when Mohammad Karim played some modes, notably *Shur*, *Chahārgāh*, and *Homāyun*, each was divided into several sections (*heseh*), which took a progressively higher tessitura and ended with a modulation back to the original mode. His performances would conclude with a *reng* (dance) followed by a *tasnif* (metred song melody) in the original mode. This kind of piece was called a *dastgāh* in Herat, though it seems the term *dastgāh* was employed more widely than in Iran, and could be used synonymously with *maqām*, another old word for mode in Herat. Although the Herati musicians do not seem to have been familiar with terms such as *radif*, *gusheh* or *forud* in a musical context, they were using these elements of form in their performances of *dastgāh* music. In a *dastgāh* with several parts (*heseh*), whose finalis (*shāhpardeh*, 'king fret') was positioned progressively higher in the pitch range, each *heseh* was called a *gāh* ('place'), and Mohammad Karim told me that the names of modes such as *Dugāh*, *Segāh*, *Chahārgāh*, and *Panjgāh* refer to the number of 'places' (two, three, four, and five respectively) they have on the neck of the *chahārtār*. This is an old explanation for the significance of these terms in Persian music.

When a group of musicians (i.e. singers and *chahārtār* players, with tabla, *sekh* and *tāl*, and possibly *santur*), performed together at a wedding party (*ʿarusi*) or a garden party (*meleh bāgh*), the *dastgāh* had the following form. They would start with a *shakl*, an introduction in free rhythm, either sung or played on the *chahārtār*. This was followed by the singing of a *ghazal* in the slow *āvāz* style of Iran. Then another singer would take over to sing another *ghazal*, then another a third *ghazal*, and so on. After several such *ghazals* there would be a *tasnif*, a song in strict rhythm (often translated in Iran as 'ballad'), and finally an instrumental dance piece called a *reng*. There were also instrumental interpolations of the type called *zarbi* in Iran.

The political and social significance of this period

A certain amount can be inferred about the social and political context of the Persian music vogue of the 1920s. In the turmoil of the nineteenth century, the Shiah merchants of Herat were an oppressed community and it seems unlikely that they would have called attention to such wealth as they had by holding lavish wedding celebrations. By about 1900 Herat was recovering from the chaos of the preceding epoch, the Shiah merchant class had re-emerged, and it was no longer necessary to take precautions against the expropriation of riches by the authorities. Weddings became lavish displays of wealth, and the venue for sophisticated musical entertainment, as they had no doubt been in earlier times. There was an increased patronage of urban music. Furthermore, in 1919 King Amanullah came to the throne of Afghanistan. The ten years of his reign were characterised by strenuous attempts at social reform and modernisation, and the 1920s was a time when music acquired a new respectability and popularity in the face of religious censure.

When the patronage of art music in Herat was re-established, a demand was created which was met by adopting music from Iran. There are several reasons why Iran should have been the source. Mashhad, the nearest Persian city, was only 225 miles from Herat, while Kandahar was 350 miles distant. Land communications at that time were slow and difficult. The Shiahs of Herat, who made up the wealthy merchant class, looked to Iran as the source of their 'Persian culture', and many visited Iran, especially Mashhad, on pilgrimage. As we have seen, Herat has a long history of shared music culture with Iran, and one might guess that the Heratis simply adopted the current style of Persian music, the *dastgāh* system. In Iran, too, music was undergoing a renaissance, with a surge of renewed interest in music making after the Constitution of 1906. Musicians such as Haidar Pineh visited Iran to collect new items of repertory. Phonographs may have been an important medium for the communication of Persian music after 1914, which could help explain why the Heratis played seemingly rather truncated versions of the *dastgāh*s and were unfamiliar with technical terms such as *gusheh* and *forud*. The popularity of Persian music in Herat at that time might be interpreted as confirming traditional cultural links with Iran. In the 1930s there was a dramatic shift in the kind of urban music patronised by the Heratis, with the adoption of the instrumentarium and art music of Kabul. These matters are discussed in the next chapter.

3 Afghan urban music in the twentieth century

Music in Kabul

Unlike Herat, Kabul is not a city of great historical importance. The first capital of Afghanistan was Kandahar, but Timur Shah, the son of Ahmad Shah Durrani and the second ruler of Afghanistan, moved the capital to Kabul in 1776 after disputes with the tribal elite in Kandahar. The population of Kabul at that time is estimated at 10,000 (N.H. Dupree 1975), and contained a sizeable component of Qizilbash, members of a Persianised Turkic ethnic group, Shiahs, who had been settled in Kabul by the Persian ruler Nadir Shah Afshar at the time of his campaigns in North India. Timur Shah was exceptional for an Afghan ruler of the time in that he tried to 'make the royal court an intellectual and artistic centre through his patronage of scholars and artists' (Gregorian 1969:50). His successors did not attempt to follow his example for nearly a century. There can be little doubt that there were musicians at Timur Shah's court, but we lack (as yet) any concrete evidence regarding their music. It is significant that we cannot discern in this period an indigenous Afghan art music equivalent to Persian or Hindustani classical music. Afghanistan was overshadowed by the musical culture of its two great neighbours and it is almost certain that music from both of them was played at the Kabul court in the nineteenth century.

According to the Afghan musicologist, A.W. Madadi, before the 1860s the principal urban and court musicians in Kabul were of Persian origin, a statement repeated by Slobin (1976:34) on the same authority. 'Of Persian origin' is a vague phrase. Where they descendants of musicians who came originally from Iran? Were they recruited from the Qizilbash community? Or were they Persians familiar with the music of the Qajar court who were engaged to play in Kabul? We cannot tell. It is understandable that the Durranis, who came originally from Kandahar, and who had much more contact with the Persian world than had the more easterly Pashtun tribes, should have enjoyed Persian music. The Qizilbash population, who constituted a wealthy and influential section of Kabul society, might also be expected to patronise the contemporary music of Iran. It seems safe to assume that Persian *ghazal* singing in the rhythmically free *āvāz* style, in Persian melodic modes, with instrumental accompaniment, was the predominant form of Persian art music at the Kabul court.

There must also have been contact with the Hindustani music of the time (Slobin 1976:34). Before the establishment of Afghanistan in 1747, Kabul and (intermittently) Kandahar were part of the Moghul Empire and Moghul governors and their officials might be expected to have patronised Hindustani music and exposed the Afghans to it. Musicians from India may have been attached to their courts or households or perhaps made visits to the region, visiting a circuit of patrons. One of the four styles of Indian *dhrupad* singing is sometimes called the *Qandahārbāni*, the 'Kandahar style', though modern scholars doubt whether it actually originated in Kandahar (Alastair Dick, personal communication). Pashtuns moved freely about Hindustan and established settlements in various places. Pashtun musicians studied Hindustani music in India, and ultimately contributed to its development. From such contact, knowledge of Hindustani music would have trickled back to Afghanistan. As early as 1829 Burnes noted, 'We had songs in many languages. The Pooshtoo is softer when sung than when spoken; but Hindoostani is the favourite language with the Afghans, having, to use their own phrase, "more salt in it".' (Burnes 1842:259). In the 1860s the Amir of Kabul, Sher Ali Khan, brought a number of Indians to Kabul as his court musicians, but it seems likely that there were performances of Hindustani vocal and instrumental music at the Kabul court long before then.

The Indian court musicians

Sher Ali Khan, who ruled Afghanistan from 1863 to 1866, and again from 1868 to 1879, is known to have brought Indian court musicians to Kabul, presumably after his two years' exile in India, so consolidating and legitimising the Afghans' interest in Hindustani music, and setting it on course to become an 'official' art music of the country, patronised by successive rulers of Afghanistan right down to the time of His Majesty Zahir Shah (reigned 1933–73), whose predilection for Hindustani music is mentioned by Neuman (1980:190).

According to an article by A.W. Madadi in *Pashtun Zhagh*, the house magazine of Radio Kabul, and based on information gleaned from Ustad Natu, then (1960s) the oldest singer on the staff of the radio station, the first court musicians from India were:

   Ustad Mian Samandar Khan, grandfather of Ustad Natu
   Ustad Shain Kot Koli Khan
   Ustad Nata Khan
   Berpur Khan
   Gamu Khan
   Rang Ali Talemand
   Qand
   Raji

The first five men in the above list were singers, Rang Ali Talemand was a tabla player, while Qand and Raji, played tabla, *sārang* and *rubāb*. The same names were given to Lorraine Sakata by Ustad Rahim Gul in 1972, who also mentioned two women court singers, possibly also from Hindustan. One has little idea of the reputation of these *ustād*s ('master musicians') in India, nor of where they came from, though later on a definite connection with Patiala in the Punjab can be discerned. We may assume they were lesser court musicians, familiar with all the genres cultivated at the courts of North India at the time. Sher Ali Khan may simply have been very fond of Hindustani music, but he perhaps also realised from his experiences of Indian court life that the rank of a ruler was measured in part by the music he could command; to establish a credible court in Kabul he would need to display the appropriate musical symbols of power. While the number of Indian musicians who migrated to Kabul, then and later, was small, their descendants flourished and made Kabul a place where Hindustani vocal and instrumental music was maintained and performed. This was a circumstance of great importance for the future course of musical developments in Afghanistan. Under royal patronage Kabul became comparable to a North Indian court and, though no recognised *gharānā* (stylistic school of Hindustani music) arose in Kabul, a type of art music was eventually produced which was distinctly Afghan in style, notably the Kabuli *ghazal*, a vocal form, and the associated *naghmeh-ye kashāl*, the 'extended instrumental piece'.

We may speculate that the music making of the Indian *ustād*s was constrained and directed by the tastes and preferences of their Afghan patrons. Hindustani vocal music (*dhrupad* and *khyāl*) may have commanded high prestige amongst the Afghans but ultimately they did not have much support outside a small circle of *aficionados* (which included the musicians themselves). One might argue that Hindustani music was too sensuous for the Afghan musical aesthetic; too florid, too drawn out. The *ustād*s were encouraged to cultivate genres that resonated more closely with the musical tastes of their patrons, Pashtuns with a love of Persian culture. Accordingly, the main vocal genre cultivated by the *ustād*s was the *ghazal*, the 'Persian ode', using the poetry of classical Persian poets from Iran, Afghanistan and India. In this respect there was continuity with the past, for the *ghazal* would have been the predominant form of the old Persian music of the Kabul court. The musical form for singing *ghazal*s in Kabul may have been adopted from India, but also bears distinctly Afghan characteristics, examined more fully in chapter 5.

We may further speculate that the Afghan *rubāb* had an important role in the creation of a new genre of Afghan instrumental art music. The Afghan *rubāb* (I follow the orthography suggested by Farmer (1931:103-4)), with its distinct shape and sympathetic strings, is not an ancient instrument. It is a member of the *rubāb* family (double chambered lutes) that includes the Indian *rubāb*, the Iranian *tār*, the Tibetan *danyen*, the Pamir *rubāb*, the Dulan *rubāb*, and the Kashgar *rewap*, with its vestigial upper chamber. Although earlier forms of *rubāb* are often found depicted in Persian miniature paintings, the Afghan *rubāb* is not, nor is it shown in miniatures of the various Indian schools. The *rubāb* is mentioned by Elphinstone (1815), presumably the Afghan type. One might guess that the Afghan *rubāb* was devised in the eighteenth century in Kandahar, Kabul, Peshawar, or some other city with a sizeable Pashtun population. The instrument is sometimes called the 'Kabuli *rubāb*', and Ghazni was often mentioned by Afghans as its place of origin. It may well have been cultivated at Timur Shah's court. The Afghan type of *rubāb* is known today in Baluchistan, Tajikistan, Pakistan and Kashmir, with variations in the number and tuning of the strings and fretting, and in the nineteenth century it was also found in certain parts of India. Willard (1834) comments, 'The Puthans are remarkably fond of this instrument, which is very common in Rampoor' (Tagore 1965:99), and Day (1891:127-8) gives an illustration and notes its high incidence in the Punjab. In India the Afghan *rubāb* was modified by Afghan musicians to become the *sarod*, possibly in Lucknow in the 1860s (Solis 1970).

The *ustād*s from India were probably already familiar with the *rubāb*, but in Kabul they would have found that this instrument, with its strong Pashtun associations, was regarded with particular favour. Abdur Rahman, Habibullah and Amanullah were three Afghan rulers (spanning the years 1881-1929) remembered as having been great lovers of the *rubāb*, and apparently both Habibullah and Amanullah played it a little (Ustad Mashal Ghori, personal communication). It seems reasonable to suppose that the *ustād*s were encouraged to develop a repertory of instrumental art music for the instrument, which accounts for the existence of two such genres in the 1970s. One, the *naghmeh-ye klāsik*, appears to be a simplified form of the *ālāp* and *gat* of Hindustani instrumental music. The other, the *naghmeh-ye kashāl*, was a new genre, possibly combining elements of Pashtun music with Hindustani compositional features. These genres are discussed further in chapter 5.

Another important contribution of the Indian *ustād*s was the introduction of a system of social organisation for hereditary professional musicians in the musicians' quarter, the

Kucheh Kharabat, which grew up around the area just outside the Bala Hisar (a fortified palace). The *ustād*s and their descendants shared the musicians' quarter with Afghan hereditary professional musicians from families of barber-musicians, who were originally players of the *sornā* and *dohol*. Over the years these two communities of hereditary musicians became to some extent integrated: the barber-musicians received training in Hindustani music from the *ustād*s, and some became masters of that style.

The *ustād*s of the 1920s and 1930s

In the 1920s, during the reign of the progressive Afghan ruler Amanullah Khan, significant steps were taken to broaden the audience for what was now established as Kabuli art music. Even in the 1920s radio broadcasting played some role in this process. The type of hand pumped portable harmonium so common in India, called *armonia* in Afghanistan (sometimes *piānu*), had come into use in Kabul by this time (presumably introduced by the *ustād*s), and became an integral part of the small ensemble used to accompany urban vocal music in Afghanistan. A photograph from 1915 published in Neidermayer (1924) shows two harmoniums being played by street musicians.

Ustad Qasem and Ustad Ghulam Husein were particularly remembered from this period. Their busts stood in the foyer of the Radio Afghanistan building in Kabul, with bronze plaques that read as follows (dates in the Islamic lunar calendar):

Ustad Qasem. Son of Sitarju. Born in 1262. Winner of gold and diamond medals for songs at the Independence celebrations. The originator of the new Afghan music. Had a good knowledge of poetry. Lived to the age of seventy-three.

Ustad Ghulam Husein. Also winner of gold and other medals. Established *tarānā* singing in Afghanistan. Son of Atar Husein, born in 1265 in Kabul. Manager and Adviser of Music at Radio Kabul. Had many professional and amateur students. Lived to the age of eighty-two.

Ustad Qasem (1882–1955) was born in Kabul; his father Sitarju (a sitar player) came from outside Afghanistan, possibly from Kashmir, and was a court musician to Abdur Rahman Khan. Qasem trained in Hindustani music in Kabul under Ustad Piara Khan, becoming a great favorite of Amanullah, and the leading singer at the court. Amanullah liked to visit the Kucheh Kharabat (the musicians' quarter) dressed incognito, and would address Ustad Qasem as 'Qasem Jan', and treated him as a personal friend. When Amunullah visited Europe in 1928 he took his collection of Ustad Qasem's gramophone records with him and listened to them whenever he had time. A letter written by Amunullah to Ustad Qasem at this time reveals their warm friendship (Reshtia, personal communication). His fame rested particularly on his excellence as a *ghazal* singer. An elder member of the Tarzi family who had been at court as a young man once described to me how Ustad Qasem had a tremendous fund of poetry at his command, which he would use to make apposite comments about everyday events at court. For instance, when the King selected a beautiful green apple from the table, Ustad Qasem would immediately produce some lines of poetry in praise of the apple.

Amanullah secured Afghanistan's independence from British domination in 1919. From then on there were annual celebrations of independence (*Jeshan*) with great festivities held in Kabul and other cities. Ustad Qasem became nationally famous at these celebrations for the *ghazal*s he performed expressing patriotic and nationalist sentiments, earning him the award of gold and diamond medals. His plaque describes him as 'the originator of the new Afghan music'; in similar vein he was often referred to as 'The Father of Afghan Music'. It seems he was largely responsible for popularising the Kabuli *ghazal* and making it the principal genre of art music in Afghanistan. He later played an important role in the creation of popular music at the radio station. Like Ustad Ghulam Husein, he was responsible for training hundreds of professional and amateur musicians. His son Yaqub Qasemi was a vocalist in the Hindustani style, but did not achieve the fame of his father.

Ustad Ghulam Husein (1885–1967) was only three years younger than Ustad Qasem but seems to have been overshadowed by him, so that his great flowering came rather later, in the 1930s and 1940s. His father, Atar Husein, apparently came from Patiala in the Punjab and was brought to Kabul as a court musician by Amir Abdur Rahman, presumably sometime in the 1880s, since Ghulam Husein was born in Kabul. He seems to have made an important contribution to music education and played a crucial role in radio broadcasting in the 1940s and 1950s, when the new popular music style was being forged. Ustad Ghulam Husein had one son, the singer Mohammad Husein, or Ustad Sarahang, the doyen of Hindustani vocal music in Kabul from the 1950s to the 1970s. Ustad Sarahang studied for seventeen years in Patiala as a boy and young man and was well known in India as a classical singer. His photograph can be found in Neuman (1980:211). He died in 1981.

The names of two other important singers should also be mentioned. Ustad Nabi Gol, who features prominently in the next part of this chapter, was from the town of Tirah, in the heart of Afridi country, today in the North West Frontier Province of Pakistan. His origins are obscure. It is possible that he was not an Afridi at all but a Dom, a member of a musician 'caste' attached to the Afridi tribe. He was originally a singer of Pashto songs and came to enjoy the rank of a great *ustād* in the Kucheh Kharabat, and he was obviously favoured by the King. He was first the student of Ustad Qasem and later of Ustad Ghulam Husein, but stylistically sang more like the latter. He also studied in India, where he collected material from a number of musicians. Another important singer was Ustad Sheida, a studnt of Ustad Ghulam Husein who also studied in India. His father was Ustad Ghorban Ali, the principal *rubāb* player at the radio station in the 1940s. Sheida was killed in a car crash in Kabul in the 1960s.

On one occasion these four *ustād*s were apparently sent to India by King Nadir Shah to make some gramophone recordings. On the record labels they were styled, in English, Master Nabi Gol and Master Sheida, and as Professor Qasem and Professor Ghulam Husein, in recognition of their relative ranking (Ustad Mashal Ghori, personal communication).

Kabuli art music is brought to Herat

In the 1920s both Herat and Kabul experienced a flowering of urban music. In the following decade the Kabuli style replaced the Persian style in Herat and the *dastgāh*s fell into disuse. An early intimation of the imminent change was the importation of the first harmonium, introduced by the entrepreneurial Haidar Pineh, who received many invitations to perform on it. As the harmonium became more common in Herat, the *chahārtār* lost favour. This shift of interest was accompanied by a change of tonal system, away from a 'Persian scale', embodied in the fretting of the *chahārtār*, with neutral seconds, to the 'Indian scale' of the harmonium, with twelve semitones to the octave. The latter was not new, for the fretting of the *rubāb* already gave approximately this scale. The adoption of the harmonium would have given the *rubāb* a new importance, and the combination of singer with harmonium, *rubāb*, and tabla soon became the standard ensemble for urban music in Herat. The repertory is not exactly clear; in part it certainly comprised old Herati and Iranian songs. Kashmiri songs were also said to have been popular at this time.

In the early 1930s Kabuli musicians occasionally found their way to Herat, and two or three singers from India also visited the city while on tour in Afghanistan. Once word got around that a visiting singer was in the city he would be invited to perform at parties of music lovers and would be well paid for his services. Such visiting singers must have created an interest in this novel music, without staying long enough to teach the Heratis how to play it. As we have already seen, it is likely that the phonograph was important. Byron describes the hotel in Herat where he stayed in 1933:

The second and third [downstairs rooms] are filled with marble-topped tables, and hung with European scenes painted on glass by an Indian familiar with the early numbers of the *Illustrated London News*. Here too are Seyid Mahmud's desk, a cabinet gramophone on legs from Bombay, and a pile of Indian records.   (Byron 1937:113)

The Heratis were becoming more familiar with the sounds of music from Kabul and India; the next stage was to learn how to play it.

During the 1930s, Ustad Nabi Gol resided in Herat for a year or two. He was an old friend of Ghulam Faruq Usman, a member of the Mohammadzai (royal) clan who was appointed Governor of Herat in 1935. Adamec (1973) notes that Ghulam Faruq was a great favourite of the Prime Minister, and 'keen on road and building development'. He was Herat's Governor for about three years, and was remembered as a great lover of music. Ustad Nabi Gol decided to visit his old patron in Herat, no doubt knowing that Ghulam Faruq would be generous with employment, and would introduce him to Herat's wealthy landowners and merchants. He made three visits to Herat, each time staying for some months. On his first two visits he brought musicians from Kabul as his accompanists, but on his third visit he came without them, for by this time he had students in Herat who were competent to play with him. These were the two elder sons of Mohammad Hasan, already mentioned as the tabla player with Rahim Khushkhan and Haidar Pineh. The elder son was Chacha Ghulam, who played the tabla, and the younger was Amir Jan, the singer and harmonium player, who played the *rubāb* as Nabi Gol's accompanist. In Herat Nabi Gol played for the Governor and also for the wedding celebrations and other parties of the richer Heratis, following the Governor's example in patronising this national music. This was the time of the construction of the new city, when powerful nationalist sentiments were being expressed in Afghanistan.

Through this training, Amir Jan and his brothers, and later their sons, collectively calling themselves Khushnawazha (The Good Players), were able to establish themselves as the *ustād*s of music in Herat, performing the art music of Kabul, vocal and instrumental. For many years they were the most successful musicians in the city and were the source of much of the information given in this study.

Radio broadcasting and the emergence of Afghan popular music

Radio broadcasting from Kabul has been of crucial importance in the creation and dissemination of Afghan popular music. The radio station seems to have taken over from the royal court as the main patron of musicians and sponsor of new developments in music. The following facts are derived from Gregorian (1969) and Qasim Reshtia, (personal communication). Radio broadcasting in Afghanistan was initiated in 1925, with a 5 k.w. transmitter, during the reign of Amanullah. For a few years radio achieved a small breakthrough, with an estimated 1,000 receiving sets in Kabul in 1928. After the reaction against social reform and modernism that followed the deposition of Amanullah in 1929, when the radio station was destroyed, there was no serious attempt to resume radio broadcasts until 1936. Radio Kabul began experimental broadcasts with a 20 k.w. transmitter in 1939 and was officially opened in the following year. The stated aims of the radio station were to spread the message of the Holy Koran, to reflect the national spirit, to perpetuate the treasures of Afghan folklore, and to contribute to public education. The government saw radio as the best and quickest way to inform the population of its policies and development programmes. Broadcasting was seriously hampered during World War II by difficulties in obtaining new equipment or spares from Germany. An effective broadcasting service that could be received in most parts of the country was not established until the late 1940s. In the early days, ownership of radio receivers was very limited, and to ensure the dissemination of radio broadcasts, receiver appliances were set up in a number of cities, including Herat, linked to loudspeaker systems in the main streets. They broadcast the news, music, and other programmes. This project was launched in 1940 and completed by 1946 (Reshtia, personal communication).

Afghan popular music originated partly in response to the need to create a music suitable for radio broadcasting. In the absence of accounts from the actual originators of the new music, only the broad outlines of the process can be discerned. The new music was created through a mixing of elements already present in Afghanistan, as we shall see in chapter 6. This development took place with the assistance of the *ustāds*, the descendants of the Indian court musicians. Their knowledge of Hindustani music theory and terminology must have been very important in organising small ensembles and large orchestras at the radio station. The *ustāds* had high standards of performance, and played a key role in training musicians, both professionals and amateurs. The early days of radio broadcasting were accompanied by an unprecedented wave of enthusiasm on the part of amateur musicians, especially singers from the educated middle, and even upper, classes of Afghanistan. Musicians from the provinces were recruited, as were barber-musicians from the Kucheh Kharabat. The *ustāds* can be likened to 'foreign experts' who had the technical expertise necessary to help the Afghans 'upgrade' and 'improve' their music. In this way their role anticipated that of American, Russian and other music advisers brought to the station in the 1960s, and their contribution seems to have been much more acceptable to the Afghans and successful in a way the efforts of the Western experts was not (see Slobin 1974:244-5).

The *rubāb* player Ustad Mohammad Omar was a good example of a musician trained within the Hindustani tradition and brought into service in the creation of popular music. Ustad Mohammad Omar was not a descendant of Indian court musicians but a barber-musician who trained in Hindustani vocal music with Ustad Qasem. He became the principal *rubāb* player at Radio Kabul in the early 1950s. Given the prestige of the *rubāb* as the national instrument, and the fact that it epitomises the sound of Afghan music, Ustad Mohammad Omar became one of the best known and most highly regarded musicians in the land. Notwithstanding his expertise in the field of instrumental art music, he proved an inexhaustible fount of instrumental compositions for popular music. When a regional singer brought a new song to record at the radio station, Mohammad Omar would often compose the instrumental section (*naghmeh*) for the song on the spot. Over the years he also composed many light instrumental pieces for solo *rubāb* or instrumental ensemble. He made certain structural modifications to the bridge of the *rubāb* and perfected the right hand technique called *simkāri* (see chapter 5). He led various ensembles at the radio station and was involved in music education, teaching other musicians at Radio Kabul and training over the years hundreds of amateur *rubāb* players who attended classes held in his house in the Kucheh Kharabat.

The history of the radio station and its personnel, and of changes in the kinds of popular music produced, is a complex matter. In the 1960s the radio station moved to new buildings placed between the city and the airport. Its name was changed from Radio Kabul to Radio Afghanistan (which is how we shall refer to it henceforth). Slobin (1974) provides a useful essay on the significance of radio music, 'one of the few manifestations of an emerging pattern of national values and expression that may eventually comprise a pan-ethnic, distinctively Afghan society' (*ibid.*: 248). Certain aspects of the activities of the radio station in the 1970s are described by Baily (1981b). Madadi (n.d.) provides valuable information, especially regarding what he terms 'the golden age of Afghan music' in the 1950s and early 1960s, when the budget was large and there was strong support for amateur music making.

Changes in the *dutār* of Herat

Once the radio station was operating, in the late 1940s or early 1950s, popular music had a profound impact in Herat. The popular music repertory was learned by those urban professional musicians already playing in the Kabuli style, who included popular radio songs in their performances at wedding parties to satisfy the demands of their audience. There was also a response on the part of amateur musicians, which is well shown by the changes that took place in the Herati *dutār* between 1950 and 1965 (Baily 1976, 1977, 1985). The essential facts are as follows.

Three kinds of *dutār* were to be found in the Herat region in the 1970s, with two, three and fourteen strings, the latter two being recent innovations. In its original two-stringed form the *dutār* was played by rural amateurs, both as an accompaniment to singing and in instrumental pieces. The two stringed *dutār* was also found in Iranian Khurasan, in Badghis and Ghor, and probably further afield. The intervals given by its system of fretting are considered in chapter 4. By about 1950 certain changes had been made to the morphology of the *dutār* in Herat: the number of strings was increased to three (giving one melody string and two drones); the material of the strings was changed from gut to thin steel; the number and placement of frets was changed to give a 'gapped chromatic scale' of whole-tones and semitones; and a metal plectrum worn like a thimble on the first finger of the right hand was now used to strum the instrument (see Baily 1976:34–7 for further details). As these structural changes took place the *dutār* was adopted as an instrument of urban music making.

The changes in the *dutār* and in its use clearly show the impact of Kabuli popular radio music in Herat. Exposure to popular song melodies in modes such as *Pāri* and *Kesturi* accounts for the change of fretting on the three stringed *dutār*, since the notes required for these modes were not given by the scale of the two stringed *dutār*. The metallic and droney sound of the Afghan *tanbur* (which was often heard on the radio) may account for the switch to steel strings and the addition of the second drone string. The metallic sound was preferred for its loudness and clarity; the metal plectrum was certainly adopted from the *tanbur*. The broadcasting of popular music from Kabul stimulated a new interest in music making and a new demand for live music in Herat, which attracted *dutār* players from the villages into the city to play in certain teahouses on market days. In the city the rural *dutār* players encountered the new radio music and modified their instruments in order to play it. They brought their rural repertory to the city and popularised it there, while they took back to the villages the latest radio songs and ideas about *dutār*-playing technique.

The names of many of this generation of three stringed *dutār* players of the 1950s were recalled for me in the city, amongst them:

Mama Ghani (Bacheh Arbab Akhtar), from Shalbafan
Ghulam Mohammad, from Baranabad
Nur Ahmad, from Gozareh
Golak Ghulam Mohammad, from Gazer Gah
Ghulam Ghaus, from Sufian
Ghulam Mohammad, from Karukh
Mojer, from Adraskan
Abdur Rahman Sarkhati, from Badghis
Amin, from Kaleh Mashau
Ayub Gong, from Urdu Khan.

All these men came from villages. Mama Ghani and Ghulam Mohammad were still active as *dutār* players in the 1970s. From about 1950 to the late 1960s the teahouse was the stronghold of the *dutār* in the city, a venue for the poorer classes to make music. Many teahouses kept a three stringed *dutār*, which the customers could play or hear performed by the proprietor, on the premises. Some became meeting places for *dutār* players and were run by men who were themselves enthusiasts. A particularly important teahouse, which seems to have been at the centre of developments taking place to the *dutār*, was run by Mama Ghani at the Darwazeh Qandahar, a bazaar area for villagers visiting the city. The teahouse as a suitable place for *musical* entertainment, as opposed to the more traditional storytellers or *Shāh Nāmeh* singers, seems to have been a new idea in Herat. Perhaps this was an attempt to copy teahouse music making in northern Afghanistan, as described by Slobin (1976). Visits by Heratis to the forty-days Tulip Festival held at the time of New Year (21 March) in the northern city of Mazar-e Sharif may well have familiarised them with Uzbek-Tajik teahouse music. Melodies for singing quatrains and instrumental dance pieces from the north were adopted in Herat, but whereas in the north the *dambura* was the basic instrument of teahouse music, in Herat the three stringed *dutār* fulfilled this role. The *zirbaghali*, a hand drum which became associated with the *dutār*, seems to have become common in Herat at about this time, again possibly adopted from the north. The *dutār* bands in the 1970s were an augmentation of this kind of teahouse group, usually with several fourteen stringed *dutār*s, *zirbaghali*, and optional harmonium or *rubāb*. Their repertory still contained a large amount of Mazari material.

By 1965 a larger type of *dutār* with fourteen strings had been devised. Most of the added strings were sympathetic strings with tuning pegs along the side of the neck. Karim Dutari, a musician from Herat who worked for many years at Radio Afghanistan, was generally credited with the invention of this instrument (Baily 1976:49–53). However, later fieldwork revealed that even before Karim Dutari went to Kabul, people had tried fitting side-strings to the *dutār*. Several reliable informants said that the true originator of the fourteen stringed *dutār* was an amateur *dutār* player, Zia Moalem, a native of Herat, and at that time a school teacher in the city. This was confirmed by Zia when I met him in Kabul in 1976. Although Zia may have originated the idea, Karim perfected the design after he had joined the *Orkestrā-ye Meli* (the 'National Orchestra') at the radio station as a three stringed *dutār* player.

Karim explained (*ibid.*: 49) the reasons why he was led to develop the fourteen stringed *dutār*: he wanted to play it punteado (single string style) but for this to be effective the loudness of the instrument had to be increased, and it was necessary to add more frets to extend its pitch range. Karim, probably motivated by the desire to claim the prestige of an Indian instrument for his invention, maintained he was inspired by the example of the Indian sitar. In reality he was probably guided by the example of the *tanbur*, a large long-necked lute with sympathetic strings, and certainly Karim's own rather individual right hand technique for the *dutār* was very like that used by *tanbur* players, the upstroke being the main stroke (Baily 1977:294). In practical terms, however, we must consider the Afghan *rubāb* and not the sitar or *tanbur* as the most important model for the fourteen stringed *dutār*, for this was an instrument that Karim actually played. Within a short time of joining the staff of Radio Afghanistan, Karim began learning the *rubāb* with Ustad Mohammad Omar. One of the principles that guided his experiments with the *dutār* was that it should be capable of playing the solo instrumental *rubāb* repertory that he was learning: *naghmehā-ye kashāl*, *naghmehā-ye klāsik* and *naghmehā-ye radiu*. This also required the development of right hand techniques to emulate the drone patterns used by *rubāb* players and the raising of the shortest sympathetic string by a small protuberance on the bridge so it could be struck in isolation (see chapter 5).

The perfection of the fourteen stringed *dutār* required certain structural modifications to the instrument. Karim Dutari worked with Joma Khan Qadir, the *rubāb* maker in Kabul, on a series of prototypes before settling on the final design. The Heratis learned about the invention of the new instrument by hearing it played over the radio from Kabul, and it may be that the prestige thus bestowed upon the fourteen stringed *dutār* explains its rapid adoption in Herat. The *dutār* makers of Herat had to examine the instrument before they were able to construct it. From the mid-1960s the fourteen stringed *dutār* became the city of Herat's principal musical instrument. The new *dutār* was played either as a solo instrument, or by a singer with *zirbaghali* accompaniment, or in a *dutār* band. It was also added to the essential core of the urban art music ensemble, singer with harmonium, *rubāb*, and tabla. The structural changes in the *dutār* reveal the process of its urbanisation and the professionalisation of the *dutār* player, as stimulated by an expansion of patronage.

Women musicians

Another very interesting development in Herat since the 1930s has been the advent of bands of women professional musicians, singing and playing the harmonium, tabla, and *dāireh*. The occurrence of women professional musicians was not without precedent; in the early part of the present century women from a barber-musician (Gharibzadeh) enclave in Pai Hisar, in the old city, were sometimes engaged as singers and dancers at women's wedding festivities.

Their only instrument was the *dāireh* (frame drum), generally used by women at weddings to accompany singing and to drum for dancing. In the 1930s an enterprising *rubāb* player called Golpasand established a women's band in Herat from amongst his own wives. He was said to have come from Sya Wushan, a large village south of the river, and it seems that he was a Chelu, a member of a small Baluch speaking tribal group, white tent itinerants, whose women were generally prostitutes, and the men pimps and musicians who played *sarinda*, *dāireh*, and *tāl* to entertain their wives' patrons (see Rao 1981 for a discussion of white tent itinerants). Golpasand bought farmland just to the north of the city, where he built a large compound (*serai*). Later his descendants and other relatives built compounds next to his, and the Kucheh Golpasandha, 'Street of the Golpasands', slowly developed as a musicians' quarter. Golpasand was married four times. Nothing was ascertained about his first wife and she perhaps had no role as a musician. His second wife, Tawus, the evidence suggests, was from the barber-musician (Gharibzadeh) enclave of Pai Hesar and perhaps had been brought up in a musician family. As Golpasand's wife she became a tabla player. Golpasand's third wife, Uzrar, had been raised as a musician. Her mother, Soghrar, played the *rubāb* and seems to have played at the court in Kabul. Uzrar brought her mother to live with her in Herat. These three women, Uzrar, harmonium, Soghrar, *rubāb*, and Tawus, tabla, and the wife of one of Golpasand's brothers, remembered simply as Madar-e Habibullah ('Habibullah's Mother'), playing *dāireh*, made up the first of Golpasand's women's bands.

Golpasand married his fourth wife, Sabo, in about 1945. She came from Shendand and her three brothers, who were barbers, moved to Herat with her, having been assured of help by Golpasand in return for their sister. Sabo was perhaps sixteen at the time, not a musician but showing promise. At first she played *dāireh* with the women's band instead of Madar-e Habibullah; later she learned tabla and harmonium. In the early 1950s Uzrar was divorced from Golpasand and departed from Herat with her mother. Sabo became band leader (*sar dasteh*), singing and playing harmonium, Tawus's daughter Negar played tabla, and Tawus *dāireh*. This band seems to have established the model for the organisation of a typical women's band, led by a woman who sang and played harmonium, with her accompanists on tabla and *dāireh*. This kind of women's group seems to have been unique to Herat. They performed popular songs from the radio repertory – the same songs as performed by male musicians – and traditional Herati songs, and they played mainly for women's wedding festivities in the city.

The subsequent proliferation of these bands in the Kucheh Golpasandha is a complex story and we need not be concerned with the details; in 1976–7 there were five bands. The bands were organised in terms of kinship groups: mother and daughters, daughters-in-law, brothers' wives, or aunts. When there was a lot of work these bands could be divided in two, and a certain amount of movement of girls from one band to another to form new combinations would then occur. Marriages amongst the Golpasandha were made to secure promising young girls to be musicians. This operated in two ways. Women who were already musicians arranged marriages for their musician daughters with husbands who were close kin and would allow them to remain in the Kucheh Golpasandha and continue working in the mother's band. Band leaders would also recruit young girls from barber-musician families as daughters-in-law. The Golpasandha differed from the rest of Herati society in that they had a strong tendency towards matrilocality.

Four of Golpasand's male descendants were also musicians, and constituted a rival family of male *sāzandeh* (hereditary professional musicians) to Amir Jan, his brother Karim, and their sons. A detailed discussion of relationships between these two families, the Khushnawazha and the Golpasandha, is given in chapter 7; here it is sufficient to mention that women in the Khushnawaz family, unlike Golpasand women, had no role as specialist performers of music or dance.

The diversity of musical phenomena in Herat

The foregoing survey of certain musical developments in Herat brings us to the time of my fieldwork. I found there to be a rich diversity of musical phenomena in Herat. Most of the categories of musician mentioned by Slobin (1976:29) could be found there, and each category was associated with a more or less distinct type of music or style of performance. By focusing on one particular type of musician, the urban male professional, and neglecting to a greater or lesser extent the others, I must inevitably arrive at a rather narrow interpretation of music in Herat. A broader approach, allowing detailed comparisons to be made between different categories, might have addressed quite different issues. I mention below some of the categories of musical phenomena *not* under detailed discussion here.

Firstly, there were the various forms of religious singing: Koranic recitation; the giving of the *azān*; the Sufi ritual known as *zikr* ('Recollection of God'), with the associated unaccompanied singing of *naʿt*s, religious and/or mystical *ghazal*s; and the *rowzeh* and *nowheh* performed by Shiahs during their Commemorations of the Matyrs. These forms of religious singing were conceptualised by Heratis as rather separate from music. As Sakata (1983: chapter 4) has demonstrated, a fundamental distinction was made in Herat between song (*āwāz*, *khāndan*) and music (*musiqi*, *sāz*). The terms *musiqi* and *sāz* referred to the organised sounds of musical instruments, particularly of melodic instruments. Indeed, both *musiqi* and *sāz* were employed as general terms for musical instruments, and *sāz* was also used as a specific name for one instrument, the *sornā*. On this basis alone, religious singing, which had no association with musical instruments, was not classifiable as music, though to the ethnomusicologist these genres are of great interest as *musical phenomena* and may be analysed in terms of the Heratis' own concepts of musical structure (e.g. scale, mode, rhythmic organisation, melody, and ornamentation). The separation of religious singing from music was most strictly observed in relation to Koranic recitation, for which a simple form was advocated in order to minimise the content of musical elements (a fact which indicates that at a more subtle level the inherently musical nature of such recitation was acknowledged).

Secondly, there was the domain of rural music, with its emphasis on the singing of quatrains (*chahārbeiti*) and *ghazal*s, sometimes within the context of story telling, possibly with *dutār* accompaniment if the singer was a man, or with the *dāireh* amongst women. There was the important category of instrumental music played on the *sornā* and *dohol* by barber-musicians (Gharibzadeh), notably for village wedding festivities, where they played dance and processional music. The village repertory consisted of two categories of group dance for men, *Atan* and *Chub Bāzi*. Each dance had its own music. The various kinds of *Atan* had names such as *Atan-e Rāsteh Qadimi*, *Atan-e Wardaki*, *Atan-e Logari*, and *Aushari*. There were also various kinds of *Chub Bāzi*, 'stick dance': *Chub Bāzi Rāsteh*, *Chub Bāzi Baluchi*, and *Chub Bazi Dālbāzā*. At more lavish village weddings a group of barber-actors might be engaged to perform the folk drama (*seil*, 'spectacle') at night, out of doors. The performance consisted of a number of short plays and involved the cooperation of *sornā* and *dohol* players, for many of the plays had specific melodies associated with them. Texts for these plays are given by Baghban (1977). The status of *sornā* and *dohol* players is discussed in chapter 7.

Thirdly, in the city there was a wealth of music making by male and female amateurs, singing and playing a variety of instruments. Men played the *dutār*, *rubāb*, harmonium, *zirbaghali*, *tanbur*, tabla, *chahārtār*, and various types of flute. Women, who probably constituted by far the largest group with practical musical expertise, played the *dāireh*, and a few also played the harmonium and *zirbaghali* (Doubleday 1982). These amateurs played mainly popular music, in private, alone or in small gatherings, for their own entertainment and for that of their friends. Some had a more public reputation as amateur musicians. A few became professional, and so moved closer to the group of musicians with whom we are primarily concerned.

In singling out professional musicians for special attention I am deliberately concentrating on one end of a continuum that extends from the strictly 'non-musical' performance of Koranic recitation to music at its 'most musical'. Both Sataka (e.g. 1983:114) and Slobin (e.g. 1972:72) have pointed out the importance of song text as against melody in Afghan music, and noted how melodic structure is inextricably tied to the form of the text. This was no doubt true of Herati rural folksong, but urban music, especially art music, could not be fully understood in Herati terms simply as a 'vehicle' for the 'delivery' of text. Music existed at one conceptual level as a domain of its own, susceptible to abstract, arithmetical, even geometrical, principles of structuring. The idea that music conforms to purely musical structural principles was expressed most clearly in the *ʿilm-e musiqi*, 'the science of music', a detailed body of music theory and terminology, known primarily to the urban male professionals. These theoretical principles are the subject of the next chapter.

4 The science of music

The ʿ*ilm-e musiqi*, 'the science of music', was the special canon of verbalised musical knowledge held by urban male musicians, especially those competent in the performance of Kabuli art music. In essence it described the melodic modes and rhythmic cycles they used. Much of the science was concerned with the two basic elements of music, *sor* and *lai*, which may be translated provisionally as 'pitch' and 'rhythm'. The elucidation of the complex semantic fields of these terms takes up much of this chapter. The science of music known in Herat had much in common with the theory of Hindustani music, from which it was undoubtedly derived, presumably via the Indian court musicians brought to Kabul in the late nineteenth century and through the adoption of Kabuli art music in Herat in the 1930s. It was a 'version' of Hindustani theory; many of the terms used were the same, applied to generally similar concepts, although certain divergences could be noted.

Knowledge of the science of music was highly skewed in its distribution. It was not a subject that was taught in school. It is probably correct to state that the only people in Herat who understood the science were a small number of male urban musicians, and amongst this group some knew much more than others. The *sāzandeh* tended to regard the science of music as something which only they knew about, part of their musical inheritance, but in some cases amateurs had also acquired this knowledge through study and performance with *sāzandeh*. Outside this group of specialists, knowledge of the science was fragmentary; a few of its terms were in common use, such as the names of certain modes, and some of its concepts more widely distributed, but overall only a handful of individuals could be regarded as speaking with any authority on the subject.

The account of the science of music given here is based largely on information collected from Amir Jan Khushnawaz, though several other musicians have assisted in building up this description. Although the science of music had a special relationship with Kabuli art music, the *sāzandeh* also used it to describe and analyse other kinds of Afghan music. The study of the ʿ*ilm-e musiqi* provides us with the appropriate language for the discussion of the music examples in chapters 5 and 6.

Sor (pitch)

The word *sor* appertained to the perceptual phenomenon of pitch and had several meanings in this respect. It was perhaps derived from the Hindi *svar*, but was also present in Persian as the verb *sorudan*, 'to sing or to play music'. As used in Herat, *sor* referred to a single sustained tone produced from a musical instrument or sung with the human voice. It was a sound with a discernible pitch. Many non-musical sounds, such as the buzzing of a bee or the creaking of a door, were said by some *sāzandeh* to have a '*sor* within them'. A number of contrasting terms were used for the two ends of the pitch continuum: *zil o bam*, 'treble/bass', *past o boland*, 'low/tall', *lok o bārik*, 'thick/thin', *bālā o pāin*, 'high, up/low, down', *pāch o boland*, 'low/high', *pāch o pur*, 'low/small'. The word *boland*, 'tall', was also used to mean 'loud' when contrasted with *tār*, 'wet', *ārām*, 'calm', 'soft' or 'comfortable', or *āhesteh*, 'slow'. In this contrast these three words meant 'quiet'.

Besides meaning a single tone, *sor* could refer to a collection of tones, with the implicit assumption that they were congruent, in the sense that they could be used together, were 'in tune' with each other; tones from which a melodic line (*āhang*) could be fashioned. Musicians liked to explain this notion of *sor* in terms of the pitches to which the side-strings of an instrument like the *rubāb* or fourteen stringed *dutār* were tuned to play in a particular mode. Here *sor* referred to the set of tones used in a piece of music – its scale. *Sor* meant 'in tune', *bi sor*, 'out of tune'.

In a closely related but still distinct sense, *sor* referred to what we might call temperament, the tuning of the musical instrument. For example, the three main strings of the *rubāb* were normally tuned in fourths, but there were alternative tunings which used a fourth and a fifth. Here a different tuning was called a different *sor*. The action of tuning an instrument was *sor kardan*. Hoerburger (1968) states that the action of strumming across the sympathetic strings on the *tanbur* is called *sor kardan* but I cannot confirm this usage; the action discussed by Hoerburger was described as *sor keshidan*, 'to pull the notes', in Herat.

The notion of *sor* as a scale leads on to the question of tonal system and of the intervals used in playing music in Herat. This issue is complicated by the fact that two tonal systems were known to Heratis: a tonal system with Persian intervals (*pardeh Irāni*) and a system based on Indian intervals (*pardeh Hindi*). Since the 1930s the latter has tended to replace the former, but in the 1970s the two systems to some degree still existed side by side and were sometimes combined in the same performance. The two tonal systems were associated with different modal systems, with certain modes common to both. Of the two, it was the Indian system which was clearer and easier to discuss.

Pardeh Hindi (Indian intervals)

This tonal system was called *Hindi*, 'Indian', or *filmi*, 'of the films', the films in question being Indian. I have even heard it called *sādeh*, 'simple', in contrast to the complexity of the Iranian tonal system with its intervals of various sizes. *Pardeh Hindi*, the 'Indian tonal system', was based on a division of the octave into twelve approximately equal intervals. This was the system inherent in the tuning of the harmonium and in the manner of fretting the *rubāb* and the fourteen stringed *dutār*.

In non-musical language *pardeh* was a common word for 'curtain', while in musical terminology the word had several meanings. It referred to a fret on instruments such as the *dutār* and *rubāb*; these were movable and consisted of gut, nylon, or wire tied round the neck. *Pardeh* was also the word for the finger-holes on the *sornā* and for the digitals of the harmonium. By extension, *pardeh* also referred to a single tone, to the sound produced from a fret, finger-hole, or digital. In this sense *pardeh* could mean the same as *sor*. *Pardeh* also meant 'note'; a musician could remark of an error he had just made: '*yak pardeh qalat shod*', 'one note was wrong'. The word *pardeh* had another, rather different, meaning, and that was for an interval of a particular size between two tones. The interval of *yak pardeh*, 'one *pardeh*', corresponded to our whole-tone (major second), while the smaller *nim pardeh*, 'half a *pardeh*',

Sor (pitch)

corresponded to our semitone (minor second). Occasional reference was also made to an even smaller interval, the *nim nim pardeh* or *rob pardeh*, the 'quarter *pardeh*' or quarter-tone, as discussed later under *pardeh Irāni*. We can see now that the term *pardeh* translates rather well into English as 'tone', with its dual connotations of a tone as a single pitch and as an interval of a whole-tone.

I never heard an explanation of why there should be twelve *sor* to the octave, for example, in terms of string lengths or cosmological relationships, and this division has to be accepted as one of the 'givens' of the music. The same basic division is employed in Hindustani music (Jairazbhoy 1971:32-3). As in Hindustani music a system of note names was in use which implied a basic scale of 2212221 *nim pardeh* intervals. The names of the tones were *Karj*, *Rekap*, *Gandār*, *Madam*, *Pancham*, *Diwāt*, and *Nikot* – very close to the names used in Hindustani music: *Shadja*, *Rishabh*, *Gāndhār*, *Madhyam*, *Pancham*, *Dhaivat*, and *Nishad*. *Karj* and *Pancham* (tonic and fifth) were thought of as invariable, while *Rekap*, *Gandār*, *Madam*, *Diwāt*, and *Nikot* could take *komal* (flattened) or *tiwra* (sharpened) forms. In cases where the names of the tones were actually sung, the syllables *Sa*, *Re*, *Ga*, *Ma*, *Pa*, *Da*, and *Ni* were used, as in North India. This normally applied only to *klāsik* ('classical music', i.e. Hindustani genres such as *khyāl*), though there were instances of popular songs where these syllables had been used. When musicians were working things out for themselves they might use these syllables, but for pedagogical purposes, to avoid confusions between *komal* and *tiwra* forms of a tone, Afghan practice gave each of the twelve tones a distinct label, as shown in figure 1.

Sa Ra Re Ga Ge Ma Me Pe Da De Na Ni Sá

Figure 1 Note names and their notation

Because it is unambiguous this is the system we shall adopt here. Musicians in Herat were aware of the existence of other notational systems. In Iran, I was told, they used Do Re Mi, a system also known to a few musicians at Radio Afghanistan who had been under the tutelage of Western advisers. These foreign experts had also succeeded in teaching Western staff notation to a small number of radio musicians.

The octave relationship was clearly recognised by this tonal system. When speaking of two tones standing an octave apart, such as *Sa* and *Sá* the Heratis spoke of low *Sa* as *Sa pāch*, and high *Sa* as *Sa pur*. Amir Jan once explained the concept of the octave to me in terms of the days of the week. *Sa pāch* he described as being like Friday (the day of rest). Each successive day of the week corresponded to *Re*, *Ge*, *Ma*, *Pe*, *De*, and *Ni*, and then it was Friday again, but another Friday, and so it was *Sa* again, but another *Sa*, *Sa pur*. Curiously, this explanation is similar to the Christian ecclesiastical meaning of the word octave, being the eighth day after a religious festival.

The English word *okteif* was also sometimes heard for octave, a term that may well have come into use with English-speaking music instructors at the radio station. There seemed to be no Persian term connoting octave, which agrees with the fact that the concept of a scale 'framed' by the octave is not an important organising principle in Persian music (Farhat 1965:36). The Hindustani musical term *saptak* was sometimes used in Herat; when musicians talked about one tone being the *saptak* of another they meant it was an octave above or below. The *rubāb* was spoken of as having three *saptak*s, which were *Sa*, *Sá* and *Sã*, spanning a range of two octaves. This was rather different to the meaning of *saptak* in Hindustani theory, where it connotes the scale of seven notes within an octave (Jairazbhoy 1971:34). Another metaphor I heard used for the octave relationship was derived from the word *lā*, 'thickness'. A *rubāb* player once compared two tones an octave apart to two strings, one of *yak lā*, 'one thickness', and the other of *du lā*, 'double thickness', sounding an octave lower. It is possible that a scientific principle relating to the laws of vibrating strings was being invoked here.

Melodic modes based on *pardeh Hindi* (Indian intervals)

Several terms were used for melodic mode, the most usual being *maqām* and *rāg*. In one sense these words were synonymous; according to the folk explanation, in the old days one said *maqām* and now one said *rāg*. Both words had other meanings, too. *Maqām* could refer to an instrumental piece (more usually called *naghmeh*), and certain instrumental pieces had the word *maqām* in their title, such as '*Maqām-e Jal*', '*Maqām* of the Lark', or '*Maqām-e Āb o Shar*', 'the *Maqām* of the Waterfall'. *Maqām* suggested a Persian mode, such as *Maqām-e Rāst* or *Maqām-e Now Ruz Sabā*. The term *rāg* might connote specifically Indian modes, that is, modes of the Hindustani musical system, but this could give rise to certain ambiguities. The mode called *Talang* has been described to me as a '*rāg Irāni*' (Iranian mode) and an instrumental piece played on the *sornā* as being in a '*rāg Herāti*' (Herati mode), whereas it was also claimed that the mode *Kesturi* was not a *rāg* precisely because it was not mentioned in the treatises on Hindustani music and could not therefore be identified as a Hindustani mode. In addition, '*rāg*' could also refer to the vocal art music genre of *khyāl*, so that *rāg khāndan* meant 'to sing *khyāl*'. *Rāg zadan*, 'to play a *rāg*', could refer to the playing of a *naghmeh-ye klāsik*, or even a *naghmeh-ye radiu*, an instrumental piece originally composed for radio orchestra and loosely based on a *rāg*. The term *dastgāh* was used by a few musicians for mode, implying a Persian mode such as *Shur* or *Chahārgāh*. Some amateur musicians with little knowledge of the science of music used the word *sor* to mean mode, rather than simply a scale. This usage was probably correct for them, for such musicians did not have the *sāzandeh*'s fully developed concept of mode, which entailed certain melodic configurations in addition to scale.

Another term sometimes used in talking about modes was *tāt* (presumably the Hindi *thāt*), which represented a superoridinate grouping of related modes. I was told that *Yemen*, *Bihāg*, and *Kumāj* were all in the *Bilawal Tāt*, or that *Kumāj* and *Bihāg* were in the *Des Tāt*. Many musicians appeared to believe that there were six *tāt*s, but Karim Dutari once explained to me that according to his *sangit* (encyclopedia of *rāg*s) there were ten *tāt*s, with several thousand possible *rāg*s in each. Karim Dutari's *sangit* was a small book written in Urdu and published in India which contained details of 157 *rāg*s and 15 *tāl*s (rhythmic cycles). There were clear notions here of a hierarchical classification of modes, as in the statement '*az hasht rāg bālā nist*', 'there are no more than eight *rāg*s', meaning no more than eight parent *rāg*s. There was a concept of 'distance' between modes, so that two modes that were closely related were spoken of as *nazdik*, 'near' or 'close', or *pahlu*, 'side by side', while two less closely related modes were termed *dur*, 'far'. A common metaphor invoked with respect to the taxonomy of modes was that of a tree with many branches. This was also a dynamic metaphor because it

Sor (pitch)

could be said that new branches were always growing, and so it was with music, developments were always taking place. A simpler, and perhaps more useful, way of classifying modes defined two basic *rāgs*: *Bairmai* and *Yemen*. In *Bairami* all those tones that could take alternate forms were *komal* (*Ra, Ga, Ma, Da, Na*), while in *Yemen* they were *tiwra* (*Re, Ge, Me, De, Ni*).

The concept of mode involved firstly a scale, a *sor*. Beyond that it consisted of an ascending scale, the *raft* ('went') or *ārui* (see Hindi *āroh*), and the *āmad* ('came') or *amrui* (see Hindi *avroh*). Tonal material was thought of as ascending in a series of steps (*zineh bā zineh*, 'step by step') away from a tonal centre to the octave above, and then returning to that tonal centre. In this respect Herati ideas were similar to Hindustani theory and quite unlike Persian notions of scale, which conceive of a finalis with steps of varying intervals above and/or below it, usually within the overall ambitus of a tetrachord or pentachord (Farhat 1965.). The *raft* and *āmad* could use five, six or seven tones (*sor*) and a mode could have a different number of *sor* in its *raft* and *āmad*. There was considerable use of additional tones in some of the modes, which were regarded as not being part of the *raft* and *āmad* but as being added for *shirini*, 'sweetness'. To some extent these additional features of the mode could be expressed in a more complex form of the *raft* and *āmad*, but the full exposition of the character of a mode could only occur in that expression in free rhythm known as *shakl*, which approximately corresponded to the Arab notion of *taqsim* and the Indian concept of *ālāp*. (A fuller explanation of the concept of *shakl* can be found in chapter 5:68.)

In deriving a mode from a scale, certain tonal functions were discerned. The most important of these was the concept of tonal centre, *karj*, described as the *markaz*, 'centre', or *jā-ye 'istgāh*, 'the stopping place'. I was offered various colourful explanations of the role of *karj*: for example, this note was compared with the President of Afghanistan; whatever went on in the country (i.e. in the music) was eventually referred back to the President. In most modes the tonal centre was *Sa*, and amongst Herati *sāzandeh* it was standard practice to take D on the harmonium as *karj*.

In certain modes *karj* (the tonal centre) lay not on *Sa* but on another tone. In the modes of *Pāri* and *Kausieh* the fourth, *Ma*, was *karj*, while in *Kesturi*, *karj* was the fifth, *Pe*. In these transpositions the tonal centre did not become *Sa*; the note names were not shifted up in relation to the harmonium keyboard or the finger-board on the *rubāb*. Again, to accommodate the vocal ranges of different singers – boys were said to sing from *karj* (*Sa*) while men sang from *Pancham* (*Pe*) – a principle of transposition was employed in which scales were moved about within the tonal framework. In talking about such transpositions one said that the position of *karj* had changed, thus '*karj Rekap shod*' meant that *Rekap* had become the tonal centre, an upward shift of a major second, while '*karj Pancham shod*' meant that *Pancham* had become the tonal centre, a shift up of a fifth. In these transpositions the system of note names was again unaltered. There seemed to be no verb meaning 'to modulate'; one had to express the idea as above. One reason given for why the intervals of *pardeh Hindi* should all be the same size was that this allowed for transposition.

Other tones within a *sor* were identified as the *wādi* and *samwādi*, terms again clearly borrowed from India (compare Hindi *vādi* and *samvādi*). The meanings of these terms were variously explained to me as tones that were used a lot, tones that were used for ending phrases or for pausing on, and crucial tones that served to distinguish two modes that were perceived as being very close. Other kinds of *wādi* were also sometimes mentioned, such as *anuwādi* and *diwādi*. But while these terms might be bandied about, no great importance was attached to them. On occasions when I asked Amir Jan what the *wādi* of a particular mode might be, he played through some phrases of the mode, or sang them to himself, and then made a judgement on the basis of his performance. In other words, the attachment of these labels was not part of a verbalised model of how the mode should be played, but an abstraction from performance practice.

Urban *sāzandeh* in Herat were familiar with many modes that they identified as Hindustani *rāg*s, but out of this repertory only about eight were in common use: *Bairami, Pāri, Kesturi, Kausieh, Yemen, Āsā, Kumāj,* and *Pilu*. The first three were particularly common (especially for popular music). I have discussed these modes in some detail (Baily 1981a), and argued that they represent, in part, the augmentation of Pashtun modal practice established by the *Pāri* and *Kesturi* modes, which could account for the use of *Kausieh, Yemen, Āsā, Kumāj,* and *Pilu*. The one mode that does not fit into this scheme is *Bairami*, the most common mode of all, which I suggested is derived from the old 'Persian' music of Afghanistan (*ibid*.: 36–7). The *raft* and *āmad* of each of the eight modes are shown in figure 2. Details of tonal combinations for the eight common modes are also given in Baily (*ibid*.). These have been assessed by an expert in current Hindustani music practice, who has pointed out a number of eccentric features of Amir Jan's tonal combinations, particularly with regard to *wādi* and *samwādi* notes. There is an overriding importance attached to *karj* and *pancham* as finalis points. The Afghan versions of these *rāg*s are less well profiled than their Hindustani counterparts, as though the small number of *rāg*s used could be distinguished by scale alone, rather than by tonal combinations. The concept of mode in Herat tended to stress scale type rather than characteristic tonal combinations. This is similar to the argument that in Hindustani music a *rāg* such as *Nat Bhairav*, which is the only representative of a particular scale type, tends to be relatively free (Jairazbhoy 1971:53). The Hindustani concept of *pakar*, the 'catch-phrase' of a *rāg*, was not very clearly articulated in Herat, while there was a notion of the characteristic terminating phrase. This concept is not really found in Hindustani music and resembles more closely the Iranian notion of modal exposition.

Although *sāzandeh* musicians in Herat regarded themselves as part of the world of Hindustani music, and were familiar with the Hindustani musical system, they were aware that in certain respects the modes they used differed from their presumed counterparts in Hindustani music. For one thing, they believed that certain *rag*s had different names in Afghanistan. They believed that:

Āsā in Afghanistan corresponded to	*Mānd* in India
Āsāwari	*Jaunpuri*
Multāni	*Sindhi Bhairavi*
Sorud	*Des*
Sandareh	*Bhimplāsi*

The modes that were commonly used for Afghan urban music were not generally thought of as being 'Afghan'. Only in the case of *Kesturi* and *Kausieh*, which Herati musicians believed were not represented in the Hindustani *rāg* system, did I find the explanation 'these are Afghan *rāg*s'; for all the others I found the claim that they were Indian modes, *rāghā-ye Hindi*. With the improvement of radio communication and increased ownership of tape recorders the *sāzandeh* had much greater access to music from India than they had had in the past. It was possible to buy locally produced cassette copies of a number of long-playing records of

Sor (pitch)

Figure 2   *Raft* and *āmad* of eight common modes

famous Indian musicians at music shops in Herat. It is interesting to see how the *sāzandeh* interpreted the perceived differences between the Afghan modes and the equivalent Hindustani *rāg*s. They did not try to justify themselves by saying that Afghanistan had its own individual way of doing things: they said that the Afghan practice was wrong.

While I was in Herat in 1976–7 Afghanistan's doyen of Hindustani vocal music, Ustad Sarahang, presented a weekly radio programme called '*Klāsikhā Musiqi*', intended as an educational programme, in which he talked about Hindustani vocal music, demonstrated, and performed in earnest. This series of programmes was listened to with great interest by Herati musicians. In these programmes Sarahang pointed out a number of respects in which Afghan modal practice was wrong by Indian standards and these authoritative statements were accepted as correct by my *sāzandeh* friends and relayed back to me. In one programme Sarahang explained that the *rāg* which was called *Bihāg* in Afghanistan was not, properly speaking, *Bihāg* at all, but *Bihāgra*, for some use of *Na*, the flattened seventh, was made. Just before this broadcast Amir Jan had been teaching me the *naghmeh-ye kashāl* in *Bihāg*. When I next went to see him he was keen to correct this version and obliterate the use of *Na* in his material, which he now understood to be incorrect. It was several months before I could persuade him to continue teaching me the original version, which was how he had played *Bihāg* in the past.

Pardeh Irāni (Iranian intervals)

The Indian-derived tonal system and its associated modes were considered by Heratis to be new in their city, and were said to have been introduced in the 1930s, during the governorship of Ghulam Faruq Usman, when the harmonium and *rubāb* became the dominant instruments for urban music. The new system replaced, though by no means completely, a pre-existing tonal system called *pardeh Irāni*.

The most characteristic feature of *pardeh Irāni* was the use of neutral second intervals, intermediate in size between a semitone and a whole-tone. Farhat (1965:25–7) made a detailed study of such intervals in Persian music, as given by the fretting of the Iranian *tār*, and distinguished two sizes of interval, the small neutral second of about 135 cents, and the large neutral second of about 160 cents. Farhat found the sizes of the neutral intervals to be very flexible, from 125 to 150 cents for the small neutral second and between 144 and 169 cents for the large neutral second, but in any particular case the two adjacent neutral seconds when added together gave an interval of a minor third, about 294 cents. Farhat also identified what he called a plus second, a major third decreased by a small neutral second, about 270 cents.

The use of neutral second intervals in Herat was demonstrated most clearly in the manner of fretting the two stringed *dutār*. Strobconn measurements of the fretting of seven such *dutār*s are shown in figure 3. Five of these *dutār*s were new instruments and were fretted by the instrument maker, two were in the hands of *dutār* players. This somewhat curious system of fretting, with whole-tones and semitones in the lower tetrachord and neutral seconds in the upper tetrachord, was found over quite a wide area, in Iranian Khorasan, in Herat Province, in Badghis, and in Ghor, and may have considerable antiquity.

On the *dutār* the two strings were usually tuned a fourth apart and only the first string was stopped; the second served as a continuously sounded drone. A note a fifth above the pitch of the open first string served as the usual tonal centre. The normal scale for playing the *dutār*

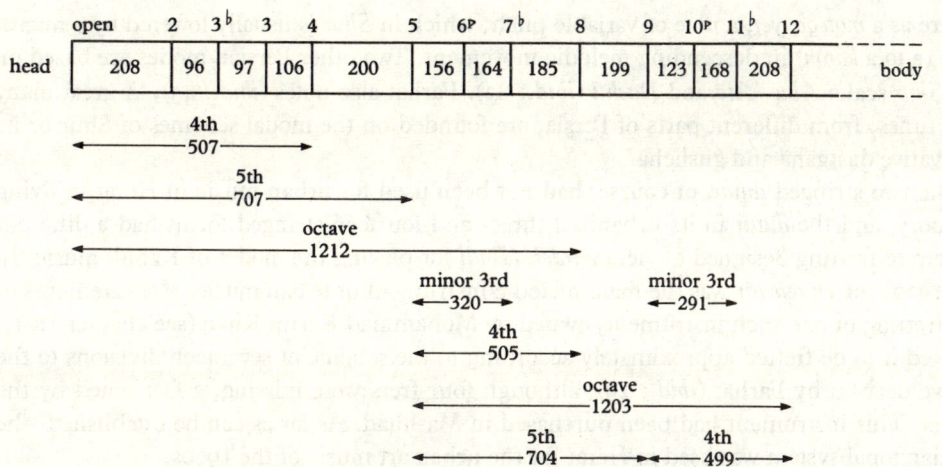

Figure 3   Fretting of the two stringed *dutār* (cents system)

extended from a whole-tone below the tonal centre to the microtonally flattened sixth above. The '*dutār* scale' is shown in figure 4. In Herat this manner of fretting was often called *pardeh rāsteh*, 'simple fretting', or 'simple intervals' (the word *pardeh* here is ambiguous), and in the 1970s urban musicians said that this *sor*, 'scale', was the scale of the Iranian mode called *Shur*, to which the Heratis later applied the name *Bairami*.

Key
M = whole-tone
n = small neutral second
N = large neutral second
TC = usual tonal centre
ꟼ = microtonally lowered note

Figure 4   The *dutār* scale

The '*dutār* scale' more or less corresponded to the intervals of *Shur* as given by Farhat (*ibid.*: 45–7) and the melodic characteristics of Herati melodies played on the two stringed *dutār* had some of the features of the *Shur* mode. The interval between the tonal centre and the second above was a small neutral second; the interval between the second above and the third above was a large neutral second; the tetrachord above the tonal centre was the focal point of melodic activity; the second below the tonal centre had importance as a starting point for ascending melodic phrases. Unlike *Shur*, the *dutār* mode did not employ the fifth above the tonal centre as a *moteqayyer*, a note of variable pitch, which in *Shur* is usually lowered by a microtone (a to a *koron*) in descending melodic movement. Two other Persian modes are based on the *Shur* scale: *Abu-ʿAtā* and *Dashti* (*ibid.*: 82). Farhat also notes (*ibid.*: 45), 'A great many folk tunes, from different parts of Persia, are founded on the modal schemes of Shur or its derivative dastgāhā and gushehā.'

The two stringed *dutār*, of course, had not been used for urban music in Herat in living memory, and the *dutār* in its urbanised three- and fourteen-stringed forms had a different system of fretting designed to yield *pardeh Hindi* for playing the modes of Kabuli music. In the 1920s the *chahārtār* was the main melodic instrument of urban music. Measurements of the fretting of one such instrument, owned by Mohammad Karim Khan (see chapter 1:21), showed it to be fretted approximately according to the scheme of seventeen divisions to the octave derived by Farhat (*ibid.*: 29), although four frets were missing, a fact noted by the owner. This instrument had been purchased in Mashhad. As far as can be established, the Persian tonal system was used in Herat for the urban art music of the 1920s.

Correspondences between Persian and Kabuli modes

Although Persian *dastgāh* music received virtually no public performance in Herat in the 1970s, Heratis continued to draw on Iranian popular music for a substantial part of their popular music repertory, though they could no longer produce the correct intervals on their instruments. In the process of adaptation they perceived correspondences between certain Persian modes and the modes of Kabuli music, once they had allowed for octave transpositions (common in Afghan musical thinking), the flattening of small neutral seconds to semitones, and the sharpening of large neutral seconds to whole-tones and plus seconds to minor thirds. Three such cases will be discussed: *Shur* and *Bairami*, *Chahārgāh* and *Beiru*, *Zaoul* and *Talang*.

In the 1970s *Bairami* was by far the most commonly used mode for urban music in Herat. A number of musicians told me that the old name for *Bairami* was *Shur* and that *Bairami* and *Shur* were almost the same, at least in terms of their scale (*sor*). The main difference was that while certain neutral seconds were found in the scale of *Shur*, *Bairami* was composed only of whole-tones and semitones. The scales of the two modes are shown in figure 5. The intervals for *Shur* are taken from Farhat (1965:45–6) and those for *Bairami* are as given by Amir Jan.

Bairami was a mode that did not 'fit' neatly onto the *rubāb*, and was usually played in the transpositions called *Bairami Rekap*, *Gandār* or *Pancham* (see Baily 1981a:31–2). In order to play *Bairami* with a more '*Shur* like' intonation on the *rubāb*, in the 1960s Amir Jan added an extra fret to his instrument, as shown in figure 6. The small interval between the first fret and this new fret was called by Amir Jan *nim nim pardeh*, 'half a semitone', or *rob pardeh*, a 'quarter-tone'. This small interval was never used by itself but was always added to the semitone (*nim pardeh*) below to yield a small neutral second, giving the scale shown in figure 7, a form of *Bairami Gandār*. One might expect to find this interval called a *seh rob pardeh*, 'three-quarter tone', but I have never heard this expression. Amir Jan told me that he had added this extra fret at a time when the Herati amateur singer Kholu Shauqi, who specialised in Iranian and Herati popular songs, often sang with his band at wedding parties. He wanted to reproduce on the *rubāb* the intervals Kholu sang. The interval given by the extra fret was a rather small neutral second, somewhere between 125 and 135 cents.

Sor (pitch)

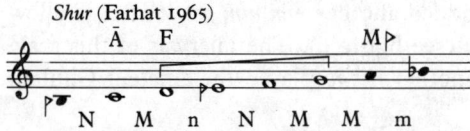

Shur (Farhat 1965)

Bairami

Key
 M = whole-tone
 m = semitone
 N = large neutral second
 n = small neutral second
 F = finalis
 Ā = *āqāz*
 M♭ = *moteqayyer*
 ♭ = microtonally lowered note

Figure 5   *Shur* and *Bairami*

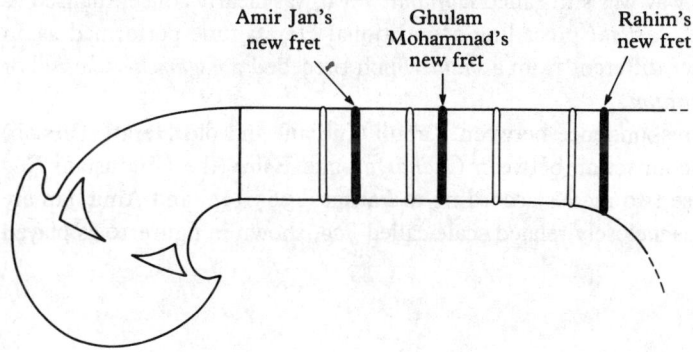

Figure 6   Extra frets on the *rubāb*

Key
 M = whole-tone
 N = large neutral second
 n = small neutral second
 F = finalis
 ♯ = microtonally raised note

Figure 7   *Bairami Gandār* with *pardeh Irāni*

Amir Jan's son Rahim, the *rubāb* player, later added another *nim nim pardeh* fret to allow *Bairami Pancham* to be played with *pardeh Irāni* (see figure 6). The intervals of this scale are shown in figure 8. In 1977 I observed that another *rubāb* player, the amateur Ghulam

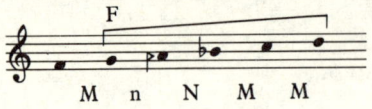

Key
M = whole-tone
N = large neutral second
n = small neutral second
F = finalis
♭ = microtonally lowered note

Figure 8 *Bairami Pancham* with *pardeh Irāni*

Mohammad Mestari, after a stay of several months in Iran, had added yet another *nim nim pardeh* fret to enable him to play *Bairami* from *karj* (*Sa*) with the appropriate neutral seconds (see figure 6). These three extra frets tied by the Heratis would in fact allow the *rubāb* to render the scale of seventeen intervals to the octave required for Persian *dastgāh* music. The *Bairami* scale altered in this way was still called *Bairami*, yet it was clearly conceptualised as separate from *Rāg Bairami*. A *shakl* preceding a traditional Herati tune performed as an instrumental piece was rather different from a *shakl* which preceded a *naghmeh-ye kashāl* or *naghmeh-ye klāsik* in *Rāg Bairami*.

A second example of correspondence between Kabuli (Indian) and old Herati (Persian) modes was manifest in the connection between *Chahārgāh* and *Beiru* (the Hindustani *Rāg Bhairav*). The scales of these two modes according to Farhat (1965:115) and Amir Jan are shown in figure 9. There was a closely related scale called *Jog*, shown in figure 10 as played

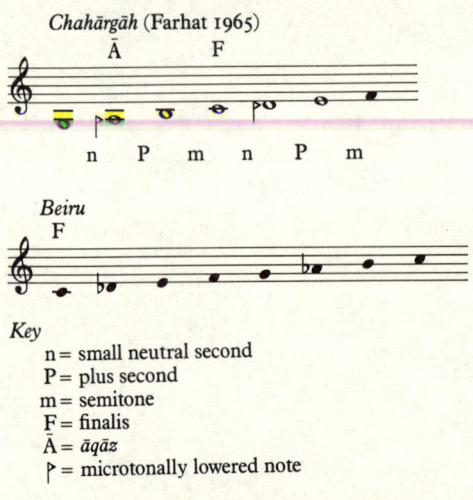

Key
n = small neutral second
P = plus second
m = semitone
F = finalis
Ā = *āqāz*
♭ = microtonally lowered note

Figure 9 *Chahārgāh* and *Beiru*

Figure 10   *Jog* from *Rekap*

from *Rekap* on the *dutār*. The tonal material of *Jog* differed from *Chahārgāh/Beiru* only with respect to the seventh degree of the scale, which was in the *komal* (flattened) form in *Jog*. *Jog* was the second most common scale for Herati music. It was also sometimes used for Iranian popular songs. The central tetrachord (E, F, G sharp, A) was a common scale for religious singing.

Some musicians associated *Jog* with *Chahārgāh* but the Persian scale that most closely resembles *Jog* is *Homāyun*. I found the name *Homāyun* was largely unknown in Herat, except by *aficionados* of Persian art music like Mohammad Karim. In any case, *Jog* was not regarded by *sāzandeh* as a fully-fledged mode with a distinct *raft* and *āmad*; it was not a *rāg* or *maqām*, but simply a *sor*, a set of tones, a scale. In fact, *Jog* could be rendered as a mode, for it was perfectly possible to play a *shakl* in *Jog*.

A third example of overlap occurred with *Zaoul* and *Talang* (Hindustani *Rāg Tilang*). A few old Herati songs and modern popular songs from Iran used a scale which Herati musicians identified as being like *Rāg Talang*. *Rāg Talang* was occasionally heard in Herat for *ghazal*s and for certain instrumental pieces played on the *rubāb*. The old name for this mode in Herat was *Zaoul*. Rahim Khushnawaz, the *rubāb* player, once gave me the *raft* and *āmad* for *Zaoul* shown in figure 11. This can hardly be correct because in *Zaoul* the note *Gandar* served as the tonal centre (*markaz*), and the *sor* is perhaps better written as it appears in figure 12.

Figure 11   *Raft* and *āmad* of *Zaoul*

Figure 12   Scale of *Zaoul*

The name *Zaoul* was probably a Herati transformation of the world *Zābol*. In Persian music, *Zābol* is a *gusheh* that appears in both *Dastgāh Chahārgāh* and *Dastgāh Segāh* (ibid.: 105-6, 120). *Zābol* in *Segāh* is closer to the scale of *Zaoul*. I have not had the opportunity to trace the Iranian originals of the popular songs which the Heratis attribute to the *Zaoul/Talang* mode. But the mode in question is perhaps *Segāh* itself, a frequently used mode of popular music in Iran, differing only slightly from *Zābol* in terms of tonal organisation (the difference lies in the note identified as *shāhed*, 'witness').

From the above discussion it is evident that the Heratis employed two tonal and modal systems in their music. *Pardeh Hindi* and the Kabuli modes represented, so to speak, the 'official system'; *pardeh Irāni* and certain Iranian modes constituted an unofficial system which did not really have a place in the science of music invoked by Heratis but was used in performance. The combination of the two systems was most obvious in playing Herati and Iranian songs. The instruments for accompaniment were tuned in *pardeh Hindi*, while the singer sang certain neutral seconds. For Iranian songs to be performed to the satisfaction of the Herat audience they had to be rendered with *lahjeh Herāti*. *Lahjeh* means 'accent', but when applied to music also has the connotation of 'intonation'. When the *rubāb* with modified fretting was played in the ensemble one could hear the harmonium playing semitones and whole-tones while the *rubāb* played neutral seconds. There is nothing particularly unusual about using two tonal systems simultaneously; it occurs, for example, in Western music, with the combination of just intonation and equal temperament, and in Indian music, where vocal microtones may be sung against the tempered tuning of the harmonium.

Great importance was attached by the *sāzandeh* and their associates to tuning and being in tune. The act of tuning was thought of as part of a performance. Karim Dutari once remarked, as he tuned his *dutār* before an impatient audience at a private party, 'Music has two parts, tuning and playing, and if I feel like it I'll spend all night tuning.'

Lai (rhythm)

The two words most commonly used in connection with the temporal aspect of music were *lai* and *tāl*. *Lai* would seem to have derived from the Hindi *laya*, which in Hindustani music theory means 'tempo' (Jairazbhoy 1971:29) or 'pace' (Fox Strangways 1914:241). It was a word that seemed to have only musical connotations, though there was a convergence with the Persian word *lā*, 'thickness' or 'layer', often applied to something like cloth. *Lai* referred to the phenomenon of musical metre, and to tempo. When music was said to have *lai*, it meant that it was rhythmically metred, in the sense of having a fixed pulse and accentual pattern. If music was said to be *bi lai*, 'without *lai*', it meant it was performed in free rhythm, though it might still have a rhythmic structure established by a poetic metre, as is the case with Persian *āvāz* (Tsuge 1970). The rural *chahārbeiti* style of singing quatrains in Herat was described as *bi lai* in this sense. The expression *bi lai* could also mean 'out of time', as when a technical error had been made, when the *lai* was temporarily lost. One might compare *bi lai* in this sense with *bi sor*, 'out of tune'. Amir Jan once remarked to me, '*Bi sor bāsh! Bi lai nabāsh!*' meaning 'be out of tune, don't be out of time', i.e. 'if you have to err, make sure it is not in your timing'.

The term *tāl* meant the same as *lai* in referring to musical metre, but was more appropriately used for instrumental performance than for singing. Music which was rhythmically metred could be said to be '*bā tāl-e tabla*', 'with the rhythm of the tabla', extending the idea of the quality of the sound (in strict rhythm) to the instrument that produced the rhythm, the tabla. The world *tāl* was also the name of the small cymbals formerly used in music making (chapter 2:19). *Tāl*, unlike *lai*, had no connection with the parameter of tempo, and, again unlike *lai*, referred to specific musical metres. *Gedeh*, *Mogholi*, and *Dādreh* were the three common *tāl*s for popular and traditional Herati music. Rhythmic cycles associated with Hindustani music had names that incorporated the word *tāl*, such as *Tintāl*, *Japtāl*, and *Ektāl*. The expression *bi tāl*, 'without *tāl*', meant (like *bi lai*) music that was in free rhythm, or a rhythmic error, but it also referred to the specific mistake of losing one's way in keeping to a rhythmic cycle like *Tintāl* in the performance of *khyāl* or a *naghmeh-ye klāsik*, most obviously manifest when the soloist and accompanist did not coincide on the first beat of the cycle at the

Lai (rhythm)

end of a melodic or rhythmic improvisation. The semantic fields of *lai* and *tāl* are mapped in figure 13.

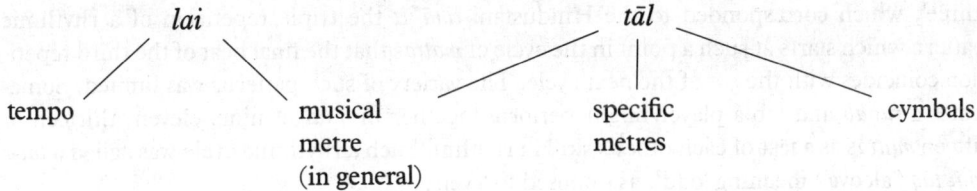

Figure 13 Semantic fields of *lai* and *tāl*

Tintāl and other rhythmic cycles

The tabla was played in Herat in the *chahārtār* bands of the 1920s. According to Karim Khushnawaz, whose own father was a tabla player of that period, 'They didn't know how to play tabla then.' In the 1930s Indian technique arrived with other aspects of Hindustani theory and practice. In the 1970s Herati tabla players used a system of onomatopoeic vocables of drum sounds, such as *Dha, Dhin, Kat, Kit, Na, Ta, Dom*, and knew the strokes to produce these sounds from the drums. These vocables were called *bol*s in Herat (cf. Hindi *bol*).

Herati musicians, especially male *sāzandeh* and their associates, used a concept of rhythmic cycle very like that described in Hindustani music. Such cycles were called *tāl*s, as in Hindustani music (cf. Hindi *tāl*). A *tāl* in Herat had a fixed number of units, which the Heratis called *matra* (cf. Hindi *mātrā*), and the *tāl*s the Herati *sāzandeh* usually knew were *Tintāl*, with sixteen *matra*s, *Ektāl* with twelve, *Japtāl* with ten, and *Rupak* with seven. *Dādreh*, a cycle of six *matra*s, is discussed later as a common metre for popular and traditional Herati music. *Tintāl* was the only one of the Hindustani *tāl*s to be in common use, for playing *naghmeh-ye kashāl* and *naghmeh-ye klāsik*. The *bol*s for *Tintāl* as given me in Herat corresponded to the Hindustani conceptualisation.

A central feature of the Hindustani concept of *tāl* shared by the Heratis was the importance attached to the first beat of the cycle as the point of resolution of rhythmic and melodic tension. In Hindustani music this beat is called the *sam*, meaning 'together'. I did not find this term at all in Herat, though it was presumably known to some musicians in Kabul. In Herat the first beat was called the *gor*. The origin of this term was unknown but a connection with the Indian term *guru* was suggested by Amir Jan. Musicians and the enthusiasts amongst their audience clearly marked the coming of the *gor* beat as the moment of release of physical tension. The head and shoulders gradually rose as the *gor* was approached, with a sudden flexion on the beat so that the head nodded down with a jerk and the shoulders dropped. It seems likely that the rhythmic cadence already existed in Pashtun vocal and instrumental music long before Hindustani music was brought to Kabul by Indian musicians in the 1860s, and perhaps explains the ready acceptance of Hindustani rhythmic concepts. The adoption of *Tintāl* and other *tāl*s can be viewed as the augmentation of Afghan rhythmic practice, just as the modes of Afghan urban music can be viewed as an augmentation of Afghan modal practice (Baily 1981a:36).

A cycle of a *tāl* in performance was called *chekār*, a 'round' or 'circuit', and melodic compositions or improvised sections could be measured in terms of the number of *chekār*s they contained. Tabla players knew various compositions which they called *qāʿida*, *porzieh*, *moreh* and *tukrā*, but the repertory of these was small. A common rhythmic device was the *seh*, the 'three', which corresponded to the Hindustani *tihāʿi*, the triple repetition of a rhythmic pattern which starts at such a point in the cycle of *matra*s that the final beat of the third repetition coincides with the *gor* of the next cycle. The variety of such patterns was limited. Sometimes a *rubāb* and tabla player might perform together in a *tāl* of nine, eleven, thirteen or fifteen *matra*s as a test of each other's skill in rhythm. Such a rhythmic cycle was called a *tāl-e tāq*, *tāq* ('alcove') meaning 'odd', as opposed to 'even'.

Common metres for popular and Herati music

There were two metres in common use for popular music; *Gedeh* and *Dādreh*. Traditional Herati music used these and, very extensively, a third metre, called *Mogholi*. These metres were short and qualitatively different from the more extended structures of *tāl*s like *Tintāl*. They were also highly susceptible to the use of rhythmic cadence devices and *gor* beats. These short metres had been codified by the urban male *sāzandeh* in terms of how they were played on the tabla, and could be represented with verbal *bol* patterns.

Gedeh

Gedeh was said to be a *tāl* of four, or occasionally of eight, *matra*s. Several tabla players gave me *bol* patterns for *Gedeh*, as shown in figure 14.

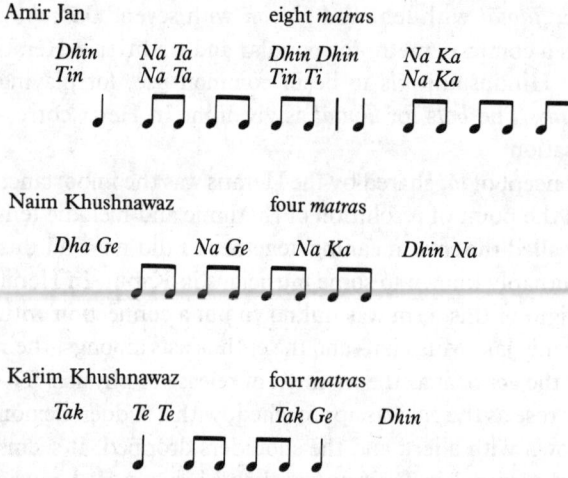

Figure 14 *Bol* patterns for *Gedeh*

Amir Jan's version was of eight *matra*s, a structure created by repeating the basic four *matra* line as a *khāli* ('empty') line, transforming the *Dhin*s to the less resonant *Tin* and *Ti*. This treatment made *Gedeh* more like the kind of *tāl* used for Hindustani music. *Gedeh* may be considered to be a form of the Hindustani *tāl* called *Kerawa*.

Lai (rhythm)

Dādreh

Dādreh was described by Heratis as having six *matra*s. An old name for this *tāl* was apparently *Qizilbashi*. *Dādreh* (cf. Hindi *Dādrā*) is very well known in Hindustani music. According to Popley (1921:76) it was sometimes also called *Pashto Tāl*.

There were two distinct metres called *Dādreh*. One was played as a slow metre of three units, the other a medium or fast metre of six. The slow *Dādreh* was demonstrated to me as shown in figure 15. Like Amir Jan's *Gedeh*, Naim made *Dādreh* into a more extended structure by repeating the basic pattern and changing the *Dhin* to *Tin*.

The second variety of *Dādreh* had a binary structure and could be written as in figure 16. It was this form of *Dādreh* which seemed to be used extensively for Pashtun music in Afghanistan. In some contexts the two varieties of *Dādreh* were mutually interchangeable and in the course of a short passage the slow form could be transformed into the fast form. Both varieties of the *tāl* were said to have six *matra*s.

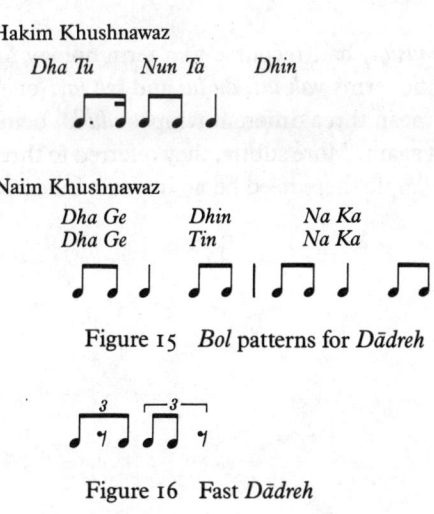

Figure 15 *Bol* patterns for *Dādreh*

Figure 16 Fast *Dādreh*

Mogholi

This term was used for a common *tāl* of seven *matra*s. The name means 'of the Moghols', and the asymmetry of this *tāl* could be construed as typically Turkic. *Mogholi* was felt as a unit of three followed by a unit of four (or of two twos). *Bol*s given by tabla players for *Mogholi* are shown in figure 17. Unlike *Gedeh* and *Dādreh* I found musicians uncertain as to the length of *Mogholi* and the significance of this is discussed below.

Tempo

Various terms were used for talking about tempo. Normal musical parlance employed terms for slow and fast that were applied in non-musical contexts, such as *āhesteh*, 'slow', 'quiet', or *tez*, 'fast', 'sharp'. *Mast*, meaning 'excited', 'exhilarated', or 'intoxicated', was a term for fast music, which might also be described as *jush*, 'boiling', or *por jush*, 'boiling over'.

54 The science of music

Amir Jan
Tin S Ta   Dhin Dhin   Ta Ta

Naim Khushnawaz
Dhin S Na   Dhin Dhin   Na Na

Karim Khushnawaz
Kat S Ta   Dhin Dhin   Dha Dha

Figure 17 *Bol* patterns for *Mogholi* (S = a silent beat)

Urban male *sāzandeh*, exponents of the *ilm-e musiqi*, had recourse to a terminology for tempo that derived from the word *lai*. They used the terms *yak lai*, *du lai* and *seh lai*, 'one', 'two' and 'three *lai*'. These terms could be used to mean three different tempos, *du lai* being twice as fast as *yak lai*, and *seh lai* being twice as fast again. More subtly, they referred to three densities of tactus, as shown in figure 18. In this example there need be no increase in tempo

Figure 18 Terminology for tactus

in the shift from *yak lai* to *seh lai*. Doubling the tactus could be said by Heratis to double the number of *matra*s in one *chekar* of the *tāl*. I was told that when *Dādreh*, six *matra*s, is played at *du lai* it has twelve *matra*s, and that *Tintāl*, sixteen *matra*s, has thirty-two *matra*s at *du lai*. These statements indicated that the Herati concept of *matra* differed somewhat from the Hindustani concept, referring to the number of regular beats in a pattern rather than to the more abstract notion of a time unit within a rhythmic cycle that can be sub-divided in various ways without affecting the length of the unit.

The term *lai* was often confused with the Persian word *lā*, meaning 'thickness' or 'layer', and *lā* was often used instead of *lai*. When musicians talked about *yak lai*, *du lai*, and *seh lai* they perhaps had the notion of a 'thickening' of the time structure; by saying it was twice as thick they meant it was twice as dense, twice as much was there. The term *lai* was therefore highly ambiguous. To say that 'the *lai* had changed' in the course of a piece of music might mean that the tempo had changed, either through a change of tactus or by a real acceleration or deceleration of the tempo, or it could mean there had been a change of metre, say from *Gedeh* to *Dādreh*. Moreover, cross-rhythms might be referred to as differences in *lai*. For playing a section in *Dādreh* ('triplets') within *Tintāl* (chapter 5:74) one said '*yak lai siwā*', 'one *lai* separated'. Other terms that *sāzandeh* had for talking about tempo were *wilampat* (cf. Hindi *vilambit*), 'slow', and *dorut*, (cf. Hindi *drut*), 'fast'. These terms could also refer to types of compositions that were usually performed at a slow or a fast tempo. The kind of instrumental composition known in India as a *razākhāni gat* was often called *naghmeh-ye dorut*, 'fast instrumental piece', in Herat.

The significance of the *ʿilm-e musiqi*

The above discussion of *sor* and *lai* clearly establishes that the science of music in Herat was a version of Hindustani music theory. This in itself is a somewhat remarkable fact; here in an Afghan city close to the borders of Iran and the USSR were musicians who invoked an Indian theoretical system. The terms of the science of music applied most appropriately to the genres of art music – *khyāl*, *ghazal*, *naghmeh-ye kashāl* and *naghmeh-ye klāsik* – that were the special domain of the urban male *sāzandeh*. The theory was further applied, less appropriately, to the genres of popular music and traditional Herati music.

When we compare the science of music in Herat with Hindustani music theory as discussed by Indian authors (which may be rather different to its representation by traditional Hindustani musicians) it has to be acknowledged that the version of the theory held in Herat was simpler and less complete than the Hindustani version. Certain changes in the use of terminology can also be noted. In part these changes may have arisen from the transmission of theoretical knowledge through a chain of individuals who were removed from the original source and unable to verify the accuracy of their knowledge. This may have led to certain simplifications and transformations in the organisation of that knowledge. Changes of this kind were observed to take place within the musician network in Herat when theoretical knowledge was transmitted from the most expert *sāzandeh*, through their amateur turned professional associates, to amateur *dutār* players. A further point is that the musicians of Herat had taken on Hindustani concepts and terminology that usefully expressed structural features that were of interest to them. Hindustani music was only a small part of Afghan urban music. The notion of *wādi* and *samwādi* constituted an example of the limits of usefulness of Hindustani terminology to Herati modal thinking. In the Herati concept of mode, the tonal centre was of such overriding importance that there was no need for the concept to *wādi*. Musicians knew the term and could attempt to identify the *wādi* of a mode, but the notion was peripheral to their practical concerns.

The adoption of Indian-derived terminology to some extent replaced older terminology in Herat. There was, for example, an old terminology for melodic modes. But it may well be that the Persian-inspired art music of the 1920s had rather little theory. Hindustani music is remarkable for its richness of terminology, of taxonomy and classification, while Persian music is notable for the paucity of verbal expression of musical concepts (at least in the nineteenth century), a gap which was to some extent filled by the adoption of French terms (such as *tonik*, from *tonique*, for tonal centre, or *gamme* for scale (Hormoz Farhat, personal communication)). If Heratis lacked a rich terminology in the 1920s, then we may ask why they had adopted one later. What did they use it for? Why did they need it?

There are undoubtedly important cognitive aspects to this question, for it touches on the nature of musical thought and the role of verbal mediation in the mental processes through which musical performance is organised. We may ask whether the science of music was an operational model that had a direct role in the control of performance, or whether it was a representational model that described what the musician already knew, but had no direct role in performance? The terms operational and representational model have been borrowed from Caws (1974) but are used here in this special sense.

The terminology of the *ʿilm-e musiqi* was used by *sāzandeh* for talking about music in several kinds of context. It was part of their 'common language', of their distinct musicians' culture. It was employed in critical listening and in wider discussions about music, and it was used in the course of training young *sāzandeh* musicians, but it was not clear to what extent technical terms were used as a teaching tool. It seems likely that young *sāzandeh* learned mostly 'by ear', through exposure to the sounds of music, imitation of musical performance, and individual trial and error in a social environment where every encouragement was given by family members. In the process of learning, the musician may have had to learn concepts and terms that were part of the *ʿilm*, and this may certainly have helped in the cognitive organisation of aural and motor learning, but the terms of the science of music did not normally constitute a medium for instruction.

The question of whether the science of music was an operational or a representational model is faced most directly in relation to the use of notation, for note names and tabla mnemonics could serve as both oral and written notation. Using notation would seem to be potentially the most obvious practical application for the science of music. It was, of course, useful for musicians to have labels for individual notes and drum sounds, so they could be pinpointed in verbal discourse. But their use potentially goes much beyond this: they could be used as written notation for storing information about particular compositions. In India, oral notation is used in a special way; ideally an instrumentalist should learn to sing the compositions being learned in *sargam* notation before attempting to play them on the instrument, and a tabla player should learn to recite new compositions by *bol* before trying to translate them into movements on the drums. This kind of practice would seem to develop very specific musical skills which involve the capacity to translate between verbal, aural, and motor representations of the structure of compositions.

Written notation was important to some professional musicians in Herat. Amir Jan, who could both read and write, often attributed his superiority as a musician to the fact that he was the student of a Kabuli *ustād* who wrote all his lessons in a notebook for him. He certainly seems to have used these notations when he was learning the material, but had probably not consulted them for many years. Forty years later this notebook was said to be somewhere in the house, but this potentially fascinating document was never produced. He also had the unique skill amongst Heratis of being able to sing *sargam*, a skill he acquired in learning to sing *khyāl*. This underlay his precise labelling of pitch and allowed him to dictate compositions with spoken note names, and to analyse *rāg*s as heard, in terms of their scales. This highly educated 'musicality' no doubt helped him to establish and maintain his dominant role amongst the *sāzandeh* of Herat.

In the case of other Herati *sāzandeh*, the evidence indicates that though they were familiar

The significance of the ʿilm-e musiqi

with oral notation, and in some cases could read (but not write) it, they did not actually learn from notation. A particular example of this occurred in 1974 when Karim Khushnawaz, Amir Jan's younger brother, wanted to learn some *tukrās* (tabla compositions) from a manuscript in my possession. Being non-literate, Karim Khushnawaz asked his friend Karim Dutari to write them down so he could teach them to Karim Khushnawaz by reading them out repetitively in private. This raised several problems. Although Karim Dutari could write the tabla *bol*s as dictated by me there was no very adequate way for him to represent the time relationships except by grouping the *bol* symbols on the paper, which made writing the rhythmic complexities of some of the material impossible. He had to learn the compositions in spoken *bol* form. The second problem was that even when Karim Dutari had learned to recite the *bol* sequences, Karim Khushnawaz still had great trouble in remembering their verbal forms. He needed to hear the patterns as played on the drums. It became clear that Karim Khushnawaz, the *ustād* of tabla in Herat, was not used to learning tabla pieces from oral notation, let alone written notation, and usually learned 'by ear', remembering patterns of drum sounds.

In our previous discussion of *lai*, tabla *bol*s for *Gedeh*, *Dādreh*, and *Mogholi* were cited. However, I do not think that the tabla players who gave me those *bol* patterns actually remembered those patterns in their verbal forms. A tabla player could discover the verbal *bol* pattern from what he played, but that was not how the patterns were represented operationally. This phenomenon recalls the way that Amir Jan would try to discover the *wādi* and *samwādi* from patterns of *shakl* combinations. A further point arises from the stated lengths (in *matra*s) of *Gedeh*, *Dādreh*, and *Mogholi*. The *sāzandeh* 'knew' that *Gedeh* consisted of four or eight *matra*s and that *Dādreh* consisted of six *matra*s, but that knowledge did not seem to be used in playing these metres. Nobody ever told me that *Mogholi* consisted of seven *matra*s. I asked this on a number of occasions and was met only by confusion, '*nagoftand kasi*', as one musican put it, 'nobody has said'. The best estimate was usually six, this being the actual number of strokes in the several *Mogholi* patterns given to me (figure 17). If I suggested it was seven then the musician might well agree. Although musicians were ignorant of the fact that *Mogholi* had seven *matra*s, this did not impede the correct performance of *Mogholi* patterns. *Mogholi* was associated with traditional Herati music, and rarely appeared in the popular music repertory, and the *ustād*s of Kabul had perhaps not given a judgement on its structure. The same can be argued for *Gedeh* and *Dādreh*; although the number of units could be correctly stated, that knowledge was of no bearing on their performance. *Gedeh*, *Dādreh*, and *Mogholi* were played by other kinds of musicians and performers who had no verbalised idea of their length in equal time units.

Taking this kind of evidence into account I conclude that for the performance of popular and traditional Herati music the science of music served mainly as a representational model. It described some of the principles for the structuring of music and formulated terminological distinctions through which the principles could be verbally articulated. It was indicative and revealing of a 'rich knowledge base', but the theory was not the knowledge itself but simply an attempt to represent that knowledge in verbal form. Only in the case of *khyāl*, Hindustani vocal music, did the science of music clearly have a more operational role, as shown in the performance of *sargam*, improvised passages sung to the note names. The role of verbalised musical knowledge in *ghazal* singing is more uncertain; probably it was a help in operational terms without being a prerequisite. It is also probable that the science of music served a more operational role for some musicians than for others, a situation found in other musical systems, including Western classical.

Paradoxically, it was not the *sāzandeh* who benefited most from the use of written notation but those amateurs and amateurs turned professional who studied with the *sāzandeh*. Gada Mohammad, the *dutār* player, had a notebook in which he had written tonal combinations for playing *shakl* in a number of *rāg*s, dictated by his band leader, Amir Mohammad from Kabul. A few other musicians had notebooks of this kind. Karim Dutari had his *sangit*. There are two reasons for the greater reliance on written notation by amateurs and amateurs turned professional. Firstly, many amateur musicians were fully literate, having attended primary school and sometimes secondary school, while very few *sāzandeh* had been to school and acquired the skills of literacy. Secondly, amateurs needed notation more than the hereditary professional *sāzandeh*, who had the advantages of receiving musical training (in the broad sense) from a very early age. What the *sāzandeh* learned by ear the non-*sāzandeh* might be able to learn with the help of notation.

Women's knowledge of the *ʿilm-e musiqi*

The terms and concepts discussed in this chapter were derived from male musicians, especially members of the Khushnawaz family. Women made very little use of this theory and terminology. They did not employ a system of note names, and while the music they performed employed a number of modes, principally *Bairami*, *Kesturi*, *Pāri*, and *Jog*, and the women clearly understood that they were dealing with different scales (what the male *sāzandeh* would call *sor*), and could easily transpose such scales to a number of different places on the harmonium keyboard, they did not know the 'correct' names for these scales. To explain the difference between *Bairami* and *Jog*, a woman musician might call the first 'the one with one black', and the second 'the one with two blacks', referring to the white and black digitals on the harmonium. One reason why the women did not need a system of note names was that they were not faced with tuning problems; the harmonium was an instrument of fixed pitch, and they did not attempt any fine tuning of the tabla. As a male musician amongst the Golpasandha explained: 'That's the difference between women's music and men's music. The women don't tune, they just bang away [on the tabla], but with the men if you have one [sympathetic] string out of tune [on the *rubāb*] they'll tell you to get in tune.'

Similar remarks apply to the domain of rhythm. Although women musicians perhaps knew that the men's word *tāl* had something to do with rhythm, they did not use the word themselves (except to refer to the small cymbals). Nor did they use the terms *Mogholi*, *Dādreh*, and *Gedeh*. They had no notion of counting beats to determine the length of the rhythmic patterns they used in playing the *dāireh* and tabla. To convey the idea of rhythm they used the term *dāireh*. Veronica Doubleday's teacher once told her to try to sing the song '*Eh del belāi delbar*' with the *dāireh* of '*Asprā awordim*'. 'You can't do it, can you, because it won't fit.' (One was in *Dādreh*, the other in *Gedeh*.) But there were no standard song titles used as rhythmic names: instead of telling her to play the *dāireh* of '*Asprā awordim*' she could have mentioned many other songs.

There were a few terms that women did use, such as words for different kinds of songs, *Irāni*, *Herāti*, and *Māldāri*. They spoke of *beit-e hāleh*, a currently popular song, literally a 'now song', or *beit-e khandeh*, a 'comic song'. Some songs were said to 'tell a story' (*qeseh*

Women's knowledge of the 'ilm-e musiqi

dāshtan). A song was considered to consist of *beit* and *pāzarb*, 'verses' and 'refrain', and *naghmehā* were clearly distinguished and called by that name. A good voice should be *shirin*, 'sweet', and *boland*, 'loud'. The contrast *zil o bam* was used for high and low pitch. But all this was a small range of terms and verbalised concepts in comparison to the 'ilm-e musiqi of the men *sāzandeh*. It is clear that verbal explanations and terminology played little part when girls learned to become musicians.

5 Kabuli art music

In this and the following chapter we shall examine the various genres of music performed by urban male *sāzandeh* musicians in Herat in the 1970s. The broad distinction that these two chapters imply between art music and popular music is in accordance with Herati thinking. The procedure adopted in this exegesis is to illustrate the various genres through the discussion of the representative examples found on the cassette that accompanies this text. A musical analysis to bring out the generative principles behind the music is beyond the scope of the present work. I have given nothing in the way of musical transcription using Western staff notation, following Bartók's aphorism that 'the only true notations are the soundtracks on the record itself' (Bartók and Lord 1951:3), except for skeletal outlines of examples 2 and 3, both performances of *nagmeh-ye kashāl*, which are of special interest as examples of specifically Afghan instrumental art music. What I have tried to do in the limited space available is to give morphological analyses of the various genres of music played in the city of Herat. The selection of examples has itself involved some sampling artifact, for I have tried to find from amongst my field recordings short examples, to allow the reader full appreciation of a piece of music as a complete entity. In a few cases items have had to be faded out in order to fit them into the time available on the cassette. Some of the musicians represented in these examples have already been mentioned by name; they are discussed in further detail in chapter 7. In the present chapter it may appear that there is a disproportionate amount of attention to those genres associated with the *rubāb*. This is because I understand this kind of Afghan music as a performer. When writing with reference to specific examples, which can be 'examined' on the cassette, I write in the present tense.*

Ghazal singing

The *ghazal* is one of the principal forms in Persian poetry. Western scholars of Persian poetry often refer to the *ghazal* as 'the Persian ode' or 'Persian lyric', or as the 'love poem'. As a poetic form, the Persian *ghazal* consists of a variable number of couplets, called *beit*. The *beit* is the basic unit in every form of Persian poetry, and consists of two symmetrical halves, called *misrāʿ*, each usually consisting of six or eight feet. In the *ghazal* form the same rhyme runs through the whole poem; the two *misrāʿ*s in each *beit* do not usually rhyme except in the *matlaʿ*, the opening couplet. The rhyme scheme is usually of the order: aa ba ca da ea etc. From the fourteenth century it became usual for the poet to insert his *takhalos*, 'pen name', in a *beit* towards the end of the poem.

The term *ghazal* also indicates a *musical* form for the singing of this kind of poetry. This form is characterised by a type of cyclical organisation with fast instrumental sections interpo-

---

* My special thanks are due to Alastair Dick for comments on the performances considered in this chapter from the perspective of Hindustani music.

lated between units of text. It would appear that the current musical form for singing *ghazal*s was perfected in Kabul in the late nineteenth or early twentieth century, when it became the principal genre of vocal art music in Afghanistan. The *ghazal* style of musical performance was sometimes used for singing poetry that was not in the *ghazal* form, and not all *ghazal*s were necessarily performed in this musical style.

*Ghazal*s were seen as constituting 'good' poetry with significant meaning, and in this respect were compared to the usually simplistic romantic poetry of popular music. As one musician expressed it to me:

Have you heard '*O Bacheh! O Bacheh!*' [On Boy! Oh Boy!] on the radio? It's rotten verse, it's not poetry. I'm going to tell you something. This poetry is rotten [*kharāb*]. It's about kissing and playing around [*bāzi*]. Now the old poetry they used to sing had meaning, it was good [*pokhteh*], like the poetry of Amir Sahib Khusro who's buried in Delhi. Or the poetry of Bedil Sahib.

'What's the difference between infidels and us?

The same light illuminates both the *Kāʿba* and the temple of the infidels.'

Now you've got to understand the meaning of this. With one lamp the temple, where they have idols, like the Hindu idols, and God's house, the *Kāʿba* [in Mecca] are illuminated. What's the difference between you and me? That means something, its from Bedil Sahib. What is the meaning of the lamp? It's the moon. It brings light to both the temple and the *Kāʿba*, but it's one lamp. Everything is illuminated by that lamp. That's poetry with meaning. Now, what's this?

'*O Bacheh! O Bacheh!* Come so we can dance the *Chā Chā Cheh* [Cha Cha dance].

Come let's dance to the Logari *naghmeh*.'

This poetry is trite [*sabok*], it has no meaning. That poetry of the poets has a lot of meaning, nobody can fully understand it. (Sultan Wardak)

Although the *sāzandeh* prided themselves on the belief that the *ghazal* texts they sang were *ketābi*, 'of the book', meaning that they were drawn from the great tradition of Persian literature, the texts of the *ghazal*s sung in Herat and Kabul were not usually poems as penned by famous authors. Afghan *ghazal* singers liked to create their own texts by taking couplets from various sources and putting them together so as to create a new song text. Amir Jan likened this to picking a bouquet of roses (*dasteh gol*), with a flower from here and a flower from there. One might be told that a *ghazal* was by a famous author such as Hafez or Sadi when it turned out that not more than one couplet in the text was derived from the stated author. Some *beit*s sung in the performance of a *ghazal* might be from the best classical authors, others by lesser 'imitators', some perhaps even created by the singer himself, possibly on the spur of the moment, for the *ghazal* as a song text allowed scope for apposite comments referring to people or events at the performance. Singers had to have a feeling for, and to have learned a good deal of, poetry, although they were often criticised by the *literati* for singing texts that were strictly incorrect.

When *ghazal*s were set to music in the Kabuli style certain procedures were observed. Firstly, there was a division of the text into verse and refrain. Generally the *matlaʿ*, the first *beit* (with its aa rhyme scheme) functioned as the refrain, while the other *beit*s served as verses, with the *matlaʿ* repeated after each *beit*. The melodies for 'verse' and 'refrain' were distinct, and termed the *antara* and the *āstāi*, the former having a higher tessitura than the latter.* A third component of the *ghazal* form was an instrumental section called *duni*, which

---

* The terms *āstāi* and *antara* are good examples of the rather free use of Hindustani terminology in Afghanistan. Most melodies for popular and traditional Herati songs have two parts, with the melody for the verse having a

was an instrumental reiteration of the *āstāi* melody. The song form was cyclical with respect to tempo: the verse (or *antara* as the *sāzandeh* called this section of the musical form) was sung at a slow tempo; with the refrain (or *āstāi* as they called this section) the tempo accelerated, and continued to accelerate in the *duni*, to reach a tempo which was approximately double that used for the *antara*. The *duni* was terminated by a rhythmic cadence and a sudden drop back to the slow tempo of the *antara*, when the next verse was sung, and so on.

Certain interpolations and other modifications were possible. The most important of these was the interpolation of extra *beit*s in slow tempo after a *duni* and before the next *beit* of the *ghazal* itself. The extra couplets were usually called *fard*, which, properly speaking, is an interpolated *misrāʿ* in a section of prose (Browne 1902:25). Sometimes a *rubāʿi*, a form of quatrain, was interpolated. Some singers used such interpolated *fard*s a great deal; I found that the Kabuli singer Haji Hamahang was a striking exponent of this highly text-orientated style. It was usual to sing a *fard* at the beginning of the *ghazal*, followed by the *āstāi* and a *duni*. Another kind of interpolation was called *ālāp*, a non-textual vocal line sung to the vowel sound [a:], often placed after a *duni* and before the succeeding *antara*.

Example 1 on the cassette is a performance of the *ghazal* '*Piram o ārezu-ye wasl-e jawānān dāram*', sung by Amir Jan, who also plays the harmonium, accompanied by two of his sons, Rahim (*rubāb*) and Naim (tabla), and Ghulam Nebi on the fourteen stringed *dutār*. According to Amir Jan, this *ghazal* used to be sung by Ustad Qasem, though to a different melody, but Amir Jan had added certain couplets himself, according to his own inclinations, 'a rose from here and a rose from there', to make a bouquet. The sentiments of the poetry were particularly apposite to the singer, in his early sixties at the time, and about to retire from singing professionally. The *ghazal* was recorded in 1974 at a dinner party (*mehmāni*) at the singer's house. The text he sings is as follows:

Text	Translation
Fard 1	*Fard* 1
Ruz-e qiāmat har kasi bar dast girad nāmeyi	On Judgement Day everybody holds a deed of their actions
Man niz hāzer mishawum taswir-e jānān dar baghal	I will also come with a portrait of my loved one under my arm
Matlaʿ (*Beit* 1)	*Matlaʿ* (*Beit* 1)
Piram o ārezu-ye wasl-e jawānān dāram	I'm old but have the desire to be united with young ones
Khāneh weirān bewad o hasrat-e mehmān daram	My house is ruined but I yearn for guests in it
Beit 2	*Beit* 2
Gar chi piram tu shabi tang dar āghusham gir	Although I'm old hold me tight in your arms at night
Tā sahārgāh ze kenār-e tu jawān barkhizam	So that at dawn I will rise from your side young again
Beit 3	*Beit* 3
Garmi-ye eshq o wasal mu-ye sar az ghoseh sefid	The warmth of love and closeness is the reason for white hair
Zir-e khākestār-e khod āteshi penhān dāram	Beneath my own ashes a fire is hidden

higher tessitura than the melody for the refrain. The former was called *antara* and the latter *āstāi*, and musicians used these terms to distinguish verse and refrain sections of the song.

Ghazal singing

Plate 4 Amir Jan, vocal and harmonium; Ghulam Nebi, *dutār*; and Naim, tabla; playing '*Piram o ārezu...*', 1974. Note the bird cage in front

Plate 5 Amir Jan and his son Rahim playing *rubāb* on the same occasion

Rubāʿi
Abru ze mā makash ke ma del shekasteim
Khākestārim bar rokh-e ātesh neshasteim
Ne khuni kardeim o ne kasira kushteim
Taqsir-e ma ham in ke āsheq-e tu gashteim

Fard 2
Agar jauhar shenāsi teghrā oriyān tamāshā kon
Tā tegh-e aslerā jauhar ze khākestār birun ārad

Fard 3
Cherāgh o dideh be rāh-e tu kardeam roshan
Be sharti un ke nasuzad ze entezār marā

Beit 4
Nist yak lahze biyad yād-e tu fāregh bāsham
Digar chi piram man o dar hāfezam noqsān dāram

Beit 5
Nemidānam kirā didam ke az khod mirawad husham
Jenun āhesteh miguyad mobārak bād dar gusham

Fard 4
Nagu ke pir shodi āsheqi nemizibad
Sharāb koneh shawad nesheh-ye digar dārad

Rubāʿi
Don't turn your eyebrow away from me for I am broken hearted
I am like ashes on the surface of something burning
I haven't drawn blood or killed anyone
My only fault is that I've fallen in love with you

Fard 2
If you can recognise the essence then look at the blade naked
Till the genuine blade is brought intact from the ashes

Fard 3
I have lit your way with a torch and with my own eyes
Provided that the lamp doesn't burn out while I await you

Beit 4
Not a moment passes without my thinking about you
Although I'm old and my memory is going

Beit 5
I don't know who I've seen that has made me lose my senses
Madness is whispering congratulations in my ear

Fard 4
Don't say that love is unbecoming to one who is old
Wine that is matured has another intoxication

The musical setting

The melodic mode is *Kesturi*, one of the Afghan urban modes that musicians acknowledged was not found in Hindustani classical music. Its anomalous *raft* and *āmad* are shown in figure 2. The *tāl* is *Dādreh*, with six *matras*. The text could be sung to different melodies in other modes, while the *antara* and *āstāi* melodies used here could also be applied to other texts.

Example 1 starts with a short vocal phrase of the kind called *ālāp*. This is followed by an introductory *fard* sung to one of the several closely related *antara* melodies used in this example. The rhythmic pattern over which the *antara* melodies are sung is a slow *Dādreh* (which the musicians call *Dādreh yak lai*), but the vocal lines of the *antara* are not structured within a set number of *Dādreh* cycles. In this sense there is a tendency for the vocal melody to be in free rhythm. The musicians consider this kind of singing to be akin to *shakl*. Then comes another phrase of *ālāp*, followed by the *āstāi*. The main text for the *āstāi* is the first *beit*

Ghazal singing

of the *ghazal*, the *matla'*: 'Piram o ārezu-ye wasl-e jawānān dāram/Khāneh weirān bewad o hasrat-e mehmān dāram'. Each of the two *misrā'*s of this *beit* is sung to a melody which occupies four cycles of *Dādreh*. During the *āstāi* the tempo begins to accelerate. Having sung the *āstāi* the instruments take over and play the *duni*. The melody for this is essentially the same as that used for the *āstāi* but with certain modifications to facilitate playing at speed. Rhythmically, the *duni* is the climax of the *antara–āstāi–duni* cycle, where the *rubāb* and *dutār* 'come into their own', using a variety of right-hand stroke patterns to create various polyrhythmic effects to build up 'rhythmic tension'. The *duni* is played four times in this instance, then one cycle of *Dādreh* is tacked on to the end of the *duni*, with the instruments finishing together on the *gor* beat, the first beat of the rhythmic cycle. The perceptual effect of this is to introduce a brief pause after the *gor* beat, and it is up to the tabla player to cue the musicians into the next *antara* in the original slow tempo. In example 1 this next *antara* consists of the second *beit* of the *ghazal*, followed by another *āstāi* and *duni*, and so forth. The overall form of example 1 is shown in table 1.

Table 1 *Morphology of* 'Piram o ārezu. . .'

Music	Text	
Ālāp		
Antara	Fard 1	
Ālāp		
Āstāi	Piram o ārezu-ye. . .	×2
	Khāneh weirān bewad. . .	×2
Duni		×4
Antara	Beit 2	
Āstāi	Piram o ārezu-ye. . .	
	Khāneh weirān bewad. . .	×2
Duni		×6
Antara	Beit 3 (2nd *misrā'* in *āstāi*)	
Āstāi	Zir-e khākestār. . .	×3
Duni		×6
Ālāp		
Antara	Rubā'i	
Āstāi	Zir-e khākestār. . .	×3
	Piram o ārezu-ye. . .	
Duni		×4
Antara	Fard 2	
Āstāi	Zir-e khākestār. . .	×3
Duni		×5
Fard	Fard 3	
Antara	Beit 4 (2nd *misrā'* in *āstāi*)	
Āstāi	Digar chi piram. . .	×2
	Piram o ārezu-ye. . .	
	Khāneh weirān bewad. . .	
Duni		×4

Table 1 (*cont.*)

Music	Text	
Antara		
Āstāi	Beit 5	
	Piram o ārezu-ye...	
	Khāneh weirān bewad...	
Duni		×6
Antara		
Āstāi	Fard 4	
	Piram o ārezu-ye...	
	Khāneh weirān bewad...	×2
Duni		×6

We may note several features of example 1 which serve to complicate the basic *ghazal* form. There is the variable occurrence of repetitions of lines, and in a few cases of parts of lines. The length of the *duni* varies between four and six reiterations of the *āstāi* melody. A *rubāʿi* has been interpolated. Different melodies are used for the *antaras*. And the poetry used for the refrain shows some interesting variations. When Amir Jan comes to *Beit* 3 he sings the first *misrāʿ* twice to an *antara* melody, then sings the second *misrāʿ* to the *āstāi* melody, using it as the refrain instead of '*Piram o ārezu-ye...*'. This *misrāʿ* is used again for the refrain sung after *Fard* 2, while after the *rubāʿi* he sings '*Zir-e khākestār...*' three times, then the line '*Piram o ārezu-ye...*', omitting all mention of '*Khāneh weirān bewad*'. He does the same thing with *Beit* 4, where the second *misrāʿ*, '*Digar chi piram...*' is used for the refrain before singing '*Piram o ārezu-ye...*'. These divergences from the underlying structural prototype are concentrated in the middle third of the song, but I cannot say whether this is significant from Amir Jan's point of view.

One of the most remarkable features of the Kabuli *ghazal* is the cyclical fluctuation of tempo. There is an alternation between tempos, with a gradual acceleration from slow to fast, and a sudden falling back from fast to slow. The accelerations of tempo occur mainly in the *āstāi* sections, and level off during the *dunis*. The average tempo in example 1 is *matra* = 167 for the *antara* and 297 for the *duni*. The perceptual effect of fast tempo is increased by a tendency to double the tactus as the *āstāi* speeds up. Figure 19 represents the 'profile' of the Kabuli *ghazal* form.

Another notable feature of example 1 is the sound of songbirds. Two canaries in cages, belonging to the musicians, had been placed in front of the band, and their singing, which occurs early on in the *ghazal* and again in the final *duni*, adds an aesthetically important component to the sound of the music (a matter discussed further in chapter 9). Although never stated by Heratis, I believe there to be a connection between the sounds produced from the high drone string (*sim-e bajgi*) on the *dutār* or *rubāb* and the sounds of birdcalls. An instance of this is provided in example 1. The fast trills of the birds heard during the second rendering of the *āstāi* are echoed by the *rubāb* in the first cycle of the following *duni*.

Naghmeh-ye kashāl

The term *naghmeh-ye kashāl* means 'extended instrumental piece'. This kind of piece consists of three main parts: the *shakl*, an extempore exegesis of the melodic characteristics of the

Naghmeh-ye kashāl

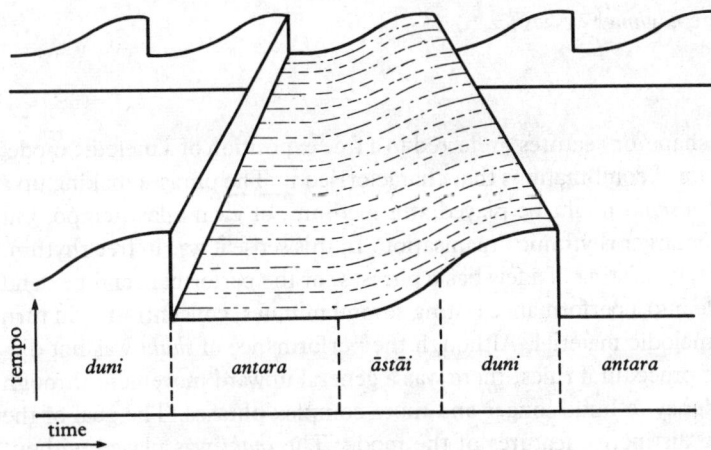

Figure 19 Profile of the Kabuli *ghazal* form

mode, in free rhythm; the *āstāi*, the main composition, repeated many times with rhythmic variations; and the *antara*, a series of short compositions played several times each, with gradual acceleration towards the end of the piece. The *naghmeh-ye kashāl* was considered to be a speciality for solo *rubāb* performance, with tabla (or less commonly *doholak*) accompaniment. It was sometimes played as a solo on *dutār* or *tanbur*, and it was also used as a group instrumental piece to commence an extended musical performance (at a wedding party or *Ramazān* concert). As a student of the *rubāb* I gave special attention to the collection of *naghmehā-ye kashāl* compositions, both in the form of recordings and in notations given me by Amir Jan. Examples were collected in the following modes: *Yemen, Yemen Kelyān, Kumāj, Pāri, Kesturi, Kausieh, Bihāg, Bairami, Beiru, Pilu, Bhupāli, Āsā, Āsāwari, Des, Bāgheshri,* and *Bhimpālasi*.

In Kabul this kind of piece was sometimes called a *naghmeh-ye chahārtuk*, a 'four-part instrumental piece'. Ustad Mohammad Omar, who taught this kind of piece in his *rubāb* class for amateur musicians, called it by that name. In his terminology the four parts of the *naghmeh* were called *āstāi, antara, bhog,* and *sanchāri*, essentially the same names employed for the four sections of the *dhrupad* form of Hindustani vocal and instrumental music, which are *sthāyi, antra, sanchāri,* and *ābhogi* (or *bhog*). Note the reversal of the terms *bhog* and *sanchāri* in the Kabuli usage. However, most examples of *naghmeh-ye kashāl/chahārtuk* have more than four parts, sometimes considerably more. It is my opinion that Ustad Mohammad Omar simplified the form somewhat for his many amateur students of *rubāb* and borrowed the terms *bhog* and *sanchāri* as convenient labels for two of the parts. No further connection with *dhrupad* need necessarily be inferred from the use of these terms. This kind of piece was the only genre of art music commonly performed by amateur musicians, and was greatly respected by musicians and non-musicians alike, who called it a *naghmeh pokhteh*, 'a well cooked *naghmeh*', or a *naghmeh sābeqdār* or *naghmeh qadimi*, an 'old' or 'ancient *naghmeh*'. According to the musicians, these pieces had been created by the great *ustād*s of Kabul, such as Ustad Qasem.

Morphology of the *naghmeh-ye kashāl*

Shakl

The term *shakl*, meaning 'shape' or 'features', referred to a free exposition of a melodic mode, using and building on the tonal combinations that characterised it. The phrases making up a particular performance of a *shakl* might be played at a medium, or even a fast tempo, but there was no overall pulse or larger rhythmic organisation. In this sense it was in free rhythm. A *shakl* could be very short, consisting of a few basic phrases, or the performer might extend his *shakl* as fully as possible into a performance lasting several minutes, concentrating in turn on various aspects of the melodic material. Although the performance of *shakl* was not dictated by an elaborate set of procedural rules, there was a general upward movement through the tonal range and a tendency to build longer and more complex phrases. The goal of the musician was to reveal the distinctive features of the mode. The *shakl* was played without tabla accompaniment but sometimes one encountered a section towards the end of the *shakl* called *āstāi-ye tabla*, where the tabla entered in slow tempo while the *rubāb* continued to play *shakl* phrases. In theory the tabla part should have been a slow *thekā* for *Tintāl*, or for some other *tāl*, but in practice it might consist of non-cyclic rhythmic patterns which occasionally joined with the *rubāb* in a cadential pattern. An instance of this is shown in example 5 (*naghmeh-ye klāsik* in *Rāg Des*).

Āstāi

In this section a fixed composition, called the *āstāi*, was repeated many times with rhythmic variations. All *āstāi* compositions that I have encountered for use in *naghmehā-ye kashāl* were set in *Tintāl* (sixteen *matras*). Some were composed across two cycles of *Tintāl* and were thirty-two *matras* in length; they were identified by musicians as old compositions. An *āstāi* composition was an abstract melodic outline which could be realised in many ways using different patterns of right hand strokes on the *rubāb*. The general tendency was to maintain a particular pattern (called *parand*) through a cycle of the *āstāi*, then change to a new pattern. Many of the stroke patterns involved the use of the short drone string (*sim-e bajgi*) found on the *rubāb* and the fourteen stringed *dutār*, in a virtuoso technique called *simkāri*, 'metal-string work'. The plectrum stroke patterns which underlie such variations are discussed in Baily (1987), where a detailed analysis of this kind of rhythmic improvisation can also be found. The rhythmic variations tended to be organised into 'episodes', each consisting of several repetitions of the *āstāi* composition. In the course of each episode there was a gradual build-up of 'rhythmic tension'. This could involve an increase in tempo, an increase in the number of right hand strokes on the *rubāb* per *matra*, an increase in the frequency of *simkāri* strokes on the high drone, and the tabla might double the tactus, playing *du lai*. The build-up of rhythmic tension was resolved with a cadence onto the *gor*, the first beat of the *tāl*, and often a fall back to a slower tempo. Sometimes an episode would end with a rhythmic cadence of the type known as *seh*, 'three', played by the *rubāb* and/or the tabla. The episodic organisation of the *āstāi* gave it a profile similar to that of the Kabuli *ghazal* (see figure 19).

Some *āstāi* compositions had an associated *antara* which was melodically related to the *āstāi* but rose to a higher part of the pitch range, and was distinct from the compositions played in

Plate 6 Karim Dutari, *dutār* and Karim Khushnawaz, tabla, recording the *naghmeh-ye kashāl* in *Rāg Pilu* in Karim Dutari's house, 1974

the succeeding *antara* section of the *naghmeh-ye kashāl*. This '*āstāi* related' *antara* was interpolated at various points in the course of the *āstāi*, between episodes, when it was played several times before a return was made to the *āstāi* composition. It was also possible to interpolate in the *āstāi* short melodic improvisations, called *paliteh*, of one or more cycles in length.

Antara

The third (*antara*) section of the *naghmeh-ye kashāl* consisted of a series of shorter compositions, each an individual *antara*. At this point the tempo doubled, and there was a gradual acceleration throughout the *antara* section. Each individual *antara* composition was usually played several times, then the musician proceeded without a break to the next composition. The successive *antara* compositions became progressively higher in pitch, then, having reached a high point, moved down again. Later, groups of these *antara*s might be repeated. For example, having played *Antara* 4 the musician might go back to repeat *Antara*s 2, 3 and 4 before proceeding to *Antara* 5. Thus there could be several journeys to and from the *antara* with the highest pitch range: several 'peaks'. There was a similarity here with certain compositions for the *tanbur* in Mazar-e Sharif (in northern Afghanistan), and known in Herat as *naghmeh Uzbeki* (see example 12 on the cassette). Comparisons within the repertory of *naghmehā-ye kashāl* show that there was a small number of prototypes from which many of the *antara* compositions derived. In the course of the *antara* section there was scope for rhythmic improvisation and the interpolation of short melodic improvisations (*paliteh*).

Example 2 on the cassette is a performance of a *naghmeh-ye kashāl* in *Rāg Pilu* played by

Karim Dutari as a solo piece on the fourteen stringed *dutār*, with tabla accompaniment provided by Karim Khushnawaz. This recording is of particular interest because Karim was prompted to perfect his adaptations to the *dutār* precisely in order to perform such items of the *rubāb* repertory. This *naghmeh-ye kashāl* in *Pilu* was very well known though Karim does not play all its *antara* variations. The form of the piece is shown in table 2.

Table 2 Naghmeh-ye kashāl *in* Rāg Pilu

SHAKL	
ĀSTĀI	18 repetitions of *āstāi* composition
Episode 1	Cycles 1–5
Episode 2	Cycles 6–8
Episode 3	Cycles 9–13
Episode 4	Cycles 14–16
Episode 5	Cycles 17–18
ANTARA	
Antara 1	×4
Antara 2	×2
Antara 1	×2
Antara 3	×5
Antara 2	×3
Antara 1	×3
Antara 2	×3
Antara 3	×2
Antara	anomalous
Antara 2	×9
Antara 3	×5
Antara 4	×10

The short *shakl* explores some of the melodic characteristics of the *Pilu* mode and shows a gradual rise through the tessitura, with a descending chromatic run towards the end of the *shakl*, which is a common feature of *shakl* in *Pilu*. The *āstāi* composition is thirty-two *matras* in length and is played over two cycles of *Tintāl* as delineated by the tabla (see transcription 1). Several *āstāi* compositions in thirty-two *matras* have this melodic shape, in *Rāgs Yemen*, *Bihāg*, *Bairami*, and *Pāri*. The repetitions of the *āstāi* show the kind of episodic organisation discussed above, though perhaps not as clearly as some performances of *naghmeh-ye kashāl*. The *āstāi* can be interpreted as consisting of five separate episodes: cycles 1–5, 6–8, 9–13, 14–16, 17–18. Episodes 2 and 4 use *simkāri* (strokes on the high drone), with an increase in the frequency of *simkāri* strokes during the course of the episode. Episode 5 also uses *simkāri*, but very sparingly. Each episode is terminated by a *seh* figure played on the tabla. In each episode there is an increase in tempo, but in this example only episode 3 falls back to a distinctly slower tempo at the end of the episode.

After the eighteen cycles of the *āstāi*, Karim plays the *antara* section, which consists of four different though closely interrelated short *antara* compositions.

Analytically, the *antara* section consists of only two compositions, *Antaras* 1 and 3; *Antaras* 2 and 4 are derived from *Antara* 1. They have been labelled separately because they were described as different by the musicians. *Antara* 1 is half the length of the thirty-two *matras astai*, but is still considered to consist of thirty-two *matras* played *du lai*, at double tempo. One *matra* is notated as a crotchet in transcription 1. After the fourth statement of *Antara* 1, Karim

Naghmeh-ye kashāl

Transcription 1 Astāi of *naghmeh-ye kashāl* in *Rāg Pilu*

plays the second half of this *antara* composition, a sixteen *matra* unit, twice. This phrase, which is labelled as *Antara* 2, reappears as an independent *antara* later in the piece. *Antara* 3 is a melodic figure which occurs at some point in most examples of *naghmeh-ye kashāl*, with modifications to fit the exact scale being used for the piece. Then *Antara* 2 is reintroduced, and so on. Finally, *Antara* 4 is played, which is simply an expanded version of *Antara* 2. The tempo of the *antara* section accelerates throughout, to more than double. Thus *Antara* 1 at the start of the *antara* section has a tempo of *matra* = 117, while by *Antara* 4 this has increased to 278.

The *naghmeh-ye kashāl* as a group instrumental

Besides its role as a solo instrumental piece, a *naghmeh-ye kashāl* was usually played as a group instrumental by the *sāzandeh* at the start of a performance of music. The act of tuning the instruments, using the harmonium as a reference point, merged almost imperceptibly into the *shakl-e sāz*, a brief interlude where the various instruments played their separate *shakl* phrases. Then the *naghmeh* began, led by the harmonium player. The stated object of playing a *naghmeh-ye kashāl* at the start of a performance was to 'warm up' the instruments; at the end of the piece there would be a brief pause when small adjustments were made to the tuning of *rubāb*, *dutār*, and tabla. Playing the *naghmeh* was also said to 'warm up' the musicians, getting them accustomed to playing in the first mode of the performance, and to 'warm up' the audience too.

In former times, when *ghazal* singing was the predominant genre in a performance of urban music (before popular music was widely disseminated through radio broadcasting), great importance was attached to performing all the items in a *chashni* in the same mode. A *chashni* was a sequence of songs (or instrumental pieces) played together as a single entity, with a clear beginning and end. In those days each *chashni* would begin with the appropriate *naghmeh-ye kashāl* played as a group instrumental piece, followed by a sequence of *ghazal*s, all in the same mode, with perhaps a few lighter songs. Having come to the end of the *chashni* the performers would rest and take some refreshment before starting a new *chashni* in another mode, beginning with the appropriate *naghmeh-ye kashāl*. This use of the *naghmeh-ye kashāl* had been largely discontinued in recent times, partly due to the much greater flexibility in moving from one mode to another within a *chashni*, and a *naghmeh-ye kashāl* was usually played only at the beginning of a performance. I observed only Ustad Rahim Bakhsh from Kabul use a second *naghmeh-ye kashāl* in the course of his performance, played after the interval in his *Ramazān* concerts.

Example 3 is a *naghmeh-ye kashāl* in *Rāg Kausieh*, played by Amir Mohammad (from Kabul) and his band, Rahim Khushnawaz on *rubāb*, Gada Mohammad on *dutār*, and Fazl Ahmad (also from Kabul) on tabla, at the start of a *Ramazān* concert in 1974. The scale of *Kausieh* is shown in figure 2 and the form of the piece is shown in table 3.

Table 3 Naghmeh-ye kashāl *in* Rāg Kausieh

SHAKL-E SĀZ	
ĀSTĀI	31 repetitions of the *āstāi* composition
Episode 1	Cycles 1–7
Episode 2	Cycles 8–17
Āstāi related *antara*	×2
Episode 3	Cycles 18–25
Āstāi related *antara*	×2
Episode 4	Cycles 26–31
ANTARA	
Antara 1	×1
Antara 2	×1
Antara 3	×2
Antara 4	×2
Antara 5	×2
Antara 6	×2
Antara 4	×2
Antara 3	×4
Antara 4	×2
Antara 5	×2
Antara 6	×1
Antara 4	×2
Antara 3	×3

The tuning of the instruments and the *shakl-e sāz* have been omitted, the example starts with the *āstāi* composed in sixteen *matra*s, which is played thirty-one times, with an *āstāi* related *antara* interpolated at two points. The *āstāi* composition is sixteen *matra*s long, as is its related *antara* (see transcription 2). The *āstāi* section consists of four episodes: cycles 1–7, 8–17, 18–25, 26–31. The use of a gradually accelerating tempo in episode building is shown

Naghmeh-ye kashāl

Transcription 2 *Naghmeh-ye kashāl* in *Rāg Kausieh*

particularly well in this example, with a marked drop in tempo at the start of each succeeding episode or *āstāi* related *antara*. Episode 4 is in *Dādreh*, with the *rubāb* playing a classic set of rhythmic variations using the *simkāri* technique (see Baily 1987).

After the *āstāi* the musicians play the *antara* section. The set of *antara* compositions played in this example is unusually long and complicated. Since I have not analysed this performance with the musicians, nor notated these compositions from Amir Jan's dictations, I am not sure how the *sāzandeh* would identify the separate compositions. According to my own analysis there are six *antara* compositions, and their sequencing is indicated in table 3. The tabla playing in the *antara* section is also notable; the performer plays patterns copied from the *doholak* as used in Pashtun music, with fast heavy flat-handed strokes.

Klāsik (khyāl)

The word *klāsik* (occasionally pronounced *klāstik*), presumably the English '*classic*' brought to Afghanistan from India, had a variety of meanings. At its narrowest it referred to Hindustani vocal music, but it was also used in a wider sense. A musician in Kabul once explained to me that *klāsik* means 'difficult', and pointed out that all countries have their own form of *musiqi klāsik*, 'classical music'. In Herat, Amir Jan once remarked when we were listening to a performance of an Iranian *dastgāh*, 'That's *klāsik* too.' On a separate occasion another musician denied this same piece was *klāsik*; he used the term to refer to Hindustani music, vocal and instrumental. In Kabul, some musicians were familiar with several genres of Hindustani vocal music, such as *khyāl*, *dhrupad*, and *tarānā*; here we are concerned only with *khyāl*. *Khyāl* is a Persian word meaning 'imagination' (cf. Hindi *khyāl*). Vocal performance of a *khyāl* or other genre of Hindustani vocal art music was termed *rāg khāndan*, 'to sing [a] *rāg*', while *rāg zadan* or *rāg nawākhtan* meant to play a *rāg* on an instrument. Here the idea was not simply of *rāg* as melodic mode but as musical form.

The main stages of a vocal *khyāl* performance as distinguished by Herati musicians were three: *shakl*, *āstāi*, and *khyāl*. The *shakl* was a free extemporisation of the melodic mode without tabla accompaniment. The *āstāi* was an optional section in the *rāg* form and was

Klāsik (khyāl)

often omitted. This corresponded to what is termed a *vilambit bandish* in Hindustan, a fixed composition with improvised sections at slow tempo. In Afghanistan the *āstāi* did not usually have a fixed composition, only a short melodic cadence onto the *gor* beat; otherwise the singer performed slow *shakl* phrases in the tabla cycle. The *khyāl* was a fixed composition in medium or fast tempo with interpolated improvised sections. In Hindustan such a composition is called *bandish* or *chiz*, but I did not come across these terms in Herat (though I imagine they must have been known to singers in Kabul like Ustad Sarahang). In Herat the fixed composition itself was called the *khyāl*.

Example 4 is a *khyāl* in *Rāg Bairami* sung by Amir Mohammad at the same *Ramazān* concert at which example 3 was recorded. It was the last item performed before the interval. Perhaps because Amir Mohammad worked in Herat much more than other visiting Kabuli musicians, and had established an excellent rapport with a wide audience, he included rather more *klāsik* in his performances than some other visiting Kabuli singers cared to risk. Example 4 shows ways in which he tailored his performance to suit the tastes of the audience, and is typical of his performance of *khyāl* at wedding parties and Ramazan concerts, in contrast to how he might perform at a private party of *klāsik* enthusiasts. He presented the *rāg* as though it was 'just another song' and the performance is short, fast and exciting, almost like an excerpt from the longer performance he was capable of giving.

The mode is a form of *Bairami Pancham* (*Bairami* taken with *Pancham* on the *rubāb* as *karj*). Amir Mohammad preceded the *rāg* with several popular songs in the scale of *Bairami Pancham*, and thus preserved a continuity of mode. But there are in this performance some quite unusual tonal combinations for *Rāg Bairami*, such as passages which use *Ge* rather than *Ga* in ascent. The morphology of this performance is represented in table 4.

Table 4 Khyāl *in* Bairami

SHAKL	single *shakl* phrase
KHYĀL	
Khyāl	over 4 cycles of Tintāl
Shakl	4 cycles
Khyāl	2 cycles
Shakl	4 cycles
Khyāl	5 cycles
Shakl	1 + 4 cycles
Khyāl	2 cycles
Shakl	1 + 7 cycles
Khyāl	7 cycles
Sargam	1 + 4 cycles
Khyāl	2 cycles
Sargam	8 cycles
Khyāl	1 cycle
Shakl	1 + 13 cycles
Khyāl	4 cycles
Shakl	1 + 5 cycles
Khyāl	2 cycles
Sargam	7 cycles
Khyāl	4 cycles
Shakl	1 + 9 cycles
Khyāl	9 cycles

After a very brief *shakl*, which consists of a single phrase of the type called *ālāp*, Amir Mohammad omits the *āstāi* and sings the *khyāl*, or fixed composition. This is in *Tintāl*, and starts on the twelfth *matra*. The melodic segment from *matra*s twelve to one would be called the *mukhrā* in Hindustani music, and is used to terminate improvised sections and to lead back into the fixed composition. The text, in Urdu, would appear to be '*Dana be-riya jo more*', 'He is a wise man to me who is without guile'.

In this performance, Amir Mohammad uses two kinds of improvised section, called *shakl* and *sargam*. In the *shakl* sections the vocal melodic phrases are like those that would be employed in a *shakl* section proper, though they are sung over the Tintāl cycle. In Hindustani music this kind of passage is called *bahlava* or *ālāpi*. In the *sargam* sections the singer sings the note names. In Hindustani music this would be called *sargam tān*. A striking feature of the first passage of *sargam* is the use of *Ge* in the ascending *Sa Re Ge Ma Pe* sequence. This 'modulation' occurs again in the second and third *sargam*s. There is a general increase in tempo during the performance. The tempo of the *khyāl* sections tends to be rather faster than that of the improvised (*shakl* and *sargam*) sections, but there are several exceptions and it does not appear that there is a regular fluctuation between two tempos as in the *ghazal*. There is no evidence of episode building of the kind found in the *naghmeh-ye kashāl*.

Overall, the performance is fairly close to Hindustani style, though the accompanying instruments are rather different, with the *rubāb* following the voice in the manner of a *sārangi*. This example of Amir Mohammad's singing must be regarded as a simple form of *khyāl*. Amir Jan's style was even simpler.

Naghmeh-ye klāsik

The *naghmeh-ye klāsik*, the 'classical instrumental piece', was the instrumental counterpart to the vocal genre of *khyāl*, and was usually played on the *rubāb* with tabla accompaniment. It corresponded to the *ālāp* and *gat* of Hindustani music. The ability to perform this genre on the *rubāb* was much more widespread in Herat than the ability to sing *khyāl*; most *sāzandeh* played the *rubāb* (even if they did not do so in public) and could perform *naghmeh-ye klāsik* to some degree. This was the closest most of them got to playing what they identified as Hindustani music.

Performance of a *naghmeh-ye klāsik* consisted of two main sections, the *shakl*, in free rhythm and without tabla accompaniment, and the *naghmeh*, the fixed composition, in a rhythmic cycle, usually *Tintāl*. There were two styles of performance of the *naghmeh-ye klāsik*. In one style, the *naghmeh* was simply repeated many times using the type of rhythmic variation already described for the *āstāi* of a *naghmeh-ye kashāl*; in the other style, short improvised melodic sections, called *paliteh* (cf. Hindi *palta*) were interpolated between statements of the fixed composition. There was often considerable use of *seh*-type figures (see page 52). In the context of the *naghmeh-ye klāsik* the term *naghmeh* could have at least three levels of contrast: it could refer to the piece as a whole; it could refer to the second part of the piece, in fixed rhythm; and it could refer to the fixed composition itself. Some fixed compositions had two parts; the *āstāi*, the main composition, and a supplementary *antara*, a related composition with a higher tessitura.

Example 5 is a *naghmeh-ye klāsik* in *Rāg Des*, played on the *rubāb* by Rahim Khushnawaz, accompanied on tabla by his brother Naim. The fixed composition is a Hindustani composition of the *razākhāni gat* type, and was described by Rahim as a *naghmeh-ye dorut*, 'a fast instrumental piece'. It is not typical of the older *naghmeha-ye klāsik* associated with the *rubāb*, and is played with interpolated melodic improvisations (*paliteh*) rather than with right hand variations (*parand*s). An analysis of the piece is given in table 5.

Table 5 Naghmeh-ye klāsik *in* Rāg Des

SHAKL	
Shakl	
Āstāi-ye tabla	
NAGHMEH	
Naghmeh	4 cycles of *Tintāl*
Paliteh + seh	4 cycles
Naghmeh	2 cycles
Paliteh + seh	6 cycles
Naghmeh	2 cycles
Paliteh	7 cycles
Naghmeh	2 cycles
Paliteh	3 cycles
Naghmeh	1 cycle
Paliteh	11 cycles
Naghmeh	4 cycles
Paliteh	5 cycles
Naghmeh	4 cycles
Paliteh	3 cycles
Naghmeh	15 cycles

First there is the *shakl*, towards the end of which the tabla enters for the optional section called *āstāi-ye tabla*. The *rubāb* continues to play *shakl* phrases; the tabla does not play a fixed cycle of beats, but the two instruments come together at the end of the *shakl* in a rhythmic cadence. The *naghmeh* proper then begins, starting with the part of the fixed composition that in India would be identified as the *mukhrā*, leading to the first beat of the cycle. This is called the *shoru naghmeh* or *shoruwāt*, 'the start of the *naghmeh*' or 'the beginning', followed by four statements of the *naghmeh*. There then follow seven alternations of *paliteh*s with statements of the *naghmeh*. The tempo accelerates throughout, but there is no evidence for any episodic organisation of the kind noted for the *ghazal* or *naghmeh-ye kashāl* in this performance. Towards the end of the piece there is a marked acceleration, so that by the final round of statements of the *naghmeh*, where the composition is repeated some fifteen times, the tempo has more than doubled.

This example is typical of both Rahim's performance of *naghmeh-ye klāsik*, when he usually played *razākhāni* compositions, and the style of *rubāb* playing of his father, Amir Jan, who learned to play in this way from Ustad Nabi Gol. Ustad Mohammad Omar also played this type of piece; indeed, the style was common amongst *rubāb* players. It is worth comparing this performance of *shakl* and *naghmeh* in *Rāg Des* with a hypothetical performance of *ālāp* and *gat* in Hindustani music, to show in greater detail the relationship between the art musics of Afghanistan and the Indian Sub-continent. There are many obvious points of similarity: the melodic characteristics of the mode called *Des* in India and Afghanistan appear to be more or less the same: there is the distinction between the introductory section in free rhythm (*shakl*, *ālāp*) and the fixed composition (*naghmeh*, *gat*); the use of interleaved melodic improvisations (*paliteh*, *tān*) and triple repetitions (*seh*, *tihāʿi*) onto the first beat of the rhythmic cycle (*gor*, *sam*); and the gradual increase in tempo to reach a climax at the end of the piece.

But the comparison reveals many differences between the two kinds of instrumental music, and it seems inevitable that the Afghan practice be regarded as musically simpler, both in conceptual structure and in execution.

1. Certain limitations arise from the instrument itself. The useful range of the *rubāb* is one and a half octaves, while that of the sitar or *sarod* is about three octaves. The fretting of the *rubāb* does not provide for microtones or glissandi, and the rapid decay of the notes from the heavy gut or nylon strings provides little scope for left hand legato other than 'hammers' and 'pulls'.
2. Performances of *naghmeh-ye klāsik* in Afghanistan rarely exceed ten minutes in length, which is very short by Hindustani criteria for live performance. While the *shakl* and *naghmeh* have the same overall organisation as *ālāp* and *gat* there are fewer discernible stages of development in *shakl* and *naghmeh*.
3. Melodic improvisations on the *rubāb* are 'in phase' with the rhythmic cycle, i.e. they usually begin on the first beat of a cycle and run to the first beat of a succeeding cycle. In example 5 most *paliteh*s end with a *seh* figure, but often in other performances this cadential device is not employed. In Hindustani music the *gat* is conceptualised as beginning with the *mukhrā*, which in the case of the *razākhāni gat* in *Des* starts on the ninth *matra*, and melodic improvisations end either with a *tihāʿi* or with the *mukhrā*. In this sense the composition and the interpolated improvisations are conceived as being 'out of phase' with the rhythmic cycle.
4. The *paliteh*s used by *rubāb* players tend to be of limited variety, with a rather constant rhythmic organisation, with one stroke per *matra*. There is a high proportion of statements of the *naghmeh* to melodic improvisation. In example 5 about forty-six per cent of the cycles in the *naghmeh* section is spent playing the fixed composition, and the proportion can be much higher.
5. While the *tihāʿi* figure of Hindustani music is employed, under the name of *seh* ('three'), in Afghanistan only the simplest figures are used.
6. The Afghans use what in India are regarded as simple, old-fashioned *gat*s, some of which are used as *lahrā*s in India, to accompany tabla solos.

The Afghans liked to hear the style of *rubāb* as exemplified by Rahim's performance of *Rāg Des*. This point was brought home to me in 1976 when I had the opportunity to listen to and record a relatively young Kabuli *rubāb* player from the Kucheh Kharabat, who played the instrument in a much more 'Indian' style, with greater use of the unfretted range, more dynamic variety, less use of the fixed composition, and more elaborate improvisations. I thought him to be an exceptional performer on the *rubāb*, but he was not usually received with praise; on the contrary, he was criticised for playing the *rubāb* 'like the *sarod*', precisely the feature that interested me about his style. I discovered from this musician that he was indeed trying to copy *sarod* players such as Ustad Ali Akbar Khan, whom he had heard on the radio, record, or cassette. His playing exceeded the aesthetic boundaries that delimited how one should play the *rubāb*.

The origins of the art music genres

The four genres of art music discussed in this chapter have been performed in Afghanistan since at least the 1920s. They are closely related to Hindustani vocal and instrumental music.

though they vary amongst themselves in this respect. Assessing the 'Hindustani contribution' to this music helps to clarify the status of the various genres and shows that a distinctly Afghan art music was developed in Kabul in the course of the last hundred years.

Of the four genres in question it is clear that *klāsik* (*khyāl*) was closest to Hindustani music. It is significant that an Afghan singer such as Ustad Sarahang was apparently quite acceptable to audiences in India, and regularly performed there at music conferences. The son of a prominent Kabuli *ustād*, he had studied in Patiala for many years. He was not alone in this respect; other Kabuli *sāzandeh* had also studied in India or Pakistan, though not for anything like as long. *Klāsik* had clearly been borrowed from India, but was often performed in a rather simplified manner in Afghanistan.

The *naghmeh-ye klāsik* clearly corresponds to the *ālāp* and *gat* form of Hindustani instrumental music. In many respects, the *naghmeh-ye klāsik*, as played on the *rubāb*, is simpler than its modern Hindustani counterpart. This might be the result of a deliberate simplification of a Hindustani genre to adapt it for playing on the *rubāb*, or it could be that the *naghmeh-ye klāsik* represents a Hindustani form as it was a hundred years ago. The style of rhythmic improvisation sometimes used for playing *naghmeh-ye klāsik* is like an archaic technique used for the *surbāhār* and sitar in India. It is perhaps revealing to note that the great Ustad Qasem's father was a sitar player at the Kabul court in the late nineteenth century.

The Kabuli *ghazal* form corresponds to the Indian *ghazal* form but bears distinct Afghan characteristics, especially in terms of its temporal organisation, in the use of gradual acceleration from a slow tempo to a fast tempo, exaggerated rhythmic cadences, and the singing of couplets in free rhythm. There is reason to suppose that the rhythmic characteristics of the Kabuli *ghazal* style derive originally from Pashtun regional music, with its interest in fast instrumental sections and rhythmic cadences. Pashtun regional music uses the *ghazal* amongst a variety of poetic-musical forms. It appears that the basic Pashtun *ghazal* form has been 'dressed up' with Hindustani elements, often sung in Hindustani *rāg*s, with Hindustani vocal performance style and ornamentation. The texts are usually in Persian, by poets of Afghan, Persian, or Indian origin. The practice of singing couplets or quatrains in free rhythm may be related to the *āvāz* style of *ghazal* singing in Iran.

The *naghmeh-ye kashāl* is the only genre of urban art music in Afghanistan which does not have a direct and obvious equivalent in India. As suggested above, the technique of rhythmic improvisation, especially using the high drone strings in the *āstāi* section, may derive from an archaic usage in India. The *antara* section is more distinctive; the separate *antara* compositions are often like very simple *gat*s (Hindustani instrumental compositions), and some are like melodies played as introductory pieces for a performance of *qawwāli* (Muslim devotional music). My own guess is that the *naghmeh-ye kashāl* is an old type of Afghan piece, its history intimately bound up with the history of the *rubāb*. Although the compositions that we have today may have been created more recently (by, for example, Ustad Qasem), they were perhaps composed in the style of a pre-existing type of piece.

By the Afghans' own account, the *ghazal* and the *naghmeh-ye kashāl* are Afghan in origin, while *khyāl* and *naghmeh-ye klāsik* have been adopted from India. The criterion of temporal organisation is one parameter that would seem to distinguish between these two kinds of art music: *Afghan* art music, as distinct from Afghan performance of Hindustani art music, is characterised by a certain kind of episodic organisation, whether it be the *antara–āstāi–duni* cycle of the *ghazal* or the use of rhythmic variation in playing *naghmeh-ye kashāl* on the *rubāb*.* This cyclical principle can be identified in other kinds of music in Afghanistan, in Pashtun regional music and in the style of popular music created and disseminated by the radio station in Kabul, which is discussed in the next chapter.

* It is perhaps necessary to state clearly the use of these various terms. By 'Kabuli art music' I refer to the art music performed in Kabul, consisting of two types: (a) Hindustani (art) music, consisting of the *khyāl* (*klāsik*) and *naghmeh-ye klāsik* genres, and (b) Afghan art music, consisting of the Kabuli *ghazal* and *naghmeh-ye kashāl* genres.

6 *Popular and Herati music*

The role of Radio Afghanistan in the creation and dissemination of a new kind of Afghan urban popular music was discussed briefly in chapter 3. It is now time to consider in greater detail the general characteristics of this music, which the *sāzandeh* of Herat were obliged to provide at most of the events at which they performed. The Herati *sāzandeh* called this *kiliwāli*, a Pashto word meaning 'of the village'. In Pashto *kiliwāli sandaray* refers to Pashtun regional music, the 'ethnic' or 'folk' music of the Pashtuns. The equivalent Persian word is *mahali*, 'local'. Both words could, in their respective languages, be used to refer to regional music as a general category, be it Pashtun, Uzbeki, Hazaregi, Herati, or whatever. The *sāzandeh* of Herat used the term *kiliwāli* in a rather special sense, to refer to the type of popular music broadcast by Radio Afghanistan. Their use of this term provides important clues as to how they regarded Afghan popular music, in contrast to art music. They saw it as unsophisticated and simple, both musically and textually, and identified it as an outgrowth of 'folk music'. This view was an accurate analysis of the origin of popular music. The world *kiliwāli* was extended even further, so that Iranian popular music (as performed in Iran) was called *kiliwāli Irāni*, and instrumental *dhun*s played on *shahnā'i* or sitar in India were described as *kiliwāli Hindi*.

The criteria for identifying *kiliwāli* as 'popular music' have been examined by Baily (1981b: 120–21). Only a short résumé of the arguments is needed here. (1) The people themselves distinguished the genre in question as a distinct category, and contrasted it with other types of music, with *klāsik* and *ghazal* singing on one hand, and with Herati regional music on the other. (2) *Kiliwāli* was closely associated with the sound broadcasting and recording media, which formed an indispensable element in the network of communication between the users of the music – the creators, performers, and audience. (3) *Kiliwāli* had a rapid turnover of repertory. The recognition of this fact by the audience was an important part of their perception and appreciation of the music and became an issue of central interest. (4) Leading exponents of *kiliwāli* in Kabul were given a special 'star' status (Slobin 1974:245–6). Particular songs were identified with known singers and there was a keen interest in a favourite singer's latest song. Familiarity with a 'star system' had come about through the Indian films shown in Afghan cinemas, the sale of postcard portraits of famous Indian actors and actresses, and magazine articles about them.

The Pashtun basis of Afghan popular music

The popular music style that developed at Radio Afghanistan, and which was adopted by the Heratis, had many characteristics in common with Pashtun music and can be regarded as having been modelled on it. Certain problems arise in making this assertion because too little research has been carried out for us to specify the precise characteristics of Pashtun music.

Within the predominantly Pashtun territories of south-east Afghanistan there was considerable regional variation in musical style, and there were important differences between rural and urban music. The situation was further complicated by the possible feedback of the radio style on Pashtun music. During a visit to Peshawar in 1985 I heard a good deal of Pashtun music, as played by both Afghan and Pakistani musicians. This aural evidence convinces me that the Pashtun urban style of cities such as Jalalabad and Kandahar forms the basis of Afghan popular music.

Traditionally, the typical Pashtun group consisted of a singer accompanied by *rubāb*, *sarinda* and *doholak*. Sometime in the late nineteenth or early twentieth century the harmonium was added to this kind of ensemble, and became indispensable. Pashtun music utilises a variety of song forms, such as *tappā*, *chahārbeita*, *ghazal*, *loba*, *rubāʿi*, and *dastān*, but discussion of the differences between them falls outside the scope of the present study. Slobin (1976:90–1) gives some details of the *tappā*, or *landay* as it is also called. The *dastān* is an epic composed of quatrains, and provides a point of overlap with Pashtun folklore and oral history (see Elphinstone's comments on page 17). There is also an important repertory of short instrumental dance pieces in Pashtun music. The Logar Valley, south-west of Kabul, was particularly famous for such tunes (see the discussion of example 11 below). What the vocal forms have in common is the regular alternation of vocal and instrumental sections, the latter played at fast tempo and terminated by heavily emphasised rhythmic cadences. The rhythmic cadence seems to be one of the dominating characteristics of Pashtun music, and may be used to terminate lines of text as well as instrumental sections. The *rubāb* is very well suited to this fast percussive music.

The generalised Pashtun song form was adopted for popular radio songs. Whatever the precise nature of the poetry sung, the text was used as though it consisted of verses and a refrain, each having different melodies. The melody for the verse section almost invariably had a higher tessitura than the melody of the refrain. *Sāzandeh* used the terms *antara* and *āstāi* for the two parts of the song, *antara* for verse, *āstāi* for refrain. The form was not unlike the *ghazal*, but instead of playing a *duni* (an instrumental reiteration of the *āstāi* melody), an independent *naghmeh* was inserted between *antara*–*āstāi* units. The texts of popular radio songs were generally in Dari. The *Pāri* and *Kesturi* modes, already important in Pashtun music, were used a great deal, but *Bairami* was by far the most common mode, which may relate to an 'older stratum' of 'Persian music' in Kabul, which probably used the *Shur* scale extensively (as in Herat, see page 46). The radio style therefore synthesised elements of the music cultures of the two main ethnic groups in Afghanistan, Pashtun and Tajik, 'systematised' and 'improved' in the light of Hindustani theory and practice. Pashtun culture provided the basic musical style, Tajik culture the poetry and the most common melodic mode.

The radio station broadcast a variety of music, from *khyāl*, *ghazal*s, Hindustani instrumental music, Indian film songs, to performances by 'folk musicians' who came to Kabul to perform over the air on their own regional instruments. The station employed many kinds of musical ensemble, from the harmonium, *rubāb*, *sarinda*, *doholak* combination of Pashtun music to large orchestras such as the *orkestrā-ye bozorg* I observed in 1977, which consisted of two *rubāb*s, two *tanbur*s, mandoline, Spanish guitar, *tulak* (cross-blown wooden flute), Boehm flute, piccolo, two tenor saxophones, clarinet, piano, string bass, tabla, sitar, and *delrubā* (Baily 1918b:110–11). Of the traditional Pashtun instruments the *rubāb* was elevated to the status of the national instrument of Afghanistan, and was generally prominent in the typical radio ensemble, while the *sarinda* remained a 'folk instrument', and was often replaced or augmented by the *delrubā* or *sārangi* (both Indian instruments). The *doholak* was likewise replaced by the tabla.

The popular music repertory derived from a variety of sources. Local songs from different regions of Afghanistan formed an important input to the radio repertory; the music of Parwan Province, immediately to the north of Kabul, seems to have been particularly important in this respect. Some songs were composed by singers employed at the radio station, notably educated middle-class amateurs who held staff positions at the station as producers, directors, and administrators. Some songs were adapted from Hindi films, others borrowed from Iran. The example of Herat shows how regional songs were adopted by the radio station, reworked in the popular music style, with a newly composed instrumental section (*naghmeh*), and broadcast with orchestral accompaniment. The singer Madadi, a Herati employed on the staff of Radio Afghanistan, made trips to Herat to collect local songs which he then recorded at the radio station, and usually broadcast at least once. A old Herati song could then become a new popular song in Afghanistan, and be given a new lease of life back in Herat. Probably the most popular song from Herat in recent years was '*Mullāh Mohammad Jān*', which was very common in the late 1960s and early 1970s (see Sakata 1983:144–5). During the time of my fieldwork there were no songs from Herat enjoying this kind of popularity.

Many singers from Herat had been to Kabul to record their songs. An examination of the sound archive at Radio Afghanistan in 1977 showed that forty-four Heratis had recordings there. Of these, eleven had recorded ten or more items, and three singers had more than twenty items: Madadi had one hundred and twenty-one, Nawak sixty-six, and Amir Jan Saburi twenty-eight. Less than half the artists were known to me; many of those I did not know had recorded just one or two items. Not all the recordings were of Herati songs. Amir Jan Khushnawaz had six *ghazal*s in the archive. Herat seemed well represented: there were eight artists from Kandahar, five from Ghazni, five from Mazar, twenty from Jalalabad, fifteen from Paktia, twenty from Logar. This high proportion, of course, reflects Herat's large population.

Genres of popular music in Herat

Much of the *kiliwāli* repertory played by the *sāzandeh* of Herat was learned from Radio Afghanistan. Iranian popular music was another important source of new songs, so were films from India and Pakistan, and other items were derived from several regional musics of Afghanistan. Few songs in Pashto were ever performed in Herat, and then usually by women theatre singers who were Pashto speakers. The various genres of *kilawāli* played by the Herati *sāzandeh* were generally labelled according to their place of origin: *Kābuli*, *Uzbeki*, *Mazāri*, *Irāni*, *Hindi*, *Shomāli*, *Logari*, etc. The following examples have been chosen to illustrate these various genres.

Kābuli

The history of urban music in Afghanistan over the last 100 years shows that innovations occurred first in Kabul and then spread to other towns and cities. By the 1970s a very modern style had developed, with the addition of instruments such as the electric organ, electric guitar, trumpet, and the *jaz*, as they called the trap drum set. Musically there was a tendency towards the use of simple chord progressions.

Example 6 on the cassette, '*Kajaki*', is an example of a song originally performed in this modern style. Very popular in 1976, it was composed and originally sung over the radio by Ahmad Zahir (son of a former Prime Minister of Afghanistan) who often played in Western-style nightclubs in Kabul (before they were closed in 1973). Ahmad Zahir sang and played the electric organ rather than the harmonium, accompanied by electric guitar and *jaz*. Here the song is performed by Ali Ahmad, vocal and harmonium; Amir, *rubāb*; Ghulam Haidar, *dutār*; and Jalil, tabla and vocal refrain. The performance took place at a large party in Ali Ahmad's compound to celebrate a circumcision. It was a mixed party with men and women together. A bandstand was erected and several male singers took turns to perform.

This example shows many of the basic features of the popular music form and style. The text and form of '*Kajaki*' are shown below.

Music	Text		Translation
Āstāi	Zing zing zing (a)	*Āstāi*	Zing zing zing
	Zinga zinga zing zing zing (b) (3 times)		Zinga zinga zing zing zing 'Little crooked one' your eyebrows are like the point of a serpent's tail
	Kajaki Kajaki Kajaki abruyat nish-e gezhdom ast (c)		
	Chi konam afsus māl-e mardom ast (d)		What can I do? Alas, you're someone else's
	Kajaki abruyat nish-e gezhdom ast (e)	*Antara* 1	Who has two intoxicating eyes? Who has two snake's tail eyebrows?
	Chi konam afsus māl-e mardom ast (d)		I'll wander in the wilderness Asking who is your guardian
Naghmeh		*Antara* 2	Oh girl, I love you, what do you say?
Antara 1	Du cheshm-e por khumāratrā ki dāre		Why haven't you talked to your relatives?
	Du abru domb-e māratrā ki dāre		I've talked to my relatives
	Begardam kuh be kuh sarā be sarā		If your people won't give you, what will you say?
	Beporsam ekhtiāratrā ki dāre		
Āstāi	a,b,b,c,d,e,d	*Antara* 3	If I had but one pain, what then?
Naghmeh			If pain was only trifling, what then?
Antara 2	Alā dokhtar turā māyam chi migi		Come to my bedside as a healer or friend
	Chirā ba qaum o khesh-e khod nemigi		If you were either of those, what then?
	Me ku bam qaum o khesh-e khod bigoftam		
	Turā bā man nemidam tu chi migi		
Āstāi	a,b,b,c,d,e,d		
Naghmeh			
Antara 3	Agar dardum yaki budi chi budi		
	Agar ghamandaki budi chi budi		
	Be bālinam tabib biā habibi		
	Az in du gar yaki budi chi budi		
Āstāi	a,b,b,c,d,e,d		
Naghmeh			

Genres of popular music in Herat

Antara 4	Du cheshm-e por khumāratrā ki dāre	*Antara* 4	same as *Antara* 1
	Du abru domb-e māratrā ki dāre		
	Begardam kuh be kuh sarā be sarā		
	Beporsam ekhtiāratrā ki dāre		
Āstāi	a,b,b,c,d,e,d		
Naghmeh			

The melodic mode is *Kesturi* and the rhythm a fast *Dādreh*. The *antara* and *āstāi* melodies are fairly typical of *Kesturi*, except the *Re Ma Pe* phrase used to sing '*Zing zing zing*'. Amateur composers like Ahmad Zahir were said by the *sāzandeh* to be ignorant about melodic modes and to frequently break their rules. The *naghmeh* is also constructed from this phrase. In the *naghmeh*s, which close with pronounced rhythmic cadences, the tempo increases, and members of the audience, many of them women musicians, clap along with the music, while the *rubāb* and *dutār* play on the high drone strings. Later in the song the clapping begins in the *āstāi* sections. Clapping with the *naghmeh* of a song was a common form of audience participation, and underlines the musical role of the *naghmeh* as an expression of rhythmic excitement. Comparison with Ahmad Zahir's version of '*Kajaki*' reveals a number of differences. Ali Ahmad has altered the tune of the *antara* somewhat, and the original does not conform to the standard *kiliwāli* form, having few *naghmeh*s, which are treated more like solos for electric guitar.

Shomāli

Shomāli refers to a densely populated region to the north of Kabul, in Parwan Province. The people are mainly Tajiks and speak Dari. Charikar is the principal town in this region, and is the centre for a local music which combines Dari texts with Pashtun musical style, one of the prototypes of popular radio music.

Example 7, '*Chahārbeiti Shomāli*', is an interesting genre, which appears to be based on a regional song style, usually performed *bi lai*, in free rhythm, like the *chahārbeiti*s of Herat region (see below), the *falak*s of Badakhshan (Sakata 1983:54–5, 156–65), and the *landay* of Pashtun areas (Slobin 1976:90–1). The *chahārbeiti* of the Shomali area, like that of Herat, is a melodic 'vehicle' for the singing of quatrains, the same stereotyped melodies being used for the singing of any number of *beit*s, selected from the singer's memory. According to Sakata (1983:53) *shomāli* is the most widely known melody-type throughout Afghanistan. Though familiar to Heratis, '*Chahārbeiti Shomāli*' was not usually sung by them. It is performed here by Amir Mohammad, vocal and harmonium; Rahim Khushnawaz, *rubāb*; Gada Mohammad, *dutār*; and Fazl Ahmad, tabla; at a *Ramazān* concert in 1974 (when examples 3 and 4 were also recorded). The complete recording lasts ten minutes, and only the first four quatrains are given here.

Music	Text	Translation	
Antara 1	Gham-e eshqat biābān parwaram kard	*Antara* 1	Sadness at love for you has made me frequent the desert
	Hawāyat morgh-e bi bāl o pāram kard		Your air has made me into a bird without wings or feathers

Āstāi 1	Marā gofti saburi kon saburi		You told me to wait, to wait
	Saburi khāk-e ālam ba saram kard		Waiting has brought me a world of unhappiness
	Chi shod gar khāter-e khoram nadāram	Āstāi 1	What would happen if I had no fresh memories
	Gham-e eshq-e tu dāram gham nadāram		I'm sad through love of you, I have no other sadness
	Agar mordam makon mātam be margam		If I die, don't mourn for me
	Shahid-e bikasam mātam nadāram		I'm a martyr without family, I have no one to mourn me
Naghmeh			
Antara 2	Marā az duriat bimāro kardi	Antara 2	You've made me ill by being far away
	Be bālinam fegandi zāro kardi		You've thrown me to languish in my bed
	Bā man ahd-e mohebat basta budi		You had a firm promise of love with me
	Cherā ai biwafā in kāro kardi?		Oh unfaithful one, why have you done this?
Āstāi 2	Az awal biwafā budi azizam	Āstāi 2	You were unfaithful from the beginning, my dear one
	Bā matlab āshenā budi azizam		You were faithful to your own designs, my dear one
	Ze bas didam khelāf-e wādehatrā		So many times have I seen your broken promises
	Be har kas āshenā budi azizam		Whoever you were faithful to, my dear one
Naghmeh			

The melodic mode is *Bairami* played from *Diwāt*, and the melodic line is sung over a slow *Mogholi* in which the third and sixth beats are stressed on the tabla. After some lines the tabla plays a rhythmic cadence onto the *gor* beat, from which the metre can be perceptually established. The poetry consists of quatrains with aaba or aaaa rhyme schemes. Two closely related but distinct melodies are used to sing the first and second members of each quatrain pair. The melody of the first quatrain, being higher in tessitura than the second, is called the *antara*, while the second is called the *āstāi*. The *naghmeh* played after each pair of quatrains is in a fast *Mogholi*. This is an example of a Logari *naghmeh* (see also example 13), and it gives '*Chahārbeiti Shomāli*' a strongly Pashtun character.

Filmi

Another source of new songs was provided by the films from India and Pakistan which were shown in the cinemas of Kabul and other cities. Since the innovation of synchronised sound film in India in the 1930s, most commercial Indian films had a strong element of music and dance. Film music became the popular music of India, with its dissemination assisted by phonographs and radio broadcasting (Skillman 1986). Gramophone records were undoubtedly an important influence in Afghanistan long before the first cinemas were established, even though gramophones were few and far between (see Byron's comments on page 29). Over the years many *filmi* songs were adopted by Afghan singers and entered the popular music repertory. Since most of these *filmi* songs were originally performed in Hindi or Urdu, their adoption posed certain problems. Sometimes the singer attempted to reproduce the

Genres of popular music in Herat

original text; sometimes a new text was written in Persian, or a pre-existing text adapted to a *filmi* song tune. Some Kabuli song-writers copied the style of Indian film songs in their compositions.

Example 8 is the *filmi* song '*Chal chal chal mere sāthi*' sung by Mahmud Khushnawaz at a wedding party in 1977, the band consisting of Mahmud, vocal and harmonium; Amir Jan, *rubāb*; Ghulam Nebi, *dutār*; Naim, tabla. The text is in Urdu, a language largely based on Persian, and partly comprehensible to Heratis, and Mahmud reproduces it with sufficient clarity for it to be understood by an Urdu speaker.

Music	Text		Translation
Fard	Nemidānam ke bāz kārwān-e khat chi āworde	Fard	I don't know what letters the post has brought
	Agar dānam ke nerkhe buse arzān mishawad		If only I knew, the rate for kisses would go down
Āstāi	Chal chal chal mere sāthi	Āstāi	Let's go go go my companion
	O mere hāthi		O my elephant
	Chal chal kātara ki chāki		Go go nervous grinding-stone
	Chali ā hato mat o banda ho motargāri		Come along, don't give way O let that motor car be a slave
	Chali ā hato mat	"Bridge"	Let's go go go my companion
"Bridge"	Chal chal chal mere sāthi		Oh oh
	O...O...	Antara 1	The delicate wafting of the flowers
Antara 1	Phulon ki nāzuk hawā		That lingers in the breeze
	Hawā men rahti hai jo		The delicate wafting of the flowers
	Phulon ki nāzuk hawā		That lingers in the breeze
	Hawā men rahti hai jo		Go on, slowly, slowly
	Āhista āhista chal		May no trouble be upon you
	Tujh ko na taklif ho		Yes, yes, come, won't you
	Hai hai ā nā jay		Yes, yes, come, won't you
	Hai hai ā nā jay		On that delicate belly let not a hair be harmed
	Us ki nāzuk kamariyā men bāl		
Āstāi	Chal chal chal mere sāthi	Āstāi	
	O mere hāthi	Antara 2	You who lifted me up
	Chal chal kātara ki chāki		How faithful you remained
	Chali ā hato mat		In the whole world
Naghmeh			Your love is true
Antara 2	Tu jo uthāyā rahā		You're mad, aren't you, mad
	Kitnā wafādār hai		You're mad, aren't you, mad
	Hotā hai sārā jahān		(Don't you realise) the whole world has changed?
	Sachā terā pyār hai	Āstāi	
	Tu paglā nā paglā		
	Tu paglā nā paglā		
	Sāri duniyā gai hai badal chal		
Āstāi	Chal chal chal mere sāthi		
	O mere hāthi		
	Chali ā hato mat o banda ho motargāri		
	Chali ā hato mat		
Naghmeh			

The mode is *Pāri* and the metre *Gedeh*. After a brief *shakl* to establish *Pāri* (after singing in *Bairami*) Mahmud starts with an introductory *fard* before beginning the song. The melodic lines are more complex than is usual with Afghan popular songs, and instantly recognisable as 'Indian'. There is an unusual feature of the musical form: after singing the *āstāi* for the first time Mahmud goes on to sing an *antara*, whereas it would be more usual to play a *naghmeh* at this point. The transition from *āstāi* to *antara* is effected by the addition of what amounts to a 'bridge passage'. The *naghmeh* is taken from the last line of the *āstāi*, and shows an increase in tempo.

Irāni

In the 1970s the direct input of Persian music into Herat was in the form of popular songs. In those years Iran was undergoing a boom in popular music, with many independent record companies releasing singles in a wide variety of popular music styles. The situation is described by Nettl (1972). New songs from Iran reached Herat either via radio broadcasts or through cassettes. A few singers in Herat made a speciality of adapting the latest Iranian 'hits' for performance in the urban Afghan style. Nawak, an amateur turned professional singer who often performed with *sāzandeh* bands, copied the Iranian singing style very closely, and was responsible for the introduction of many Iranian songs. These were often recorded for Radio Afghanistan by Herati singers, and sometimes taken up by Kabuli artists. It seems that such songs were often identified as Herati songs in other parts of Afghanistan, and it is clear that of all the regional styles of Afghanistan Herati music was most like Persian music. In 1971-2 the most popular song in Herat was '*Āmineh*', originally sung by the Iranian singer Aghasi.

Example 9 is the Iranian song '*Fereshteh jān qashangi*' performed by Amir Mohammad, vocal and harmonium; Rahim, *rubāb*; Gada, *dutār*; and Jalil, tabla; at a wedding party in 1976. This song became popular in Herat in that year.

Music	Text		Translation
Fard	Zenhār maiyāzār ze khod-e delirā	Fard	God forbid that you offend another heart
	Ke hich deli nist ke rāhi ba Khodā nist		There is no heart that lacks a way to God
	Kherāj-e molk bā gonjeshk midahad shāhbāz		Or a falcon would pay tribute to a sparrow
	Zamāneh ba tu nasāzad tu bā zamāneh besāz		If circumstances don't suit you, you have to adapt to them
Āstāi	Fereshteh jān qashangi, belāi	Āstāi	Dear Fereshteh, you are pretty, naughty teaser
	Makon tu digar az man jedāi		Don't go away from me again
	Fereshteh jān qashangi, belāi		I love you oh Fereshteh
	Makon tu digar az man jedāi		Your anger and your fights oh Fereshteh
	Man ke turā dust dāram ai Fereshteh		
	Ghāhr-e tu o jang-e tu ai Fereshteh		
	Man ke turā dust dāram ai Feresh(teh)		
	Ghāhr-e tu o jang-e tu ai Feresh(teh)		
Naghmeh			

Genres of popular music in Herat

Antara	Gol-e mekhak-e man barāyat kharidam	*Antara*	I bought you a carnation
	Be har jā ke raftam turā man nadidam		Anywhere I went I didn't see you
	Tā bezanam be sinehat Feresh(teh)		So that I could place it on your breast
	Tā bezanam be sinehat Feresh(teh)		
	Tā bezanam be sinehat Feresh(teh)		
	Tā bezanam be sinehat Feresh(teh)		
Āstāi	Fereshteh jān qashangi, belāi		
	Makon tu digar az man jedāi		
	Man ke turā dust dāram ai Fereshteh		
	Ghāhr-e tu jang-e tu ai Fereshteh		
Naghmeh			
Antara	Gol-e mekhak-e man barāyat kharidam		
	Be har jā ke raftam turā man nadidam		
	Tā bezanam be sinehat Fereshteh		
	Tā bezanam be sinehat Feresh(teh)		
	Tā bezanam be sinehat Fereshteh		
	Tā bezanam be sinehat Feresh(teh)		
Āstāi	Fereshteh jān qashangi, belāi		
	Makon tu digar az man jedāi		
	Man ke turā dust dāram ai Fereshteh		
	Ghāhr-e tu o jang-e tu ai Feresh(teh)		
	Man ke turā dust dāram ai Feresh(teh)		
	Ghāhr-e tu o jang-e tu ai Fereshteh		

The mode is *Jog* and the metre is *Dādreh*. This example shows the application of Pashtun musical style to a Persian song presumably performed originally in a quite different manner. It is short, and was sung in response to a request at the end of a *chashni*, hence the emphatic closing section at the end. It may be that the singer forgot the other verses and so repeats the *antara* he has already sung. The song is prefaced with an introductory *fard*, with more weighty poetry than found in the rest of the text.

Example 10 '*Eh del belāi delbar*' is another example of an Iranian popular song, in this case performed by a band of women *sāzandeh*: Anar, vocal and harmonium; Bibi Jan, tabla; and Urak, *dāireh*. The occasion was the same circumcision celebration at which example 6 was recorded, and the song was collected by Veronica Doubleday before the women joined the men.

Music	Text	Translation	
Antara 1	Maram az duriat bimāro kardi delbar	*Antara* 1	You made me ill by being far away darling

	Be bālinam fegandi zāro kardi delbar		You've thrown me to languish in my bed darling
	Be man ahd-e mohabat basteh budi delbar		You had a firm promise of love with me darling
	Cherā eh biwafā in kāro kardi delbar		Oh unfaithful one, why have you done this darling?
Āstāi	Eh del belāi delbar bālā belāi delbar	Āstāi	Oh heart, you're a teaser darling, up there you're a teaser darling
	Eh del belāi delbar bālā belāi delbar		
	Dar entezāram key az dar dar āyi delbar		I'm waiting for you to come in the door darling
	Dar entezāram key az dar dar āyi delbar		
Naghmeh			
Antara 2	Shabi az del ze del goftam qalamrā delbar	Antara 2	In the night I told my pen from the bottom of my heart, darling
	Biā tarif konim ghamhā delamrā delbar		Come, let's boast about the sorrows of my heart darling
	Shabi az del ze del goftam qalamrā delbar		
	Biā tarif konim ghamhā delamrā delbar		
	Qalam gofte buro bichāreh āsheq delbar		My pen said go, you poor love-lorn thing darling
	Nadārum tāqat-e in kuh-ye ghamrā delbar		I don't have endurance for this mountain of sadness darling
Āstāi	Eh del belāi delbar bālā belāi delbar	Antara 3	At night I'm up on the wall like a pigeon darling
	Eh del belāi delbar bālā belāi delbar		By God I'm wakeful through love for you darling
	Dar entezāram key az dar dar āyi delbar		So long as you're not unfaithful darling
	Dar entezāram key az dar dar āyi delbar		By God, I'm your love until Judgement Day darling
Naghmeh			
Antara 3	Kebutar sar-e diwālet hastam delbar		
	Ba wullāh āshuqi bidāret hastam delbar		
	Age az tu nayāye biwafāyi delbar		
	Be wullāh tā qiāmat yāret hastam delbar		
Āstāi	Eh del belāi delbar bālā belāi delbar		
	Eh del belāi delbar bālā belāi delbar		
	Dar entezāram key az dar dar āyi delbar		
	Dar entezāram key az dar dar āyi delbar		

The mode is *Bairami* and the metre *Dādreh*. One of the features of the women's style of performance is the joining of several voices together. The leader sings the first half of a line, and others sing the second half, producing a type of antiphonal singing. The tabla style is also noteworthy, using flat handed strokes on the two drums. During the *naghmeh*s the audience clap along, and there are also abrupt accelerations of tempo at these points.

Genres of popular music in Herat

Mazāri

Some of the popular songs performed in Herat derived from the Mazar-e Sharif region of northern Afghanistan, where one of the putative tombs of Ali was located. Such songs were associated with the forth-day Tulip Festival (*Meleh-ye Gol-e Sorkh*) that took place every springtime, and they would appear to derive from the Uzbek-Tajik teahouse music of the north (Slobin 1976:161–75).

Example 11 '*Seil-e gol-e sorkh be Sekhi Jān-e*' is from this repertory. It is performed by Amir, vocal and harmonium; Ahmad, *dutār*; Kholek Sauz, *dutār*; Bolbol Hairawi, *zirbaghali*; and Ghulam, *duzangeh*. The occasion was a *meleh* at Pul-e Malan in Herat in 1977. The group is what I term a *dutār* band, even though the leader is a singer and harmonium player (whereas in the typical *dutār* band the singer usually also plays the *dutār*). There are two *dutār*s in the group, with *zirbaghali* rather than tabla, and the addition of a pair of rattles called *duzangeh*, which are designed to imitate the sound of the bells worn by dancing boys.

Music	Text	Translation	
Āstāi	Seil-e gol-e sorkh be Sekhi Jān e	*Āstāi*	The sight of the red flowers at Ali's shrine
	Ai shahr-e Herāt borde mehmāne		Has brought guests, oh city of Herat
	Seil-e gol-e sorkh be Sekhi Jān e		The sight of the red flowers at Ali's shrine
	Ai Shahr-e Mazār karde mehmāne		Has made guests come, oh city of Mazar
Duni			
Naghmeh 1			
Antara 1	Tufān karde gol sabze dar jush e	Antara 1	The flowers and greenery are blooming like a storm
	Dasht o biābān namad gol push e		The desert and wilderness are covered with flowers like a felt rug
	Gar suy-e chahār bāgh gole bā jānim		Going to the park wearing a flower
	Ziyārat bekonim chi jam o jush e		We'll pay homage at the shrine which is all bursting with people
Āstāi 2	Seil-e gol-e sorkh be Sekhi Jān e	*Āstāi* 2	The sight of the red flowers at Ali's shrine
	Ai shahr-e Mazār borde mehmāne		Has brought guests, oh city of Mazar
	Meleh-ye gol-e sorkh be Sekhi Jān e		
	Ai shahr-e Herāt borde mehmāne		
Naghmeh 2			
Naghmeh 3			
Antara 2	Meleh gol-e sorkh ruz-e Now Ruz e	Antara 2	The red tulip festival, it's New Year's Day today
	Golhāye lāleh chi del afruz e		The tulips – how bright the heart is!
	Biā be Mazār o nafas jānim		Let's go to Mazar oh dearest
	Ziyārat mikunim duniā seh ruz e		We'll pay our devotions at the shrine, life is short
Āstāi 3	Meleh gol-e sorkh be Sekhi Jān e	*Āstāi* 3	The red flower festival at Ali's shrine
	Ai shahr-e Mazār karde mehmāne		Has made guests come, oh city of Mazar
	Meleh gol-e sorkh be Sekhi Jān e		
	Ai shahr-e Mazār karde mehmāne		
Duni			
Naghmeh 4			
Antara 3	Rowzeh Sekhi Jān fakhr-e bimāri	Antara 3	Ali's tomb takes pride in healing the sick

	Daur-e gombade jome nafari		There are crowds of people around the dome
	Kheil-e kaftarhā be sar-e gombad		
	Bāshad bāsafā ham chu wāri		A flock of pigeons on top of the dome
Āstāi 4	Seil-e gol-e sorkh be Sekhi Jān e		
	Ai shahr-e Mazār borde mehmāne		May it be revered just like this
	Seil-e gol-e sorkh be Sekhi Jān e	Āstāi 4	The sight of the red flowers at Ali's shrine
	Ai shahr-e Mazār borde mehmāne		
Duni, leading into *dutār* solo and next song			Has brought guests, oh city of Mazar

The melodic mode is *Bairami* and the metre is *Mogholi*. The song melodies are simple and short, typical of Afghan folk music. The performance shows several points of interest. There is the usual division into verse and refrain sections. Note the use of *gor* beats at the end of the *antara* sections. Two types of *naghmeh* are played: those which are like a *duni*, that is, a repetition of the *āstāi* melody as a fast instrumental piece at an accelerating tempo; and independent *naghmehā*, of the Logari type, led by the *dutārs*, which are noticeably out of tune to *sāzandeh* ears. This example gives a good idea of the general 'rawness' of *dutār* band music. The rattles provide an excellent guide to the changing rhythmic density, as the music proceeds from *antara* to *āstāi*, *duni* or *naghmeh*.

Naghmeh Uzbeki

A number of instrumental pieces, usually played on the *dutār* (three- or fourteen-stringed versions of the instrument) were described as *Uzbeki*. The Uzbeks are a large Turkic speaking ethnic group living mostly in northern Afghanistan. The origin of such pieces is obscure; clearly there is a relationship with northern teahouse music, traditionally associated with the *dambura*, but these pieces were cultivated by *tanbur* players in the city of Mazar-e Sharif, and were originally learned by Heratis from them, either directly or through audio cassettes.

Example 12, 'Uzbeki', is an example of such a purely instrumental piece, played on the fourteen stringed *dutār* by Gada Mohammad, accompanied by Naim on tabla. The mode is *Bairami* and the metre is *Gedeh*. This excerpt comes from the end of a sequence of tunes in *Bairami* played as a single *chashni*, and consequently is not prefaced by a *shakl*. The *Uzbeki* tune is played twice. Each rendering consists of a sequence of phrases, each usually repeated several times, which show a gradual ascent through the pitch range, and then a gradual descent. This is reminiscent of the *antara* section of the *naghmeh-ye kashāl* (see page 69). Gada follows this *Uzbeki* piece (one minute and fifty-three seconds into the recording) with the tune of the song 'Jom Jom Ki', variously classified as a *Mazāri* or *Uzbeki* tune. Although I have been told this song derives from an Indian film it is certainly like a teahouse song from the north and in Herat was used for the singing of quatrains, often by two or more singers taking turns to sing verses. Although tunes like example 12 were often played in the context of dancing boy parties, Gada Mohammad also played this kind of piece in his solo spot at *Ramazān* concerts.

Naghmehā-ye bāzi

Naghmehā-ye bāzi constituted a repertory of dance tunes associated with dancing boys and played for their dance performances (*bacheh bāzi*, 'boy play', see chapter 8). *Sāzandeh* musicians did not openly admit to playing for dancing boys – more usually such accompaniment was provided by a *dutār* and *zirbaghali* duo – though there is no doubt that on occasion they were hired for such parties. At wedding parties, solo dancing was also performed by young men from amongst the guests, who danced to the same music as dancing boys, 'quodlibets' of dance tunes (as Slobin (1976:169) has called such sequences in Afghan Turkestan), played one after another. Some were purely instrumental pieces, others were old song melodies that had passed into the dance repertory.

The creative selection and stringing together of discrete dance and song tunes had much in common with improvising a song text from memorised couplets, and with the way the *ghazal* singer constructed his texts (see chapter 5). Some of the tunes played for *bāzi* were derived from the *Uzbeki/Mazāri* repertory. Another important source was the Logar region, south-west of Kabul. *Logari* tunes were short and ended with emphatic rhythmic cadences, followed by prolonged pauses, particularly suitable for stringing together in long sequences. The pause was an important structural element for the dancer, who froze at this point until the music started again. *Logari naghmeh*s could be described as quintessentially Pashtun in spirit. They existed in the modes of *Pāri*, *Kesturi*, and *Bairami*, and many of those that were in current use in Herat in the 1970s were created by Ustad Duray Logari, a singer and harmonium player who achieved great prominence at Radio Afghanistan.

Example 13 consists of a set of such tunes played for a dancer at a wedding party by Mahmud (on the same occasion at which example 8 was recorded) and is an extract from a performance of dance music lasting for about half-an-hour. The sequence of dance pieces is shown below.

Naghmeh Logari 1
Naghmeh Logari 2
Naghmeh Logari 3
Mazāri/Uzbeki
Naghmeh Logari 1
Naghmeh Logari 1
'*Aushāri*' – '*Baleh Bābā Mizrā Maʿshalā*'
'*Aushāri*' played very fast
Naghmeh Logari 1

The sequence starts with three well known *Naghmehā-ye Logari* in *Bairami*. The rhythmic metre is *Mogholi*. *Naghmeh* 1 is a classic short *Logari* piece ending in a strong rhythmic cadence, and reappears three times later on. *Naghmeh*s 2 and 3 are also very common, and can be prolonged, as they are here, by the multiple repetition of a phrase in the middle of the tune. In Pashtun music rhythmic accompaniment was usually provided by the *doholak*, and Naim plays *doholak*-like patterns in this part of example 13.

The *Mazāri/Uzbeki* piece that follows is a standard tune for singing quatrains. The mode is still *Bairami*, the metre is now *Gedeh*. *Naghmeh Logari* 1 is played again, twice, at the end of the *Uzbeki* tune.

In the next piece there is a change of mode to *Jog*. This piece is played in response to a request for '*Irāni*' by the dancer. The band plays '*Aushāri*', a village dance usually performed by a group of men to music of the *sornā* and *dohol*. Sakata (1983:137–40) discusses several performances of '*Aushāri*' in Herat. At least two distinct '*Aushāri*' compositions were played by *sornā* and *dohol* musicians, one in *Bairami*, the other in *Jog*, both in *Dādreh*. *'Aushārī'* was one of the few traditional Herati tunes that were regularly performed by the *sāzandeh*, usually as music for dancing. In this performance *'Aushārī'* merges without interruption into a modern Herati song, *'Baleh bābā Mirzā Ma'shalā'*, composed by the singer Ghulam Nebi Zendeh Del, and broadcast by him over the radio. The mode and metre of *'Aushārī'* are maintained in this piece.

'Aushārī' is then played again at a very fast tempo with a good deal of *shukh*, 'mischievousness', from Amir Jan on *rubāb*, who plays on the *sim-e bajgi* throughout, Ghulam Nebi, who strums the strings *below* the bridge of the *dutār*, and Naim, who plays very exaggerated patterns on the tabla, similar to drum patterns played in *sornā* and *dohol* music.

The excerpt closes with another statement of *Naghmeh Logari* 1.

Herati music

The Heratis distinguished certain genres of music as *mahali*, 'local', by which they referred to what they considered constituted the old music of Herat, or new music composed in the Herati idiom. *Mahali Herāti* embraced a complicated set of genres, including rural folksong, unaccompanied *na't* singing by Sufis, wedding songs, and *sornā* and *dohol* music (itself consisting of dance music, pieces for the folk drama, and *naghmeh*s associated with the *naqqārak-hāneh*). Some people described the old Persian music of the 1920s as *mahali*, and I even heard the claim that Iranian *dastgāh* music originated in Herat.

To some extent the Heratis had a 'folkloristic' attitude towards their own music, due in part to the intervention of Radio Afghanistan. *Fokloristik* and *foklorik* were terms used on the radio and by educated speakers, deriving presumably from French. The presentation of Herati musical folklore was fostered by the Herat Nanderi, a theatre run by the local office of the Ministry for Information and Culture. When Sakata worked in Herat in the early 1970s a second theatre, the Behzad Nanderi, was also active. Most of Sakata's (1983) examples of urban Herati music derive from the two theatres. This was quite appropriate for the purpose of her study, which was to examine Herati music, as distinct from the music played in Herat. *Mahali* was not the major part of the song repertory of the theatre, but it did form a substantial component, and Herati songs which were hardly ever performed anywhere else were performed there. Sakata's examples from the theatre (Sakata 1983: examples 1, 3, 4, 5, and 6) are songs with texts by contemporary poets, performed in the urban popular music style, by singers who were otherwise not instrumentalists.

The folkloristic attitude to Herati music was manifest in the apparent 'urbanisation' of genres of rural Herati music, such as the melody-types for the singing of quatrains in free rhythm. These were commonly called *chahārbeiti*, a term which refers both to a poetic form, the quatrain (though the appellation is actually incorrect, see *ibid*.: 54) and a musical form for the performance of the poetry. This may be compared with the dual meaning of *ghazal* (see page 60). *Chahārbeiti* was also an important rural genre in Iranian Khurasan (Blum 1972). In the villages the two stringed *dutār* was used to accompany the singing of quatrains in free rhythm, and for playing the melodies as *dutār* solos. Probably the best known of these songs was *'Chahārbeiti Siāhmu wa Jalali'*, with a text on the theme of unrequited love. The quatrains sung in this *chahārbeiti* were said to have been composed by Jalali. Siahmu was still alive in the 1960s, when a small book of Jalali's quatrains was published in Kabul. The song was first broadcast by the Herati amateur Karim Shauqi, with orchestral backing, and later by other Herati singers. This established an urban style for the performance of the Herati *chahārbeiti*.

The process of urbanisation is well illustrated by Sakata (1983:126–37) and requires no further elaboration here. Her examples range from unaccompanied quatrains by rural singers to the rendition of '*Chahārbeiti Shirin Dokhtar-e Māldār*' by Zainab Hairawi (*ibid.*: example 8). This shows various features of urban music: the performance begins with a *shakl* played on harmonium and *dutār*, followed by a section sung in free rhythm without rhythmic accompaniment, then a refrain (*pāzarb*) with tabla accompaniment, followed by a brief *naghmeh* played *du lai*, of a typically Herati kind, ending with a rhythmic cadence. Sakata's example 7 shows the same *chahārbeiti* (also often called '*Chahārbeiti Koshki*' or '*Chahārbeiti Chakhchurāni*' (both place names)), played as a solo for fourteen stringed *dutār*. Sakata shows clearly how the phrasing of the melodic lines of the section in free rhythm is related to the metre of the poem, as though the musician had the poem in mind while playing (*ibid.*: 127–9). Karim Dutari seems to have had some role in the urbanisation of the *chahārbeiti* as a solo piece for *dutār*, for he often broadcast this type of piece. The *chahārbeiti* was seen by Heratis to refer back to the Persian music of the 1920s, when the Persian *āvāz* style of singing was important. Sakata (*ibid.*: 129) has made the same connection.

Very little in the way of Herati songs or tunes were performed by the *sāzandeh* in the performance contexts in which I was primarily interested, and Sakata's treatment of Herati music renders further discussion unnecessary. It is, however, worth looking at some marginal cases.

Wedding songs

This category includes a small group of songs: '*Heinā ba kārā*', '*Olang Olang*', '*Bādā Bādā*', and '*Āhesteh Buro*'. The first three might be performed by male *sāzandeh* at wedding festivities (see chapter 8), and all four were performed by women musicians. The one indispensable song was '*Heinā ba kārā*'.

Example 14 on the cassette is a version of '*Heinā ba kārā*' sung by Mahmud at the same wedding party at which examples 8 and 13 were recorded, during the central ritual of the *takht-e dāmād*, when henna was bound to the little finger of the bridegroom's right hand (see chapter 8). The total performance runs for five and a half minutes, but only the first part is examined here.

Text	Translation
Az āmadanet agar khabar midāshtum hai	Had I known about your arrival
Heinā biyārim ba dastesh bemāl(im)	Let's bring henna and rub it onto his hand
Pish-e qadamat kharman-e gol mikāshtum hai	I would have strewn a pile of flowers in your pathway
Heinā biyārim...	Let's bring henna...
Gol mikāshtum gol-e golāb mikāshtum hai	I would have strewn flowers, rose flowers
Heinā biyārim...	Let's bring henna...
Khāk-e qadamat bā didane war dāshtum hai	I would have raised the dust from your pathway to my own eyes
Heinā biyārim	Let's bring henna...
Emshab chi shab-e shab-e murād ast emshab hai	Tonight what a night, a night of fulfilled wishes
Heinā biyārim...	Let's bring henna...

In khāneh por az sham o cherāgh ast emshab hai	This house is illuminated with lamps and with light tonight
Heinā biyārim...	Let's bring henna...
In khāneh por az sham o cherāgh ast emshab hai	This house is illuminated with lamps and with light tonight
Heinā biyārim...	Let's bring henna...
Mastam ze gham-e eshq-e tu mastam mastam hai	I'm crazy with the grief of being in love with you
Heinā biyārim...	Let's bring henna...
Del dar talab e wasl-e tu bastam bastam hai	I have tied my heart in wanting to join with you, tied, tied
Heinā biyārim...	Let's bring henna...
Guyando marā āsheqi badnām tui hai	They say to me "You are the infamous lover"
Heinā biyārim...	Let's bring henna...
Monker natawān bud ke hastam me hastam hai	I cannot deny that I was, and I am
Heinā biyārim...	Let's bring henna...
In jashn-e shab-e heinā mobārak bāshe hai	Blessings upon this evening henna festival
Heinā biyārim...	Let's bring henna...
(Fade out)	(Fade out)

It is notable that the song is not performed in the popular music form: the song is strophic, with no differentiation into *antara* and *āstāi* sections. There is no use of instrumental sections or of cyclical changes of tempo. The text is drawn from several quatrains and couplets, with the refrain '*Heinā biyārim ba dastesh bemāl(im)*' sung after every line, with Amir Jan joining his voice with his son's. The mode is *Pāri Pancham* and the metre is *Mogholi*.

'*Heinā ba kārā*', like other wedding songs, was widely known by musicians but rarely played outside the wedding situation. There was no injunction against this, for musicians were quite ready to play wedding songs in a recording session, but there was no demand from their audience for such songs at other times. Wedding songs were an essential part of wedding rituals. Sakata (1983:140-4) analyses two versions of '*Heinā ba kārā*'. Both use a different melody to the one adopted by Mahmud, and are in *Pilu*. The texts of the three versions are quite different.

'*Heinā ba kārā*' was probably widely disseminated in Afghanistan. In the case of another wedding song well known in Herat, '*Āhesteh Buro*', Slobin (1976:175-6) compares a Kabuli version sung by women amateurs with a version by professional women musicians from a small town in Afghan Turkestan. He also reports that '*Āhesteh Buro*' was recorded for Radio Afghanistan by Hamahang, a leading Kabuli *ustād*. 'In this case a specifically feminine and ceremonial song has been transmuted into a generalized sentimental "asexual" component of the mass media' (*ibid.*: 177).

Example 15, '*Olang olang*', is an example of a wedding song that was more specifically Herati. It is sung by Amir Jan, who also plays the harmonium; his younger son Mahmud, then aged about twelve, also singing; and his elder sons Rahim and Naim playing *rubāb* and tabla. It was recorded at Amir Jan's house in 1974. The complete performance lasts over seven minutes; only the first part is given here.

	Text		*Translation*
Verse 1	Hai barg-e darakhtān-e sabz	Verse 1	A leaf from green trees
	Hai amān hai delbar		Oh alas sweetheart
	Dar nazar-e hushyār		From the point of view of an intelligent person

Herati music

	Jān āghā jān	Dear Lord
	Har waraqash daftar e	Each one is like a page in a book
	Hai ma'arefat-e kerdegār	Introducing the omnipotence of God
Refrain	Hai olang olang hai olang	Refrain Oh meadow meadow, oh meadow
	Hai amān hai delbar	Oh alas sweetheart
	Bolbol-e mast yār yār	Intoxicated nightingale, dear
	Yār āghā jān	Dear Lord
	Khodā mobārak kone	May God give his blessings and congratulations
	Hai bar hame kas yār yār	
Verse 2	Hai khāle be rokhsar e yār	Upon everyone dear
	Hai amān hai delbar	Verse 2 There is a beauty spot on the beloved's cheek
	Por araq ast yār yār	
	Yār āghā jān	Oh alas sweetheart
	Hosne chi yak ja dārad	Her face is covered with sweat, dear
	Hai zār waraq ast yār yār	Dear Lord
Refrain		Beauty? It's all in her
Verse 3	Hai dowlat-e jān parwar e	Like gold leaf, dear
	Parwar ast delbar parwar e	Refrain
	Sohbat-e āmuzegār	Verse 3 Money sets the trend for one's behaviour
	Jān āghā jān	
	Khelwate bi modā e	Sets the trend sweetheart
	Hai sofreh-ye bā entezār	The discourse of a learned person
Refrain		Dear Lord
Verse 4	Hai sabat-e por gol-e me	Who has retreated without any claims on him
	Gol-e me delbar gol-e me	
	Khāli shode yār yār	Is like a feast waiting for guests
	Yār āghā jān	Refrain
	Yārak-e jāhel-e man	Verse 4 My basketful of flowers
	Hai rāzi shode yār yār	Flowers, sweetheart, flowers
Refrain		Has been emptied, dear
		Dear Lord
		My naive little darling
		Has accepted my love, dear
		Refrain

Like example 14, the performance is strophic, with no instrumental sections apart from the brief *shakl* and the song melody played as an introductory *naghmeh*. The mode is unusual, with the scale shown in figure 20. Amir Jan called this '*Bayāt-e Rāst*'. I have come across song melodies in the same scale in the town of Obeh, eighty miles up river from the city, accompanied on the two stringed *dutār*. The metre is a slow *Dādreh*. Mahmud singing along with his father illustrates how he learned to perform.

It is remarkable that the wedding songs known in Herat were not in the modes one normally associates with Herati music, *Bairami* and *Jog*. '*Heinā ba kārā*' could be sung in *Pāri*

Figure 20   Scale of '*Bayāt-e Rāst*'

or *Pilu*, '*Olang Olang*' was in *Bayāt-e Rāst*, '*Bādā Bādā*' was in *Pāri*, while '*Āhesteh Buro*' was in *Pilu*. The significance of this fact is open to several interpretations. If they conformed to the usual pattern of ritual songs, one might expect the wedding songs to be amongst the oldest in the Herati repertory, which adds weight to the idea that modes like *Pilu* and *Pāri* were known in Herat for vocal music long ago (see page 18). One thing is clear, however: although Heratis regarded these songs as 'old Herati local songs' some of them were widespread throughout Afghanistan.

Other Herati songs

The two remaining examples of Herati music considered here illustrate several points of interest.

Example 16 is '*Hai Rebābeh*' sung by Ghulam Nebi Zendeh Del, vocal and *dāireh*, and Gada Mohammad, fourteen stringed *dutār*, at a recording session at my house. '*Hai Rebābeh*' seems to have derived originally from Iran but had been sung in Herat for long enough to have become identified as a Herati song. The Herati singer Kholu Shauqi originally popularised it on the radio.

Music	Text		Translation
Antara 1	Hey, dutā yāre gereftim dar jawāni	Antara 1	We took two sweethearts in our youth
	Hai Rebābeh jān del kebāb e		Oh Rebabeh, dear, my heart is burning
	Yaki Re- yaki Re- yaki Reshti yaki Māzenderāni		One from Rasht and one from Mazendaran
	Hai Rebābeh jān del kebāb e		Oh Rebabeh, dear, my heart is burning
	Be ghorbān be ghorbān be ghorbān-e sar-e Reshti begardam		Sacrifice me for the head of the one from Rasht
	Hai Rebābeh jān del kebāb e		Oh Rebabeh, dear, my heart is burning
	Ke delrā ke delrā ke delrā ke delrā ke delrā mibore Māzenderāni		I hoped to win the heart of the Mazenderani
	Hai Rebābeh		
Āstāi 1	Hāl-e del kharāb e		
	Jigaram kebāb e	Āstāi 1	My heart is broken
	Hai Rebābeh		My liver is burnt
	Jān del kebāb e		Oh Rebabeh
	Hai Rebābeh		Dear, my heart is burning
	Jān del kebāb e		
Naghmeh		Antara 2	We are two sweethearts who fell in love
Antara 2	Dutā yārim ke bā ham khod pasandim		One of us is short and the other tall
	Hai Rebābeh jān del kebāb e		Oh God, Oh God, burn down the house of the cruel
	Yaki ku- yaki ku- yaki kutāh yaki mā qat balandim		Oh can't we stay together?
	Hai Rebābeh jān del kebāb e		
	Illāhi illāhi illāhi khāneh-ye zālem besuze		
	Hai Rebābeh jān del kebāb e		
	Nemimā- nemimā- nemimāne ke del ham bebandim		
	Hai Rebābeh		

Āstāi 2	Qāmatam kamān i	Āstāi 2	I have graceful stature
	Qadr-e man nadāni		You don't appreciate me
	Rang-e man khazān e		My colour is (sick as) autumn yellow
	Dar jawāni hai		Oh youth!
	Dar jawāni hai		Oh youth!
	Dar jawāni		Oh youth!
Naghmeh			
Antara 3	Kolāh-ye sor-e tur bālā konam man	Antara 3	Let me take off your dark karakul hat
	Hai Rebābeh jān del kebāb e		Let me see your black hair
	Be kāko- be kāko- be kākolhay siāh negāh konam man		This dust which falls from your head
	Hai Rebābeh jān del kebāb e		I will use for eye-kohl to blacken my eyes
	Ham un gar- ham un gar- ham un garde ke az kākol berize	Āstāi 3	As for Āstāi 1
	Hai Rebābeh jān del kebāb e		
	Be jā-ye- be jā-ye- be jā-ye sormeh bā cheshmhā konam man		
	Hai Rebābeh		
Āstāi 3	Hāl-e del kharāb e		
	Hāl-e del kharāb e		
	Jigaram kebāb e		
	Jigaram kebāb e		
	Hai Rebābeh		
	Jān del kebāb e		
	Hai Rebābeh		
	Jān del kebāb e		

Ghulam Nebi was from the village of Fushenj, near Zendehjan, and was essentially a rural singer who made up new *beit* and new song melodies. He had recorded a number of these for Radio Afghanistan, accompanied by a large radio orchestra. In Herat he operated largely outside the sphere of the *sāzandeh* (see chapter 7), and would perform either solo, to his own *dāireh* accompaniment, or with a *dutār* player or small group.

This example shows several features of an older Herati style, in terms of scale and rhythmic organisation, as distinct from the urban popular song style. The mode is *Bairami*, and the singer uses a noticeably sharp minor second above the finalis, identifiable analytically as a small neutral second (see chapter 4), a characteristic interval of Herati rural song. The fretting of the fourteen stringed *dutār* does not yield this interval, as can be heard. It was to overcome this problem that Amir Jan added an extra fret to the *rubāb* (see page 46). The musical form is partly that of the urban popular song, with *antara-āstāi-naghmeh* units, but though the *dutār* produces a cadence at the end of each *naghmeh*, Ghulam Nebi does not back this up with his *dāireh*, and keeps on drumming across the break.

Example 17, '*Mui Talāi*' ('Golden Hair'), is played by Rahim on *rubāb*, accompanied by his brother Naim on tabla, at a recording session in 1974 in a hotel in the main bazaar of the new city at which I specifically asked for old Herati tunes. '*Mui Talāi*' represents a body of half-remembered 'old' songs and *naghmeh*s. I never heard '*Mui Talāi*' sung. The melody is in the mode the musicians called *Zaoul* (see page 49), but deviates from the usual *Zaoul* scale in using a major third for one of its melodic lines. The performance starts with a *shakl* in *Zaoul*. From listening to the piece it is not possible to say whether the melodies played are

Plate 7 Ghulam Nebi Zendeh Del, vocal and *dāireh*, and Gada Mohammad, *dutār*, recording '*Hai Rebābeh*' in the author's house, 1974

all for singing, or whether there is a *naghmeh* here as well. There is little influence of the urban popular music style in this performance; no fast sections or rhythmic cadences. Rahim plays as he conceives 'Herati music' should be played, without fluctuations in tempo and density. The metre is a slow *Dādreh*, typical of many Herati songs. The songbirds are the same as those heard in example 1 and were brought along to the recording session on the initiative of the musicians.

7 The social organisation of musicians

The musician in Herat had a clearly differentiated social identity; Sakata (1983:92) suggests that the clarity of the musician concept was 'imbued in the minds of Heratis because the hereditary professional musician has been a traditional part of the Herat scene for many centuries'. The general term for a hereditary professional musician was *sāzandeh*, and this included men and women, and urban and rural performers. The complex of perceived attributes and associated attitudes that constituted the Herati concept of musician was closely bound up with the Herati concept of music as the product of playing musical instruments (*ibid*.: 41–53). The English word *musician*, when contrasted with *singer*, has the same connotation. The term *musiqidān*, 'one who knows music' (from *dānestan*, 'to know'), seems to have been the only word used in Herat to refer exclusively to musician as a general category, and was limited to educated urban speakers. Being a 'knower of music' implied the possession of instrumental performance ability, some degree of mastery over a highly technical motor skill. Heratis believed that some people had a particular innate ability (*estedād*) for musical performance, and the concept of the musician certainly included the notion of possession of this ability.

Much has been made of the distinction between amateur (*shauqi*) and professional (*kesbi*) status amongst musicians in Afghanistan (Slobin 1974, 1976; Sakata 1983; Baily 1979). Slobin (1976:33) makes it clear that the distinction was based on two criteria: economic support – the *shauqi* played because of a love of music, the *kesbi* to make a living; and recruitment – the *shauqi* was a self-taught enthusiast, the *kesbi* a hereditary musician trained in that role from an early age. As Slobin notes, this seemingly neat conceptual dichotomy did not fit the facts, for there were many musicians in Afghanistan who were *shauqi* by recruitment but became *kesbi* through dependence on musical performance for their economic support (*ibid*.). Sakata (1983:76, 81) found the difference to be conceived of mainly in economic terms, but she also points to the feature of birthright, and notes the lack of a specific term for the amateur musician who became a professional.

Likewise, I found that the Herati distinction between *shauqi* and *kesbi* was an acknowledged simplification that chose to ignore those individuals who fell between the two poles of a continuum that extended from the 'true' amateur to the hereditary professional. It was the status of those in the middle of the continuum that was in question. Some had another main occupation but also played music for money ('semi-professional' status), while others had become full-time economic specialists, completely dependent upon music for their livelihood. Some amateurs who had become professional claimed to be *shauqi*, pointing out that their fathers were not musicians before them, and that they were not from hereditary musician families. Others described themselves as *kesbi* precisely because they took money, and this seemed to be the common judgement of non-musicians. '*Pāiseh ke gereft, kesbi shod*,' as one man put it, 'by taking money he has become a *kesbi*'. A *shauqi* might argue that the rules about *shauqi*s and money had changed in recent times, and nowadays it was legitimate for the *shauqi* to accept payment, although he did not *negotiate a fee in advance*, to which others might reply that those amateurs who took money were fooling themselves when they said they were *shauqi*; really they were *kesbi* but were ashamed to admit the fact.

The terminology is confusing; meanings change according to the underlying assumptions of the standpoint adopted. In terms of recruitment there were two types of professional musician: hereditary professionals and amateurs turned professional. As we have seen, there was no clear and unambiguous term that described the latter. In Baily (1979) I elected, for the sake of clarity, to restrict the term *kesbi* to hereditary professional musicians. Sakata (1983:85) points out that while, 'Strictly speaking, the definition is correct...[the term *kesbi*] was often used to refer to a *shauqi* musician who had publicly "gone professional".' This point should be respected. As one amateur turned professional explained to me, '*Kesbi hastam, sāzandeh nistam*', 'I am *kesbi*, I am not *sāzandeh*.' *Kesbi*, as I shall use the term now, refers to any professional musician; while *sāzandeh* refers to a hereditary professional musician (and more specifically, in the context of this study, to an urban male hereditary professional musician).

The importance of *shauqi* and *kesbi* status amongst musicians was symptomatic of a high degree of participation in public music making by amateurs, who wished to dissociate themselves from the traditional, male hereditary musicians of Herat, players of the *sornā* and *dohol* (the oboe and drum pair so typical of the music of the Muslim world). *Sornā* and *dohol* players embodied a particular stereotype of the musician, with many negative connotations, and occupied a particularly low rank in the social order. This stereotype provided a reference point against which other musicians could be compared by Heratis.

In Herat the *sornā* and *dohol* were played only by members of a small ethnic minority who called themselves Gharibzadeh and who followed a number of low ranking professions, most typically that of barber. Some, in the city of Herat, had barber shops, whilst in the villages (and in parts of the city) this service was provided out of doors. They cut hair, trimmed moustaches, beards and eyebrows, and shaved heads and faces. The Heratis employed two terms for barber, *sālmān* and *dalāk*. The former was a term of rather higher rank, and referred to the barber with a shop; the *dalāk* was more a street barber. Some barbers were also specialists in performing the operation of circumcision (*khatnasuri*). A number of barbers also worked as *sornā* and *dohol* players, and a few were actors in the Herati folk drama. These musical and theatrical performers were known by the name of *ustā* (derived from the word *ustād*).

Hafizullah Baghban, a native Herati, made a detailed study of the folk drama (*seil*) performed by members of the Gharibzadeh. Baghban (1977: chapter 2) contains important ethnographic information, although much of it is about actors rather than musicians. The term Gharibzadeh means 'foreigner', or 'stranger', and the Gharibzadeh had various origin myths to explain their status as outsiders (*ibid*.: 83–4). The Gharibzadeh were pejoratively called *Jat* by the rest of Herati society, a word with many negative connotations and well known across Afghanistan. Rao (1981) lists the connotations of *Jat* amongst Kabulis: to be of low morals, to be dirty, to be of violent temperament; people called *Jat* were thought of as bad Muslims, stealers of children, practising prostitution, and necrophagy.

The barber's low social rank in Afghanistan (as in many other societies) is discussed at some length by Slobin (1976:31–2) and Sakata (1983:78–81). Drawing on the writings of Barth, Clebert, and Centlivres, they conclude that this low rank was related to the barber's

Sāzandeh and their associates in Herat

handling of human products like hair and nails, which were viewed as magical and powerful, having a 'life of their own' (because they continue to grow for some time after death), and also a result of the fact that barbering involved breaching the personal privacy of the client. The barber-musician, player of the *sornā* or *dohol*, had an even lower rank. The work of the barber at least had *sawāb*, 'religious merit', for the barber carried out Islamic prescriptions. But music was regarded with suspicion by orthodox Islam, and according to the traditional view, was sinful, though permissible and appropriate on festive occasions (see chapter 9). *Sornā* and *dohol* players were feared and mistrusted, held to be liars and petty thieves, morally lax, their women accused of prostitution, and their sons thought to be dancing boys. It was in the field of economic transactions that Herati people most directly experienced difficulties with them; they found the musicians demanding, with an insatiable appetite for payment, abusive when dissatisfied, using ridicule against those who offended them. Although the *sornā* and *dohol* players worked mostly in villages, where they provided dance and processional music for wedding festivities, they were well known in the city too, where they toured from house to house and shop to shop during the festivals of *'Eid* and *Now Ruz*, playing and demanding money.

Sornā and *dohol* players conformed closely to the classic description of the musician given by Merriam (1964). They combined a low social rank with providing a service that was of crucial importance to the community: music for ritual occasions (birth, circumcision, marriage, but not death). They were given a special licence to engage in verbal abuse and to behave in other ways that deviated from the general norms of society. The last thing that amateur or amateur turned professional musicians wanted was to be identified with such people. Hence their attachment to their *shauqi* status, which emphasised their love of music, their merits as 'self-made' musicians, and their disdain for financial reward. The urban *sāzandeh*, performers of art music, also sought to distance themselves from the *Jat* stereotype, but in this case they aspired to the status of a high ranking hereditary musician, like the Kabuli *ustād*.

Sāzandeh and their associates in the city of Herat

The number of male musicians, *shauqi* and *kesbi*, who lived in the city of Herat probably numbered several hundred. They ranged from true amateurs who had no financial interest in music to those who were full-time economic specialists. They played a variety of instruments and in a variety of styles. Within this network of musicians it is possible to define a group of about thirty-five individuals who constituted a 'professional musician social group'. This consisted of the urban male *sāzandeh* and the amateur turned professional musicians who played in their bands. In one sense this group defined its role as the performance of Kabuli art music. The boundaries of the group were not precisely defined, mainly because the amateur turned professional associates of the *sāzandeh* also sometimes played with other musicians outside the group. One test of membership was to be invited when the *sāzandeh* gathered together, at the wedding celebrations of a *sāzandeh*, or when someone accepted a new student in the string tying ceremony.

The *sāzandeh* formed themselves into bands, consisting of a singer/harmonium player, accompanied by *rubāb*, *dutār* (always played by an amateur turned professional), and tabla, with the occasional addition of the *delrubā*, *tānpurā*, and *sormandel*. In 1976–7 there were four sāzandeh bands regularly operating in Herat. Their personnel included several sāzandeh musicians from Kabul. The members of the professional musician social group and their organisation into bands is shown in figure 21.

Amir Jan's band

Amir Jan had been active as a professional musician in Herat for nearly fifty years, much longer than anyone else. In that time he had played in, and led, many bands, and most of the members of the professional musician social group had played with him at one time or another. He and his brother Karim and their sons called themselves Khushnawazha, 'The Good Players'. In the 1960s Amir Jan formed a family band with his two elder sons as accompanists, Rahim on *rubāb* and Naim on tabla, supplemented by various *dutār* players after the fourteen stringed *dutār* had become established in the *sāzandeh* ensemble. Amir Jan's third son, Salim, worked in the motor vehicle repair business as a body sprayer and also played the tabla as a semi-professional. If necessary he could stand in for Naim in the family band, and he was sometimes engaged by amateur musicians to play at their soirées (*shau nishini*). Mahmud, Amir Jan's youngest son, was trained as a singer and harmonium player. He had been going out with the band for some years, singing with his father, and taking over as the singer/harmonium player for part of the programme. Amir Jan and his gifted sons were something of a special attraction. Another member of Amir Jan's household was Ghulam Sekhi, the son of Amir Jan's elder brother, Chacha Ghulam, a tabla player, who had died young. Ghulam Sehki, married to Amir Jan's second daughter, ran a motor body repair shop and was the highest earner in the household. A genealogy of the family is shown in figure 22. Amir Jan's brother Karim is discussed below.

In 1976 Amir Jan gave up singing in public, and Mahmud (then aged about seventeen) took over as the band's singer and harmonium player. Rahim, who had been increasingly committed to Amir Mohammad's group, quarrelled with Amir Jan, who took over himself as the *rubāb* player in the family band, of which he remained leader. Ghulam Nebi, who also ran a teahouse, was Amir Jan's *dutār* player in this period. Another occasional member of Amir Jan's band was his son-in-law Mohammad Ali, a *delrubā* player, one of Ustad Nabi Gol's five musician sons, who sometimes lived in Herat. Mohammad Ali was not on good terms with Amir Jan and Amir Jan's sons. During the period in question he was busy training and promoting two boy musicians, the brothers of a theatre courtesan.

As a professional musician Amir Jan made most of his income from playing at wedding festivities: *shirinikhori*s and *'arusi*s (chapter 8). At the annual independence celebrations (*Jeshan*) he was often employed by one of the guilds. In the past he had played at nightly concerts during *Ramazān*, but did not do so during the period of my fieldwork. He also played at dinner parties and garden parties, and when he was younger he sometimes played for dancing boys. Until the arrival of Amir Mohammad in the early 1970s, Amir Jan and his group were the best paid and the most prestigious musicians in Herat. By the mid-1970s, when Rahim had left and the young Mahmud had taken over as singer, they were getting between 1,500 and 2,500 *afghāni*s to play at a wedding party, while Amir Mohammad was getting 2,500 to 4,000 *afghāni*s. Still, Amir Jan had a large house in a good area of the old city and had managed to concentrate the earnings of his band on his own household; only the *dutār* player, and sometimes his son-in-law Mohammad Ali, represented money 'lost' by the household.

Sar dasteh (leader)				
Ali Ahmad (v, h) Golpasand	Amir Mohammad (v, h) Kabul	Amir Jan (r) Khushnawaz		Ghulam Salwar (v, h) Shauqi Mohammad Karim (t, r) Khushnawaz
Ghulam Mohammad (r, h, v) Golpasand	Rahim (r) Khushnawaz	Mahmud (v, h) Khushnawaz		Hakim (v, h) Khushnawaz
Qader (t) Golpasand	Gada Mohammad (d) Shauqi	Naim (t) Khushnawaz		Azin (t) Khushnawaz
Jalil Ahmad (t, h, v) Golpasand	Fazl Ahmad (t) Kabul	Ghulam Nebi (d) Shauqi		Fata (d) Shauqi
Sultan Wardak (r) Shauqi		Salim (t) Khushnawaz		Mirza (d) Shauqi
Haidar (d) Shauqi				
Ghulam Dastegir (r) Kabul				

Amir (v, h) Golpasand	Mohammad Ali (del) Kabul
Ghulam (t) Golpasand	Karim Dutari (t, h, d) Shauqi
Bismillah (t) Golpasand	Kholek Sauz (d) Shauqi
	Ahmad (d, v) Shauqi
	Ghani Landai (r) Shauqi
	Seid Gol (d, v) Shauqi

v = vocal, h = harmonium, r = *rubāb*, d = *dutār*, t = tabla, del = *delrubā*

Figure 21 *Sāzandeh* and their associates in 1976–7

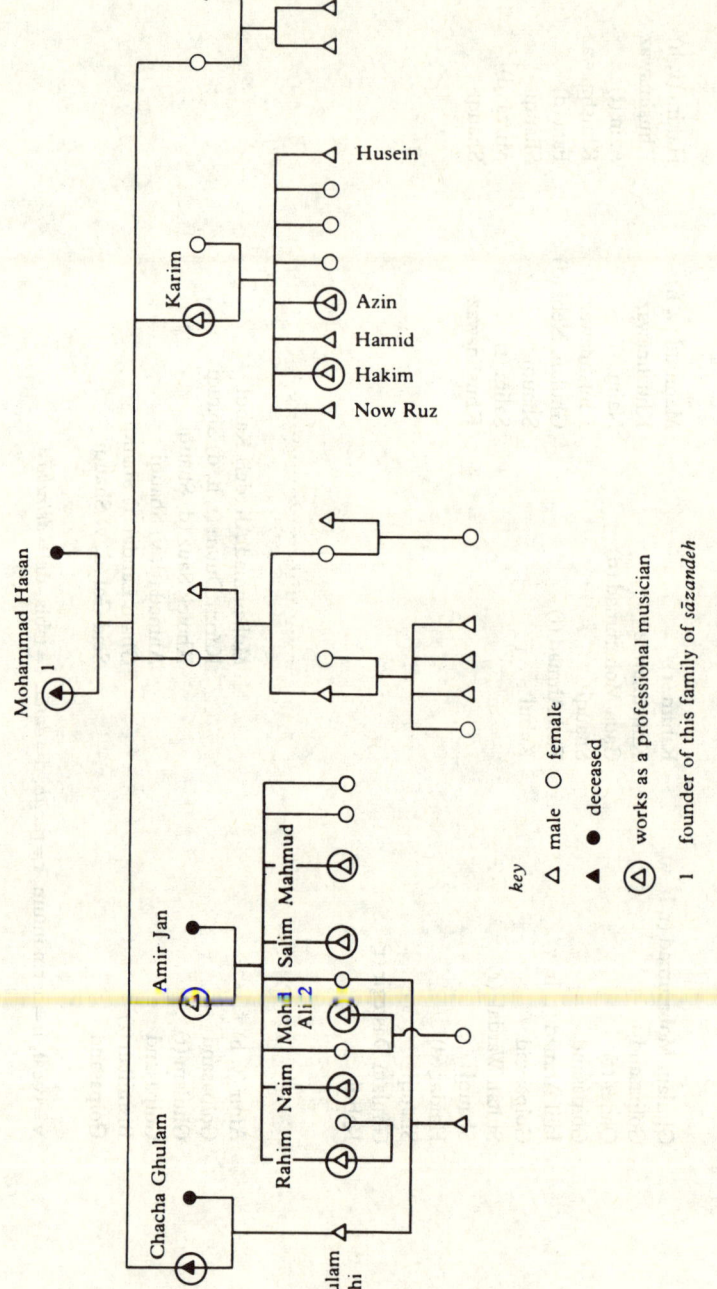

Figure 22 Genealogy of the Khushnawazha

The Golpasand band

Four of Golpasand's male descendants became *sāzandeh*, two sons and two grandsons, the grandsons being considerably older than the sons. The grandsons were Ghulam Mohammad (who styled himself *Shabāhang*, 'Night Music'), a singer, harmonium, and *rubāb* player, and Qader, player of the tabla and *delrubā* and generally considered rather untalented as a musician. They were in their mid-forties during the time of my fieldwork. Ali Ahmad (who styled himself *Delāhang*, 'Soul Music') and Jalil, his younger brother, Golpasand's two sons by his fourth wife, were also singers and harmonium players, though by 1976 Jalil was specialising as a tabla player. Although considerably younger than Ghulam Mohammad and Qader, they were senior (*kalāntar*) to them. Despite his youth (he could not have been more than thirty in 1977), Ali Ahmad, Golpasand's eldest son, was the head of the Golpasand *qaum*. They had worked in many different groups over the years, and it was only in the 1970s that they could provide the essential core of a *sāzandeh* group from amongst themselves, with Ali Ahmad singing and playing harmonium, Ghulam Mohammad on *rubāb*, and Jalil on tabla. Before this they recruited additional band members from outside the family, including Amir Jan's brother Karim. The Golpasand band that Sakata observed in 1972 consisted of Ghulam Mohammad Shabahang (vocal and harmonium), Sultan Wardak (*rubāb*), Abdul Ghani Landai (*rubāb*), Ghulam Haidar (*dutār*), Qader (*delrubā*), and Karim Khushnawaz (tabla) (Sakata 1983:86–7). Sultan Wardak, a Pashtun from Wardak, Ghani Landai, whose name also suggests Pashtun descent, and Ghulam Haidar, a Tajik, were amateurs turned professional. Another *rubābi* who often played with the Golpasandha was Ghulam Dastegir, a *sāzandeh* singer from Kabul who married two Golpasand women and lived in the Kucheh Golpasandha. Other *dutār* players besides Haidar had played regularly in Golpasand-led bands. The Golpasandha and their associates constituted a pool of musicians who would play in various combinations and could, if necessary, field two bands at the same time.

Two other male musicians amongst the Golpasandha were Amir, a singer and harmonium player, and Bismillah, a tabla player. They had a low rank amongst the male Golpasandha *sāzandeh* and rarely played with them. Amir in particular was the object of public ridicule and contempt from Ali Ahmad and Jalil, who often pointed out his limitations as a performer and lack of knowledge of *rāg*s and musical terminology. They teased him about his inability to sing *ghazal*s, and in a sense he was not permitted to perform this genre. As a musician he played not with the Golpasandha but in *dutār* bands with amateurs turned professional. Bismillah was sometimes called on to play tabla if the Golpasandha needed to form two bands. Neither Amir nor Bismillah were direct descendants of Golpasand. Bismillah's father was Golpasand's kinsman, his mother from a barber-musician family, while Amir was the orphaned nephew of a barber whose aunt was Golpasand's fourth wife. These relationships are shown in figure 23.

In the mid-1970s the band's main source of income derived from playing at wedding parties, where Ali Ahmad and his accompanists could command a fee of about 2,500 *afghāni*s. In the past they had worked for long periods as theatre musicians, but this was poorly paid work. At the spring fairs of 1974 a Golpasand band played in a tented teahouse, and in the same year a band of Golpasandha played a season of *Ramazān* concerts. But the incomes of the 'core' Golpasand *sāzandeh* (Ali Ahmad, Jalil, Ghulam Mohammad, and Qader) did not derive from their work as musicians alone. These members of the Golpasand *qaum* were com-

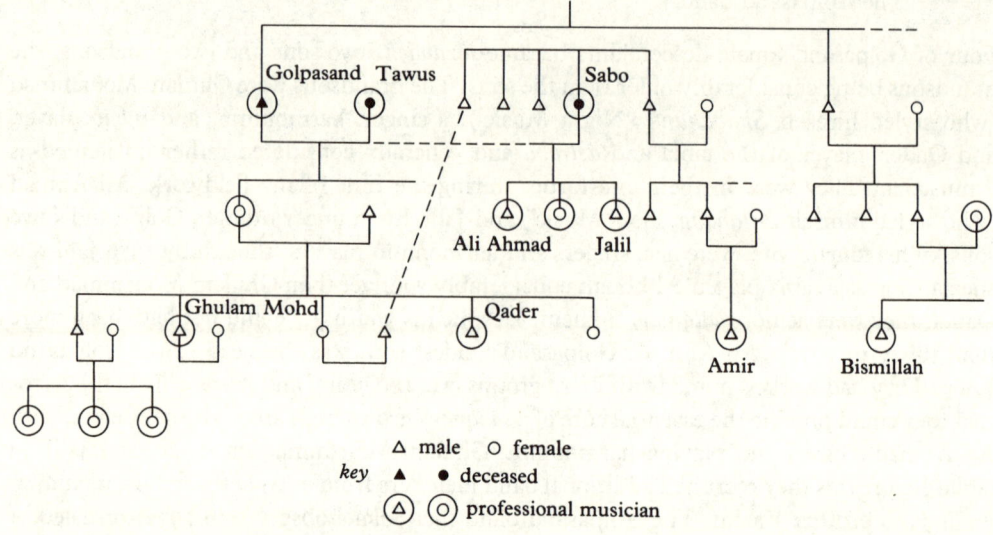

Figure 23 Genealogy of male Golpasandha *sāzandeh* (Tawus was Golpasand's second wife, Sabo his fourth)

paratively wealthy, and their family fortunes probably derived initially from running bands of women *sāzandeh*. They were astute businessmen and had used their money to invest in motor transport, owning trucks for the trade with Iran, and operating taxis. More peripheral non-musician barbers in the Golpasand *qaum* owned barber shops (*sālmāni*) in the new city. There must have been good reasons for the male Golpasandha to continue as musicians. No doubt the income it provided was significant but I think it more likely that, like Amir Jan, they enjoyed the life of music and were aspiring, to some extent successfully, to be high ranking *sāzandeh* like the *ustād*s of Kabul, a status achieved by some barber-musicians in the Kucheh Kharabat.

The Karim-Salwar partnership

Amir Jan's brother, Karim, ten or fifteen years his junior, had played tabla with Amir Jan for many years, but had eventually been replaced by Amir Jan's son Naim. Since then he had played tabla in various bands with the Golpasandha, sometimes in the theatre. He left them in 1976 and went into partnership (*shirikat*) with Ghulam Salwar, an amateur turned professional singer and harmonium player, who led the band at the Herat Theatre. Salwar counted himself a student of Haji Hamahang of Kabul, and had spent several months studying with him. Karim played in the theatre or sometimes went to play at wedding parties with Ghulam Salwar. Their partnership relied on maintaining a pool of musicians, and could, if necessary, put up two bands. To do this required bringing in one or two musicians who only occasionally played with *sāzandeh*, such as Bolbol Herawi, the singer and *zirbaghali* player, normally employed in the theatre, or Ghulam Mydin, a weaver who also played *dutār* and *tanbur*. Such musicians were too peripheral to the professional musician social group to be included figure 21.

Karim lived in a different part of the old city to Amir Jan and his sons, in the Darwazeh Iraq, another predominantly Shiah area. His sons were younger than Amir Jan's and not all of them worked as musicians (see figure 22). The oldest, Now Ruz, was a tailor. The second, Hakim, was apprenticed as a shoemaker and worked at this craft in 1973–4 but in 1976–7 he was working full time as a singer and harmonium player within the Karim–Salwar partnership. The third son, Hamid, was also a tailor, while the fourth son, Azin, was a tabla player. In 1976–7, aged about fourteen, he was working full time as a musician, usually within the Karim–Salwar partnership, sometimes with other groups. The youngest son, Husein, aged about five in 1976–7, showed a keen interest in tabla playing. It seems that Karim was on the way to establishing his own family band, with Hakim as singer and harmonium player, Azin on tabla, and himself on *rubāb*, for, like Amir Jan, he could play several instruments.

Amir Mohammad's band

In the mid-1970s the outstanding singer in Herat was not Herati at all, but a Kabuli, Amir Mohammad, from one of the barber-musician families in the Kucheh Kharabat. His father was a barber and the brother of two well known Kabuli musicians, Ustad Mohammad Omar, the *rubāb* player, and Ustad Mashin, a *sārangi* player. Amir Mohammad's teacher was Ustad Mohammad Omar, who trained him in the art music tradition of Kabul as a performer of *khyāl* and *ghazal*.

In 1971 he came to Herat for the month of *Ramazān* to play nightly concerts with a group of musicians from the Golpasandha. After this he started receiving invitations to perform at more lavish wedding parties in Herat and began his intermittent residence in the city. He maintained his house in Kabul and his wife and children were usually there, but during the mid-1970s, he lived for several months each year in Herat, staying for extended periods when work was plentiful. In 1972 or 1973 he formed a stable band with Amir Jan's son, Rahim, on *rubāb*, and Gada Mohammad on *dutār*. Often he brought a tabla player with him from Kabul, either Latif, a son of Ustad Nabi Gol, or Fazl Ahmad, from an *ustād* family; otherwise he would use a Herati tabla player. In 1973–4 Naim Khushnawaz sometimes played tabla with him, while in 1976–7 Jalil from the Golpasandha, who had married Amir Mohammad's daughter in 1975, fulfilled this role when necessary.

Amir Mohammad's reasons for being in Herat were clearly economic; he could make more money than in Kabul, where there was great competition between the various bands and a much larger supply of singers of *khyāl* and *ghazal*. There was also competition from bands manned by amateurs turned professional in Kabul, offering a more modern form of popular music to that played by the *sāzandeh*. Amir Jan told me that Amir Mohammad could command about 2,500 *afghāni*s for an engagement in Kabul, while more famous singers from the Kucheh Kharabat could get 5,000, 6,000, or even 7,000 *afghāni*s for playing at a wedding party. In Herat, Amir Mohammad could charge about 4,000 *afghāni*s in 1973–4, but was going out for less by 1976–7. Out of a 4,000 *afghāni*s' fee he would take 2,500 *afghāni*s and give his three accompanists 500 *afghāni*s each. Not only could he charge more than in Kabul but he also worked more often. Living in Herat, separated from his family, was inconvenient, but it was worth it.

Other members of the professional musician social group

Reference to figure 21 shows a number of musicians who were not working regularly with *sāzandeh* bands during the period in question, though they had in the past, and were clearly to be included in the group.

Karim Dutari, who worked as a semi-professional musician in Herat, sometimes played in ensembles with Ghulam Salwar and/or Karim Khushnawaz. Kholek Sauz had played *dutār* with Amir Jan and with Golpasand bands in the past. In 1976–7 he often worked with Amir, of the Golpasandha, and Ahmad, a former dancing boy. Ghani Landai used to play with the Golpasandha but had branched out on his own with a dancing boy, Seid Gol used to play *dutār* with the Golpasandha, Ghulam, a tabla player from a Gharibzadeh family with dancing boy traditions, sometimes played with the Golpasandha. These musicians in particular had a marginal status in the professional musician social group, for they often formed *dutār* bands or other small ensembles with semi-professional and professional musicians outside the group.

In addition to instrumentalists there were a number of semi-professional or professional singers in Herat who were also outside the social group formed by the *sāzandeh* and their associates. Typically, they did *not* also play the harmonium. A few had become well known radio singers, such as Kholu Shauqi (who died a few years before my fieldwork), and Madadi. The singer Ghulam Nebi Zendeh Del occupied this sort of position in Herat in 1976–7. He was from the village of Fushenj, towards the Iranian border, and was considered to be a *mahali* ('folk') singer. He was a tailor by profession, and had a small shop in the city. Most of the tailoring work was carried out by his wife in Fushenj. As a singer he accompanied himself on the *dāireh*, generally considered an instrument for women. He was a song maker in the Herati idiom, and had recorded many songs for Radio Afghanistan, usually accompanied by a large radio orchestra. In Herat he might perform alone, or with musicians from the professional musician social group like Gada Mohammad, the *dutār* player. He was unpopular with the *sāzandeh*, who disapproved of his frivolous attitude to the serious matter of music. Another such singer was Nawak (grandson of the famous Rahim Khushkhan), who mainly sang modern Iranian popular songs.

Musical ideology of the *sāzandeh*

The urban male *sāzandeh* of Herat perceived themselves as an extension of the *sāzandeh* of Kabul, playing the same music on the same instruments and sharing a common value system in which Hindustani music occupied a central position. Links with the Kabuli *sāzandeh* had been established through teacher–student relationships, through marriage, and through performing together.

One of the main values and interests that the *sāzandeh* of Herat had in common with the *sāzandeh* of Kabul concerned Hindustani music (*klāsik*). From their point of view this was the only music that mattered, the only music worth playing. It is difficult to convey the reverence with which they regarded it, and the respect they afforded those skilled in its performance. They saw it as a music that was difficult both to perform and to learn. The *sāzandeh* talked about Hindustani music as a sea of limitless possibilities, an ocean without shores, a tree on which new branches were always growing. The greatest *ustād* was but dipping a glass into that ocean, leaving it undiminished. They would have agreed entirely with Amir Khusro's words:

Musical ideology of the *sāzandeh*

Indian (Hindu) music, the fire that burns the heart and soul, is superior to the music of any other country. Foreigners, even after a stay of thirty or forty years in India, cannot play a single Indian tune correctly. (Bhanu 1955:16)

I often sat with *sāzandeh* listening to tapes of recordings of musicians from India and Pakistan, and saw the enthusiasm and serious attention these performances received, the exclamations (*wah wah!*), the tutting and head shaking, the sighs, the earlobe pulling, and even the tears. Their sense of identity as musicians was bound up with this music; it provided a justification for being a musician when the economic rewards were small and social prejudice against one was still in evidence. It would be wrong to say that Hindustani music was a religion to them, yet the metaphor is not inappropriate given that many *sāzandeh* professed at least a sympathy for the Chishti Sufi Order, whose adherents placed great value on the spiritual experience of listening to music in the *samāʿ*, the 'spiritual concert'.

One sometimes heard the claim that Hindustani music originated in Afghanistan, in the city of Balkh, and was taken to India by Amir Khusro Balkhi. He was an important literary figure at the thirteenth-century courts of the Delhi Sultanate who is often credited in legend with various innovations in Hindustani music, such as the invention of the sitar and tabla, and the creation of the vocal genres of *khyāl* and *qawwāli*. His tomb in Delhi is a sacred shrine. According to the Afghan view, music prospered in the more tolerant religious climate of India, while in Afghanistan the mullahs held back its development. In more recent times Hindustani music had been returned to its rightful place of origin. It was sometimes stated that the music of Afghanistan, India, and Pakistan was one, and Hindustani music was sometimes spoken of as an 'Indo-Afghan' music. Importance was also attached to the belief that this was a Muslim music, created by Muslim musicians. This folk view indicated an awareness of certain strands in the history of Hindustani music, especially the contribution of Muslim culture, transmitted via Afghanistan. These grand claims to Hindustani music also fit well with the kind of nationalist ideology that emerged in Afghanistan in the 1930s, consistent, for example, with the claim that Pashto is the purest and oldest Aryan language and that 'the Avesta and the earliest Vedas were the greatest masterpieces of Afghan and Pashto literature' (Gregorian 1969:347).

The *sāzandeh* admiration for Hindustani music was not shared by Herati audiences. Although they might respect and even admire *klāsik* for its technical virtuosity, no one outside a small group of connoisseurs would make an effort to get to hear it. On my return to Herat in 1976 I soon learned that when Ustad Sarahang had recently performed at a Herati wedding party some of the audience had found his singing hilarious, laughing particularly at his vocal *gamak* (a type of ornamentation). Sarahang had refused to continue his concert and the supporters of *klāsik* in the city felt he had been gravely insulted. Imitations of Hindustani vocal music were sometimes used for comic effect and constituted an item in the repertory of 'funny sounds' of certain singers known for their *shukh*, 'mischievousness'. At *Ramazān* concerts I observed a marked reluctance on the part of Haji Hamahang, a visiting Kabuli *ustād*, to perform *khyāl*. He liked to confine himself to *ghazal*s and popular songs in this performance context. In the middle of one concert he invited me to make a request. I asked for a *rāg*. He prefaced his performance with an apology to the audience, saying that since a foreign guest had made the request he was obliged to comply. A year later, when Hamahang was again playing in Herat at *Ramazān* I sent up a postcard with a request for another *rāg*.

He kept this to the very end of the concert. When he started it was noticeable how many people got up and left, while the clicking of stop buttons from the usual collection of cassette recordists near the bandstand told its own story. *Khyāl* and instrumental forms of *klāsik* were very much 'musicians' music' in Herat.

One of the essential institutions of the *sāzandeh* as a social group was the *ustād–shāgerd* (teacher–pupil) relationship. Not only did it dictate the ideal relationship for learning music, and a manner of imparting that knowledge, but it was in itself an important determinant of rank. According to the *sāzandeh* ideal, as explained to me by Amir Jan and supported by statements from many other musicians, there was a great difference between the person who learned music through taking lessons and the person who learned by ear, simply by listening to music. To learn music correctly one needed to be taught by an *ustād*, a master musician, who understood the '*ilm-e musiqi* and could play all the instruments, and who had been the *shāgerd* of an *ustād* in his turn. The teacher should be *chekideh*, someone who had 'completed' himself in music, and he was necessary as a guide (*rāhnemā*) for the pupil. Those who learned music without a teacher did not understand music 'scientifically', and what they did learn by ear they usually learned wrongly. The correct way to learn music was by *not* (notation, the *sargam* system).

A teacher was also important because he gave the student authority to play the pieces he had learned in public. The *ustād* had some control over the performance of his *shāgerd*, and he might forbid the student to play publicly until he had reached a certain standard. This control also had stylistic aspects, for by and large, the *ustād* wanted his student to sound like himself. A *sāzandeh* musician who learned compositions simply by hearing them, but not being shown them within a teaching relationship, was described as someone who had *dozd kard*, 'stolen', or *gadāi kard*, 'begged'. In a sense he had no right to play them. Musical knowledge (theory and repertory) was treated as something of great value and the musician had to consider carefully to whom, how, and in return for what, he transmitted that knowledge. This helps to explain many of the problems I had in learning compositions from the *sāzandeh*.

The notion of the *ustād–shāgerd* relationship was by no means confined to music, it was a general principle of learning through apprenticeship. A craftsman would refer to his apprentices as his *shāgerd*s, and to his employees in the same way, provided they were young. A musician might talk about other musicians as his *shāgerd*s even if he had not actually taught them anything. This implied that they were inferior to him and that they could study with him to advantage. The notion of *shāgerdi*, 'apprenticeship', extended beyond the actual learning of music; the social role of servant and henchman was also important. When he became Ustad Nabi Gol's student, Amir Jan had found, to his disappointment, that a lesson consisted of only a few minutes' teaching, and that not every day. The rest of the time he was serving Nabi Gol, going to the bazaar to do the household shopping, attending to the water pipe, serving tea to guests and, later, taking his *ustād*'s children out for walks.

The nature of *sāzandeh* social organisation resembles in several respects the organisation of a Sufi Brotherhood in Afghanistan (Utas 1980). I am indebted to Richard Tapper for pointing this out. An *ustād* corresponds to a *pir*. Both inherit their musical or religious powers from their fathers, and hand them on to their sons. Both are usually charismatic figures, who have a number of followers, students or disciples, who are like servants. Both are men of advanced knowledge and understanding, and impart their knowledge to their students or disciples. New students or disciples are initiated by the tying of a band around the wrist or a girdle round the waist. The *ustād* gives permission to the student to perform certain compositions once mastered, the *pir* likewise allows his disciples to take part in the *zikr* to the stage appropriate to their training. The analogy between hereditary musicians and local Sufi chapters is not confined to Afghanistan; it applies in India to an even greater degree. Amongst the descendants of Muslim court musicians in India, musical practice (*riyāz*) has something of the aura of spiritual discipline in a Sufi method of purification. This is encountered most explicitly in the *chilla*, a period of intense and isolated devotion, either to music or to religion. The practice is called *chilla* ('the forty [days]') by both musicians and Sufis, but often far exceeds that period; in musician lore twelve years is often mentioned as the length of a *chilla* (Kippen, 1985).

Musical training amongst the *sāzandeh*

Despite the *ustād-shāgerd* ideal, amongst the Herati *sāzandeh* only Amir Jan had had the benefit of this kind of training in the fullest sense. Ustad Nabi Gol had taught him many things. He gave him compositions written in *sargam* notation in Amir Jan's notebook. He instructed him in the science of music, and taught him to sing *khyāl* and *ghazal*, and to play the *rubāb*, and gave him permission to play on that instrument what he had learned to sing.

It is important to consider how other members of the Khushnawazha had learned to perform. Amir Jan held the idea, common amongst Heratis, that children learn skills quickly and easily, and that learning becomes progressively more difficult as one gets older. He and other *sāzandeh* thought that young children should be exposed to the sounds of music as much as possible, both around the house, and by sitting up on the bandstand at musical engagements. It was thought especially beneficial for children to fall asleep to the sound of music. The boys had become interested in a particular instrument between the ages of six and ten, and were allowed to experiment with it and learn to play it by ear. From about the age of ten, training became rather more deliberate; the child had acquired the basics and now had to learn specific pieces properly, as well as learning something of music theory. Sometimes, when occasion arose, the young apprentice would have to play in front of an informal group of his elders, when mistakes would be pointed out and encouragement given. By about the age of fifteen, sometimes earlier, the young *sāzandeh* musician started going out to play at engagements with family members. Frequent public performance provided the practice necessary to perfect his technique. *Riyāz*, devoted practice for many hours a day over a period of many years, described in India so well by Neuman (1980:31-43), was not pursued in Herat. Although the importance of *tamrin* or *praktis*, 'practice', was clearly articulated, the notion was more in the nature of 'experience' rather than the deliberate cultivation of 'practice sessions'.

Amir Jan claimed to have taught his sons through the medium of notation, and no doubt oral notation had played some part in their training. But it was also clear that he had not given them the kind of training that he considered they should have received. He complained to me that they had been too proud to learn properly from him, and although they had *khub dast*, 'a good hand', i.e. good technique, they did not know much about the science of music. I had numerous opportunities to see that he had superior knowledge to theirs. It is not clear whether this failing was due to a reluctance to teach all he knew to his sons, so as to retain some ascendancy over them, or because they had fallen out with him before they were ready for more advanced instruction.

Other musicians besides the Khushnawazha had received instruction from *ustād*s in Kabul, but in each case the amount of teaching was small. A musician might go and stay in Kabul for a few weeks and receive some instruction, and that would constitute his apprenticeship. In this way a musician would learn certain compositions and acquire the status of attachment to an *ustād*, a necessary condition if he were to aspire to high rank amongst the *sāzandeh* and their associates.

The Golpasand men *sāzandeh* had received a rather different kind of musical training. As children they had accompanied their mothers when they played at wedding parties, and they received the same kind of early exposure to musical performance as the girls who later became musicians. They had all learned the women's style of tabla playing when young and occasionally lent a hand with the women's music at weddings. Nearly all of them were said to have been dancing boys between the ages of about twelve and seventeen. As a boy, Ali Ahmad used to be sent to sit on the bandstand with Amir Jan so that he would become familiar with his music, and Ghulam Mohammad was at one time Amir Jan's *rubābi*. Qader and Jalil received some instruction for tabla from Karim Khushnawaz when he was playing with the Golpasandha. Ali Ahmad and Ghulam Mohammad later became students of Ustad Sarahang, who usually stayed at their house on his rare visits to Herat. According to one rather malicious account, Ghulam Mohammad's mother gave Sarahang a valuable jewelled necklace to accept them as students, but Sarahang had later confided that 'they could not learn anything'. It was true that Ali Ahmad and Ghulam Mohammad did not sing *khyāl*, but they had become highly competent urban *sāzandeh*, specialising in *ghazal* singing and performing popular and dance music. And in one way or another they had learned a good deal about the science of music.

The criticism of learning music without a teacher was levelled most directly against amateur musicians, who were generally self-taught. If the hereditary professional was a *darsei*, one who had learned through lessons (*dars*), the amateur was a *shenidigi*, who learned through listening to music (from *shenidan*, 'to hear'). An amateur did not inherit music as an established family profession. He might be anybody who had a love of music and the ability to learn to perform. My research with a sample of *dutār* players in 1973–4 showed that, according to their own accounts, they learned by copying another performer, usually a relative or friend, without revealing what they were doing; listening and watching and then practising in private. They lacked the exposure to music as children that the *sāzandeh* enjoyed, and were often actually discouraged from learning to play by their families. *Dutār* players in general were proud of being self-taught; they had overcome all obstacles. Some *dutār* players had at a later stage taken lessons with *sāzandeh*, a few on a quite regular basis, for which they paid, often considerable sums. Those who played regularly with the *sāzandeh* obviously learned a good deal from them about technique, compositions, the intricacies of the *ghazal*, and the science of music.

Social ranking amongst professional musicians

The professional musicians of Herat were much concerned with ranking amongst themselves. Very crudely, three tiers could be identified: the Khushnawazha, the Golpasandha, and the amateurs turned professional. But the position was more complicated than that. The entry of Amir Mohammad into the Herat arena had altered things, as explained below.

Social ranking amongst professional musicians

A senior Golpasand like Ali Ahmad had a higher rank than a junior Khushnawaz like Hakim. Certain non-hereditary professional musicians like Karim Dutari and Gada Mohammad also had relatively high rank. Ranking was not static, and changed over time and as the result of competition between members of the group. The criteria that were invoked for this internal ranking were various; they are considered below, along with a description of the ways in which ranking was expressed, maintained, and challenged. From them we can learn how the musical ideology of the *sāzandeh* was translated into action.

Ranking between Khushnawazha and Golpasandha

The Khushnawazha maintained themselves in a rank above their rivals, the Golpasandha, by invoking the following arguments:

1. The Khushnawazha were collectively the long term *shāgerd*s of Ustad Nabi Gol, a relationship that began in the mid-1930s. This gave the Khushnawazha status as legitimate performers of Kabuli art music. The Golpasandha had no such long term connection with a Kabuli *ustād*, though two of them had become students of Ustad Sarahang in the last few years.
2. As a result of this training, the Khushnawazha possessed the best performers of Kabuli art music. Amir Jan was considered the only competent singer of *khyāl*, his brother Karim was acknowledged as the master of tabla in Herat, his son Rahim was regarded as the best *rubāb* player. The Khushnawazha knew more about *rāg*s and *tāl*s. Amir Jan claimed that what the Golpasandha knew about music they had learned from him, by playing in his band or simply being with him on the bandstand.
3. The Golpasandha were stigmatised by their ancestry, being of mixed Chelu-Gharibzadeh descent, and could simply be dismissed as '*Jats*', with all the stereotyping of general bad character conjured up by that label. Amir Jan's father, on the other hand, was an amateur turned professional, although from the poorer artisan class of the city. His father had been a baker, and his father's seven brothers followed trades such as water carrier, carpenter, and caretaker at the Tekieh Mirza Khan (a religious gathering place for Shiahs).
4. Golpasand women worked as *sāzandeh*. Their activities were considered quite wrong by Amir Jan and the general populace. The women did not observe strict purdah and they were vulnerable to sexual approaches by men involved in organising the wedding celebrations where they played. In Amir Jan's view it was *harām*, prohibited by Islam: the activities of the Golpasand women brought the music profession into disrepute. Khushnawaz women had no role as musical performers outside the domestic environment.
5. The Khushnawazha had given a bride to one of Ustad Nabi Gol's sons, while the Golpasandha had several links with Kabuli barber-musician families and in 1975 Jalil married Amir Mohammad's daughter. It appears that the *sāzandeh* of Herat had reproduced the cleavage that existed in Kabul's Kucheh Kharabat between the Indian court musician descendants (*ustād*s) and families of Afghan barber-musicians.

The difference in ranking between the Golpasandha and the Khushnawazha was apparent to many people in Herat. The Golpasandha were well known on account of the women's bands, and were associated with prostitution and dancing boys. They would sometimes be described as *Jat*s, although it was not well known that some members of their *qaum* who lived in the Kucheh Golpasandha actually were barbers, and their more distant relatives played the *sornā* and *dohol*. The activities of their women were sufficient to warrant the pejorative label. Over the years Amir Jan had done his best to advertise the fact that his women had nothing to do with the performance of music, and he had succeeded in creating an image of comparative respectability for himself and his family. Amir Jan presented himself as a pious Muslim and during the months of *Muharram* and *Safar* (the months of mourning) appeared in the bazaar unshaven and in his oldest clothes, and allowed no music to be played in his house.

The Khushnawazha and the Golpasandha coexisted in Herat in a state of low-key rivalry. Amir Jan felt threatened by the Golpasandha and jealous of his position as the senior *sāzandeh* in Herat. They were wealthier than he was, but it was a wealth acquired by disreputable means. They were on the way up, he on the way down. Sometimes members of the two families cooperated in forming bands, and they celebrated certain rituals together, but there was often a degree of tension when they were in the same company. I was present at one encounter between the two families that occurred in May 1977. We had driven with Amir Jan, his sons Naim and Mahmud, and several of his daughters and young grandchildren, to spend the day at Shayda'i, a beauty spot with formal gardens and running water some miles from the city. A day out in the country was a rare treat for the women. When we arrived we found a group of unveiled women around the fountain at the centre of the gardens. They were immediately identified as musicians from the Kucheh Golpasandha. The outing appeared to be ruined. Amir Jan's problem was that he could not let his daughters into the gardens with the Golpasand women walking about brazenly unveiled. Someone might see them fraternising together, which could be bad for his reputation. Moreover, he was embarrased because my wife Veronica was spending a good deal of time in the Kucheh Golpasandha where she was learning singing. His solution was to hire the pavilion in the garden from the caretaker for a small sum; his daughters spent most of the day inside while the men sat out on the verandah.

We sat gloomily listening to a tape of Iranian popular music. When the women had brewed tea, spirits lifted a little. There was no sign of any Golpasand men. After a while a bleary-eyed Ali Ahmad came along to pay his respects, saying he had just woken up. The Golpasandha were on an outing to celebrate the forthcoming marriage of Ali Ahmad's great-nephew to a girl from a Kabuli barber-musician family. Ali Ahmad left and Jalil arrived, more cheerful and full of flattery for the Khushnawazha, saying at one point, '*Shomā kalān hastid, mā khordim*,' literally meaning 'you are big, we are small', and in this context, 'you are senior, we are junior'. He left, but this remark had brought about an obvious change in the mood of Amir Jan's party. Later on, Ali Ahmad, Jalil, and Amir came to sit with Amir Jan's group, drink tea and listen to tapes of Hindustani music. This put the gathering of rival musicians into a good mood and they talked and joked and told uncomplimentary anecdotes about another musician in Herat. The outing was a success after all, at least for the men. The Khushnawazha has asserted their seniority over the Golpasandha; the Golpasandha had come to them to pay their respects, and they had affirmed their inferior rank in front of me.

Amir Mohammad's rank

The presence of Amir Mohammad in Herat had disturbed the balance between the rival *sāzandeh* families. He was the highest ranking musician, though out of his hearing members of the Khushnawazha might dispute this. He deferred to Amir Jan in public but observations of social interaction between musicians on many occasions left no doubt that Amir Mohammad was in a rank of his own. He had superior skill and knowledge as a performer, especially of *klāsik*, was well known as a singer of *ghazal*s and *kiliwāli* on Radio Afghanistan, and was a Bacheh Kharabat, 'a boy from the Kharabat'. Although a barber-musician, his uncle was a government-appointed Ustad, and through him Amir Mohammad was heir to the teaching of Ustad Qasem, a court musician of the highest rank and a 'friend of Kings'. In Herat he was able to promote the Golpasandha in their rivalry with the Khushnawazha, treating them as his protégés, and in 1976 Jalil started to play tabla with Amir Mohammad, Rahim, and Gada. Amir Mohammad upset the status quo because he was a 'barber-musician' who outranked the '*ustāds*' of Herat.

Amir Mohammad played the part of the high ranking Kabuli *ustād*, but sometimes situations arose that threatened his carefully cultivated image. At one wedding party, when the time came for lighter entertainment and dancing, Amir Mohammad was asked whether the band would play for a dancing boy (transvestite with ankle bells) who had been hired. He refused. His patrons persisted. He insisted he was *honarmand*, an 'artist', and did not play for dancing boys, a morally reprehensible activity. Finally Gada said he would play and Amir Mohammad left the bandstand. Gada played the *salāmi*, the dancing boy entered the courtyard and danced for several minutes to the *dutār* and tabla. Gada stopped abruptly at a signal from Amir Mohammad amongst the seated guests, where a crowd gathered round as he angrily denounced the infamy of what was going on. The boy left and Amir Mohammad returned to the bandstand, still muttering, and resumed playing music for the guests to dance. Yet in a more discreet and private setting Amir Mohammad might have agreed to play for a Chelu dancing girl, a far more reprehensible activity. At another wedding two young men sitting by the bandstand started to smoke a cigarette spiked with hashish. Amir Mohammad leaned over in the next *naghmeh* and reprimanded them roundly, telling them to go and smoke it elsewhere. They stopped but did not leave. He addressed the next song directly to the miscreants, condemning them in the *fard*s:

> Rudeness spoils a good gathering
> We've got past the intoxication of wine and *bhang*
>
> Being a human being means having a good character
> Nothing in the world can equal it.

It is instructive to speculate about some of the considerations that faced Amir Mohammad when he decided to base himself in Herat. Herat might have represented an area of rich pickings but it also posed problems in dealing with the Herati *sāzandeh*. They might consider that he was poaching on their territory, yet he needed the best Herati musicians to be his accompanists. There was the complication of the rivalry between the Khushnawazha and the Golpasandha. The Golpasandha, who had close links with the barbering business, might be expected to be his natural allies, but it would not have been congruent with his high social rank as a Kabuli '*ustād*' to operate from the Kucheh Golpasandha. He needed to share in the prestige of the Khushnawazha as high ranking purveyors of art music. It was clear that Amir Mohammad was faced with delicate social negotiations, especially with Amir Jan. I observed that he would apologise ostentatiously if Amir Jan happened to be present when he performed, saying, 'You are the *ustād* of Herat and I cannot sing in front of you.' Amir Jan would tell him it did not matter and to go ahead. Ingratiating himself with the Khushnawazha might explain why he often brought Latif from Kabul as his tabla player for, as a son of Ustad Nabi Gol, Latif was probably more acceptable than another outsider.

Much significance can also be attached to Amir Mohammad's choice of accompanists from Herat. Rahim was a great asset as a *rubāb* master and Amir Mohammad had a written agreement with him that he would employ no other *rubāb* player, not even in Kabul, so that when he played in his home city it was to the accompaniment of two or three *delrubā* players and sometimes Gada Mohammad on *dutār*. Rahim composed many *naghmeh*s for the Iranian popular songs that Amir Mohammad learned in Herat, and he provided a contact with the wealthy Shiah merchant class who patronised high ranking musicians to play at their weddings. Gada Mohammad, the amateur turned professional *dutār* player, was also a great asset, but in a rather different way. He was a virtuoso performer on his instrument, with a tremendous fund of *naghmeh*s and song tunes at his disposal, but he lacked the kind of musical training that Rahim had received. He had the advantage of having been to school up to the sixth grade and was fully literate. This enabled him to write down the texts of new popular songs for Amir Mohammad to learn. Both accompanists were important in making sure that Amir Mohammad sang the newest songs from Iran as they became popular in Herat.

Gada Mohammad was acknowledged as Amir Mohammad's student in a way that Rahim was not. Though Gada Mohammad never went through the string tying ceremony with Amir Mohammad, in 1975 he became the official student of Ustad Mohammad Omar, Amir Mohammad's teacher. Gada Mohammad kept a notebook in which he wrote down Amir Mohammad's lessons, mostly tonal combinations for various *rāg*s. Gada Mohammad was also very much Amir Mohammad's henchman; he was with him every day in the new city hotel room which he used as his base. As a well known *dutār* player Gada Mohammad had his own circle of patrons and acquaintances, and he could advise Amir Mohammad about local conditions for engagements, where places were, their accessibility, the standing of potential patrons, and so on, and assist in negotiations for contracts. Rahim did not wait on Amir Mohammad in the same way; their relationship was more egalitarian.

Role and status of amateurs turned professional

The distinction between amateur (*shauqi*) and professional (*kesbi*) status was respected by both the *sāzandeh* and their amateur turned professional colleagues. It was a boundary that was maintained by both sides, and both sought to gain advantage from it. The *sāzandeh* stressed that they acquired their profession and professional skill *az pedari*, 'from their fathers'. They were brought up to be musicians, were exposed to music from an early age, and trained in performance by their relatives. They were *ma'lumdār*, 'knowledgeable', *sor fahm* or *sor shenāsi*, 'knowing about notes'; they knew about the *'ilm-e musiqi*, the 'science of music', the special professional knowledge of the *kesbi*. In a nutshell, according to the *sāzandeh*, the *kesbi* was *pokhteh*, 'cooked', while the *shauqi* was *khām*, 'raw'.

Amateur turned professional musicians on their part saw great value in their *shauqi* status, and used to stress that they did not derive from those low-class fellows who played music as an inherited profession. They were proud to be self-taught, perhaps precisely because training in music was associated with being a hereditary musician. While they might have a low ranking within *sāzandeh* circles, amongst their own amateur musician network they disavowed having *ustād*s, for then they did not have to respect anyone else. I found *dutār* players unwilling to name their betters; the game of social rank did not seem to interest them. They could even find a virtue in their own shortcomings as musicians, as though these proved their

Social ranking amongst professional musicians

shauqi status. Those who rejected the *sāzandeh* ideal of the *ustād–shāgerd* relationship placed themselves outside the professional musician social group.

It is not surprising to find that the non-hereditary musicians usually had a low rank amongst the social group of professional musicians. The way the *sāzandeh* treated their originally amateur colleagues was an extension of their attitude towards amateurism in music in general: they were dismissed as *shenidigi* ('hearers') who knew nothing about music. The *dutāri*s who had worked with Amir Jan's band were often the butt of jokes that exaggerated their amateurishness. Gada Mohammad, the highly successful *dutār* player, came in for a good deal of ribbing. Even his name, Gada, could evoke mirth, for *gadā* means 'beggar'. '*Salām gadā*,' they would say, and cackle with laughter, for this is how one addressed a beggar in the street. My cook once told me I should address him as Gada Mohammad, but Gada, who was present, just laughed and said it did not matter, everyone called him that. His village dancing to *sornā* and *dohol* music was well known to the *sāzandeh*, who occasionally had the opportunity to see him in action, but far from admiring his tremendous stamina and skill as a dancer, they laughed and said that Gada was flirtatious (*nāz kardan*) when he danced. At a gathering of musicians for Naim's betrothal, Amir Mohammad told the assembly during a break in their performance, 'I heard Gada singing the other day. . . .'. Gada blushed, no doubt anticipating the next move. 'Come on Gada, let's have a song!' So he had to sing for them, to their laughter and delight, just as though he was some *shauqi* singer forced to perform at a wedding party. When his voice cracked on a high note they dissolved in laughter and at the end their applause was enthusiastic. On other occasions, when Gada might happen to lead a *naghmeh* in a series of *Logari* pieces, the others in Amir Mohammad's band would grimace and nod their heads vigorously in silent but obvious laughter, as though to say, 'Look at him!'

In 1974 Gada had gone to great trouble to have a wonderful new *dutār* made, to an especially flamboyant design devised by Paindeh Mohammad, the *dutār* maker. It was also very large, perhaps the biggest *dutār* ever produced in Herat. Gada, a tall man, had no difficulty in playing it, but the other members of the band found it took up too much room in the taxi when they went to engagements. One night Amir Mohammad told him to take a saw and shorten the neck. Gada had to get a smaller instrument; the joke about the *dutār* remained. The Golpasandha treated him in the same way, teasing him, making jokes about him, laughing about his village dancing, kneeing him playfully in the groin when they met in the Kucheh Golpasandha. Despite the jokes the *sāzandeh* were very fond of Gada and greatly admired his *dutār* playing. He performed an important role in smoothing out the rivalries between the *sāzandeh*. Laughing about Gada was something they could all join in, it transcended their differences, and since they were being united in a spirit of humour and laughter this helped to make everyone feel good.

Karim Dutari had a special status amongst the professional musicians because of his expertise on the *dutār*. He knew a good deal about Hindustani music and was the only man able to perform *naghmeh-ye klāsik* on this instrument. He had not become anybody's student in a string tying ceremony in Kabul but had learned a great deal from playing in radio ensembles and from taking lessons with men like Ustad Mohammad Omar. The Herati *sāzandeh* respected his many years of service at Radio Afghanistan and acquaintanceship with the musicians of the Kucheh Kharabat. He once told me he had resigned his job in 1971 after seventeen years at Radio Afghanistan because the government would not give him a scholarship to study music in India. Back in Herat Karim ran a shop selling paraffin and old clothes, and his daughters wove carpets. As a semi-professional musician he played the *rubāb* or harmonium, only rarely the *dutār*. He also gave music lessons.

Ghulam Haidar was particularly well integrated with the Golpasandha, lived in a room in Ali Ahmad's compound, and acted as their servant in various ways. He had played with them for many years. Lack of musical knowledge was a constant point of criticism for the other *dutāri*s. If a *dutāri* made a statement about music in the presence of *sāzandeh* they would be likely to tell him to pipe down, saying, 'You are just a *shauqi* and you don't know anything about music.' The *dutāri* might be given menial jobs, such as carrying the heavy harmonium to the engagement while the singer carried the *dutār*. The *sāzandeh* would laugh at their *dutāris*' mistakes in performance. Perhaps the best indication of the rank of *dutār* players in the professional musician social group was their very low rate of pay. For example, in 1975 when Amir Jan's band (four persons) was going out for a minimum of 1,500 *afghāni*s, the *dutār* player (Mirza) was getting 100 *afghāni*s per engagement. Amir Jan told me that his *dutāri* had been complaining that he needed more money so he was going to raise it to 150 *afghāni*s. With his next *dutār* player, Amir Jan had a written agreement that he, Ghulam Nebi, would not play with anyone else without Amir Jan's permission. Karim Dutari, Gada, and Haidar were the *dutāri*s who had broken out of this low pay mould. It is hardly surprising that some professional *dutār* players did not want to play with *sāzandeh*; they could do better on their own, and avoid being bullied.

Apart from their joking relationship with Gada, the Golpasandha seemed to treat their non-hereditary associates rather better than did the Khushnawazha. Perhaps this was because they had in the past been more dependent on them to form their bands. I found, for example, that Ali Ahmad treated the *rubāb* player Sultan Wardak with great kindness and consideration. In the mid-1970s he was old and going blind; sometimes illness or bad weather prevented him from getting to an engagement, but whatever the circumstances (he told me) Ali Ahmad would still pay him his full share of the takings.

Ranking behaviour

The system of ranking amongst musicians was partly established and maintained through encounters. In some kinds of encounter two musicians competed informally to establish seniority, in others their behaviour endorsed an already agreed seniority. The question of who was addressed as *ustād*, if anyone, often gave important clues as to the ranking of those gathered. It also depended very much on context, for musicians who were quite low in rank might be addressed as *ustād* by outsiders. Another guide to the hierarchy in any given situation was to see who controlled the tuning of the tabla and stringed instruments; the prerogative of the 'best' man amongst them. The importance of precise tuning to the urban male *sāzandeh* was discussed in chapter 4. To criticise a musician for his tuning was an easy way to undermine him and to call his musicianship into question.

When *sāzandeh* gathered together for their own recreation – eating at a fellow musician's house, or engaged in their own rituals – they took turns to perform. It was considered necessary that each performer should ask the permission of the senior exponent of his instrument present before playing. When I returned to Herat in 1976 I soon heard that Amir Jan's son, Salim, had had a serious quarrel with his uncle, Karim, because at a *mehmāni* ('dinner party') he had failed to ask his uncle's permission before playing the tabla. The musicians referred to this incident for several months after, acknowledging that Karim had been right to be affronted. In this situation Salim had acted as a *cheshm sefid*, a 'white eye'. The expression *cheshm sefid* referred to someone who thought he knew better than his elders, and did not pay them due respect. The precise meaning of the metaphor is unclear; it might refer to someone who is blind (to social convention), or it may be that the person of inferior rank does not adopt the normal submissive downward posture of the eyes, but looks the person of senior rank squarely in the face, so that the white of his eyes are visible. Amir Mohammad apologising to Amir Jan – 'You are the *ustād* in Herat and I cannot sing in front of you' – could be interpreted as carefully avoiding the fault of *cheshm sefidi*.

The examples given so far show ways in which the hierarchy amongst the *sāzandeh* was expressed. There were also ways in which musicians could compete with each other, to establish at least a temporary dominance. These were clearest in 'battles' between two musicians, say a *rubābi* and a *tablegi*, but competition could also occur in group playing. At its simplest, two musicians might compete in terms of tempo, to see who had the greater stamina, or a *rubāb* player might try out some new *naghmeh* he had learned in a *tāl-e tāq*, an unevenly numbered *tāl*, such as eleven, thirteen, or fifteen *matra*s, trying to confuse the tabla player. Musicians might engage in *chapeh* playing, stressing normally unaccented beats, trying to throw each other off the *tāl*, 'hiding the *gor* beat' as they put it. This was regarded as a legitimate musical device to create excitement between the players and for their audience, who might also be confused. It could be called *bāzi*, 'play', similar to playing a game; or even *shukh*, 'mischievousness'. Perhaps to avoid some of the humiliation of defeat in a musical competition, perhaps just out of modesty, musicians often claimed to be out of practice.

Musical competitiveness between *sāzandeh* was shown in other ways. If one person knew some obscure fact about music theory, such as the term for a *rāg* with five tones in its ascending and descending scales, or the details of some rare *rāg*, it put him one up on the person who did not. Even the best Herati *sāzandeh* were aware that they did not know as much about music as the 'big *ustāds*' in Kabul. Little wonder that they valued every scrap of knowledge they could muster, and were so guarded about imparting that knowledge to others except via the teacher–student relationship. Ustad Sarahang was the final arbiter of knowledge. Musicians would invoke his name with statements such as, 'Only Ustad Sarahang knows', 'Not even Ustad Sarahang knows', or, 'Not even Ustad Sarahang would say it's wrong'. But even Sarahang was not above reproach. When he was giving his weekly radio programmes about *klāsik* in 1976–7 and criticising many Afghan musical practices (see chapter 4:44), Amir Jan commented that Sarahang was jealous and wanted to reinforce his superiority over all other musicians in Afghanistan. It was the ultimate ploy in 'playing the *ustād*'.

The string tying ceremony

During my time in Herat I attended a number of social events where *sāzandeh* were gathered: ritual occasions related to marriages of *sāzandeh*, a circumcision party amongst the Golpasandha, and a number of lunch and dinner parties. The largest gathering I observed was in 1977 when Ghulam, a young tabla player of barber-musician origin became the *shāgerd* of Naim Khushnawaz. This ceremony was called *gorbandi* in Herat and corresponds to the *ganda bandhan* of North India, where a string is tied around the wrist of the new student. Twenty-five professional musicians gathered together in the house of one of Ghulam's relatives. An unusually grand luncheon was served. Before and after the meal the musicians played in a number of different combinations. Amir, the much-abused musician from the Kucheh Golpasandha, acted as master of ceremonies, calling on various singers to perform in turn. Eight combinations of musicians played, as shown in table 6. Karim Khushnawaz and

Table 6 *Combinations of musicians at string tying ceremony*

1 Mahmud (v, h), Amir Jan (r), Ghulam Nebi (d), Naim (t)
2 Salwar (v, h), Amir Jan (r), Kholek Sauz (d), Azin (t)
3 Ghulam Dastegir (v, h), Rahim (r), Karim Dutari (d), Fazl Ahmad (t)
4 Hakim (v, h), Karim Dutari (r), Kholek Sauz (d), Salim (t)
5 Ali Ahmad (v, h), Rahim (r), Karim Dutari (d), Fazl Ahmad (t)
6 Rahim (r), Fazl Ahmad (t)
7 Seid Gol (v), Amir (h), Karim Dutari (r), Haidar (d), Ghulam (t)
8 Amir Mohammad (v, h), Amir Jan (r), Karim Dutari (d), Fazl Ahmad (t)

Note: v = vocal, h = harmonium, r = *rubāb*, d = *dutār*, t = tabla

Jalil were both absent from Herat at the time. Apart from the first band, and the *rubāb* and tabla solo, these were all novel combinations of musicians to me. Some singers were listened to with more attention than others; Salwar and Hakim rated low in this respect. Ghulam Dastegir, the Kabuli *rubāb* player with the Golpasandha, sang a *khyāl* with competence, to warm applause. Amir Mohammad performed last and was received with rapture. Amir Jan played *rubāb* with him and for the first time ever I saw him really appear to enjoy Amir Mohammad's singing, jealousy forgotten in the passion of the moment.

The *sāzandeh* clearly enjoyed playing in these unusual groupings. They were affirming their self-perceived superior musical abilities, their sense of being *pokhteh*, 'cooked, matured', as though to say, 'We *sāzandeh* can play together in any combination, even if we have not accompanied this singer, have not played that *ghazal* or *naghmeh* before. Because we are *sāzandeh* we can do it.' Another point which emerged very clearly, and which confirmed statements I had already heard about what went on at such a ceremony, was that with only one exception all the singers performed Kabuli *ghazal*s or *khyāl*, or in the case of Rahim's *rubāb* solo, a *naghmeh-ye klāsik*. For once, they were playing the kind of music they wanted to play, not what a musically uneducated audience might want. In this way they celebrated their love of art music. The one exception, Seid Gol, sang two old Herati songs, and received a considerable amount of praise. A further point was the careful asking of permission from senior exponents before performing: Amir Mohammad for vocal, Amir Jan for *rubāb*, Karim Dutari for *dutār*, and Fazl Ahmad for tabla.

The string-tying itself, which took place at the end of the *majles*, after the music making, posed an interesting dilemma. To start with there was a good deal of discussion about the propriety of Naim becoming Ghulam's *ustād*. Amir Mohammad pointed out that there were other (and better) tabla players in Herat, like Karim Khushnawaz and Fazl Ahmad, Amir Mohammad's accompanist from Kabul. Naim said that he had tried to tell Ghulam that he, Naim, did not know anything. There seemed to be an impasse; it was like a committee faced with a difficult regulation. Naim was too 'junior' to become an *ustād*, a teacher. This was finally resolved by Ghulam Dastegir's suggestion that Naim should become Ghulam's *ustād* for *kiliwāli*, popular music. Amir Jan prepared a thread of seven colours and tied it around

The string tying ceremony

Ghulam's wrist, a silk gown was presented to Naim on behalf of Ghulam, the musicians joined in a quick prayer, and immediately departed. I did not remain in Herat long enough to see how this relationship developed but in 1985 I learned from Amir, in Peshawar, that Naim had failed to give Ghulam any lessons and several months later Ghulam revoked his *shāgerdi* and reclaimed the silk gown.

8 Social contexts of musical performance

The *sāzandeh* derived their income as professional musicians from performing in a variety of social contexts. Their main earnings came from wedding parties (*majles*) for men, and this was the social context for which their repertory and style of performance were specifically tailored. Groups of *sāzandeh* often made up the pit band in the Herat theatre, and sometimes played at the country fairs held in the spring. They also gave nightly concerts during *Ramazān* (the month of fasting), when bands of *sāzandeh* from Kabul also appeared in Herat. Besides these public performances, often to large audiences, they played in the more intimate surroundings of the *mehmāni*, 'dinner party', *shau nishini*, 'night sitting', and the *meleh bāgh*, 'garden party'.

The amount of work for the *sāzandeh* varied greatly during the course of the year. It is not really correct to speak of an 'annual cycle' of music in Herat because the solar calendar (marking out the seasons) and the lunar calendar (marking out the cycle of religious observances) were out of phase with each other, with the result that the religious calendar moved forward approximately eleven days every year. The interaction between them determined the precise form of the 'cycle' of music for the year in question. The data examined below were mostly collected between September 1976 and September 1977.

For the musicians the two main periods of intense activity were during the spring, when the country fairs took place, and summer, when wedding festivities could be held outside at night. The most favoured time for large wedding celebrations was after the harvest, when landowners had money from their crops, and food was cheap. These seasonal considerations were modified by two periods in the religious calendar: *Muharram*, two months of mourning observed by Shiahs, and *Ramazān*, the month of fasting, observed by Shiahs and Sunnis alike. Shiahs would not hold wedding parties during *Muharram*, and abstained from playing or listening to music at this time. *Ramazān* was not a very suitable time for wedding festivities because of the difficulties of the fast. In 1976 *Muharram* started on 22 December and lasted until 17 February 1977, a period of fifty-eight days. Because it fell in the winter it did little to disrupt the seasonal cycle of music. The spring country fairs had already begun by the end of *Muharram*. In 1977 *Ramazān* began on 15 August, and there was a rush of wedding parties during the preceding weeks, for after *Ramazān* it would soon become too cold for outdoor celebrations at night. The theatre was the only place where live music was performed all year round, and even that was closed during particularly bad spells of wintry weather.

The two main religious festivals were the two *'Eid*s, one immediately after *Ramazān* to celebrate the end of the fast, the other three months later to coincide with the culmination of the pilgrimage to Mecca. *'Eid* was a time for putting on new clothes and visiting friends and relations. *Sornā* and *dohol* players and Chelu musicians toured the bazaars and residential areas performing outside the shops and houses for donations of money or goods. *Sāzandeh* musicians with their instruments would visit their patrons in the city and play for them, also receiving presents of money.

Wedding festivities

Marriage in Herat was a protracted affair, and passed through a number of stages. What is described here is the typical marriage amongst the relatively wealthy middle class; traditional and lavish. There was some degree of variation in this idealised account, and certain stages, such as the *nakh o suzan* and *fātehkhāni* were sometimes telescoped together. The marriage process took many months to complete, and could be even further drawn out.

1. *The search for a bride.* The family of the prospective groom (*dāmād*) made inquiries amongst members of their *qaum* to discover a suitable bride (ʿ*arus*).
2. *Negotiations with the family of a possible bride.* The women of the groom's family made a number of visits to a possible bride's family to negotiate the marriage. These visits were called *khāsruni* or *khāsgāri*. The results of negotiations were reported back to the men of the two families.
3. *Signing the marriage contract.* Once the bride's family accepted the proposal they engaged a mullah to draw up a marriage contract (*talebān*) specifying the bridewealth (*pichkash*) to be paid to her father, and jewellery and clothes for the bride. The contract was sent to the groom's family to be signed, usually by his father.
4. *The betrothal party (nakh o suzan).* This small party was held at the house of the bride, where the men and women of both families gathered separately. The *nakh o suzan*, 'thread and needle' (a large brass or gold needle, with threads of different colours twisted together and decorated with beads), was presented by the bride's family to the groom, symbolising their betrothal. In return the groom's family presented part of the *pichkash*. The following day the women of the groom's family returned to the bride's house with gifts for her, the *jawāb nakh o suzan*, 'the reply to the thread and needle'.
5. *The engagement party.* This was a large party, or *majles*, ('reception') held at the bride's house, called *fātehkhāni* ('reading prayers') by Sunnis, and *shirinikhori* ('eating sweetmeats') by Shiahs. This celebration was usually held at the same time as the legal marriage (*nekāh*).
6. *The legal marriage.* This took place at the bride's house. A mullah came to question both parties about their agreement to the match, and read particular passages from the Holy Koran. Once the religious ritual had been enacted the groom was led to the women's gathering by his father and after a series of rituals the bride and groom retired to a private chamber for the night. The couple were now legally married but the bride continued to live with her family, where the groom sometimes visited her at night.
7. *The wedding* (ʿ*arusi*). This was held at the bridegroom's house, a large *majles* to celebrate the conclusion of the wedding process, when the bride finally took up residence with her husband in his family home. This occurred once all the *pichkash* had been paid to the bride's family, and was by far the largest and most lavish of the succession of wedding parties. It is considered in more detail below.

The successive events in the marriage process became progressively more elaborate, and the amount of music making that occurred at them also increased. During the *khāsruni* visits no music was played; to do so would have been to invite misfortune on the prospective marriage. At the betrothal party the women sang and played the *dāireh* and danced. The music was provided by the women of the groom's family, for they were celebrating (*shādi kardan*) the acquisition of a bride, while the bride's family mourned the loss of their daughter. At the *fātehkhāni/shirinikhori* a group of women *sāzandeh* from the Kucheh Golpasandha would often be hired to play for the women's party, while, less frequently, men *sāzandeh* might be hired to entertain the men. The women musicians had certain ritual duties; they played wedding songs at certain points, and displayed the presents from the groom to the bride.

126 Social contexts of musical performance

Plate 8   The author, Amir Jan, Rahim, his bride, and Mohammad Ali descend for the display of gifts at Rahim's *shirinikhori* in 1974

At the ʿ*arusi*, both male and female *sāzandeh* were hired. In addition, there were opportunities to hold other smaller parties for women, where they provided their own entertainment. Marriage formed a focus for women to engage in musical activity, as Slobin has noted (1974:241).

The reception for men at the ʿ*arusi*

The ʿ*arusi* served as a display of wealth and rank. The hosts hired the best urban musicians they could afford and invited several hundred guests, sending out written invitations a few days in advance. A meal was served to all the guests and a number of rituals were enacted. The staging of a *majles* involved the co-ordination of a number of specialists. A large area,

Wedding festivities

usually a courtyard, was carpeted with a patchwork of rugs hired from a carpet dealer. The walls of the buildings round the courtyard were decorated with bolts of highly coloured fabrics hired from a cloth seller. The fabric was pinned to wooden struts put up by a carpenter. A generator was hired to power the strings of brightly coloured light-bulbs (from an electrical shop) that illuminated the courtyard, and for the public address system used by the musicians (from a radio repair shop). A bandstand for the musicians (*takht-e sāz*) was erected and decorated with cloth. Cooks were engaged to prepare the meal for the guests, and dishes, cutlery, tea glasses, and small brass trays were hired from the appropriate shops. The men of the groom's family waited on the guests, bringing tea from the samovar and serving the meal. Careful attention was paid to the seating of the guests according to their social ranking. Important guests sat in rooms overlooking the courtyard, the less important sat in the courtyard itself, while a crowd of young boys would sit directly in front of the musicians.

The musicians hired to play at such a reception were usually the *sāzandeh* bands led by Amir Mohammad, Amir Jan, and Ali Ahmad, and less frequently Ghulam Salwar. A prior agreement was made with the groom's family specifying the duration of the performance and the fee, and a deposit was paid. The course of the typical *ʿarusi* viewed as a performance event is set out in table 7.

Table 7 *The ʿarusi as a performance event*

1	First *chashni*, lasting 2–3 hours
2	Three quarters of an hour's break while musicians ate
3	Second *chashni*, followed by dancing and comic acts
4	The *takht-e dāmād*, the central ritual of the *majles*
5	More dancing and comic acts (optional)
6	Third *chashni*, mainly religious *ghazal*s

The first part of the evening consisted of one long *chashni* (set of pieces) lasting two to three hours, without a break. First the musicians tuned their instruments, a process which merged into the *shakl-e sāz*, the collective playing of *shakl* phrases, each man giving his own rendition of the mode, in free rhythm, with occasional rhythmic phrases from the tabla (*āstāi-ye tabla*). Adjustments to tuning were still made at this stage, and there was no clear boundary between tuning and playing the *shakl-e sāz*. They then played a *naghmeh-ye kashāl*, followed by several *ghazal*s, and then a programme mainly of popular songs and *ghazal*s. The modes used at this stage of the performance were normally *Yemen*, *Kausieh*, *Pāri*, *Kesturi*, and *Pilu*. At the start of each new song the singer sang a *fard*, a couplet of poetry which was appropriate to the following song. The items in the programme were presented without a break; as one song ended the singer started with the *fard* to introduce the next song. The audience could make written requests which were handed to the singer, but the request system was much less important than in the theatre or at a *Ramazān* concert.

The first part of the *majles* was a serious and dignified affair. If, as was common, the music started at six o'clock in the evening, guests would still be arriving one or two hours later. As they arrived they were greeted by members of the groom's family and shown to the area where they were to sit. They were served tea and sat quietly listening to the music, perhaps talking amongst themselves in small groups. To the outsider they might have appeared passive, even bored, but they were listening in the approved manner, without overt physical response. They applauded at the start of their favourite songs (which were usually from the popular music repertory), rather than at the end. In other words, they approved the choice rather than the performance.

At about eight thirty or nine o'clock the men of the groom's family prepared to feed the guests, bringing round ewers and basins for them to wash their hands. They then served the food on large metal dishes (*quri*) heaped with rice and meat, with bread and vegetable side dishes. The guests sat three to a *quri* and ate with their hands. Food was served in order of precedence, important guests first, the boys sitting by the bandstand last, eating five or six to the dish. The women's party was held in an adjoining courtyard, and they were normally served after the men. The musicians continued with their concert, eating in a private chamber after all the guests had been fed.

Once the musicians had returned to the bandstand the guests were ready for more music and then lighter entertainment. The band retuned to the *Bairami* mode and performed a second, shorter, *chashni*, starting with a *ghazal* and followed by a number of popular songs. Then a space for dancing was cleared in the middle of the courtyard. First, a group of men, mostly from the groom's close kin, danced an urban version of the *Atan*, the national dance of Afghanistan, usually played in *Pāri*. There were three parts to the dance: it started with the *Rasm o Gozasht*, a 'march', played in *Gedeh*, in which the men walked in a circle; then the *Atan* proper, played in *Mogholi*, with spinning movements by the dancers; then '*Aushāri*', in *Dādreh*, also with spins. The melody for '*Aushāri*' played as part of the *Atan* at an urban wedding was quite different from the Herati tunes called '*Aushāri*' (see chapter 6:93) and was in the *Kesturi* mode. The music gradually accelerated in tempo and continued for five to ten minutes, when the dancers were exhausted.

Following the *Atan* the most common form of entertainment was solo dancing by young men from amongst the guests, who performed dances such as *Shishkebābi*, *Turisti*, and *Ghamzagi*, also part of the dance repertory of young women and girls. These dances were performed with much hip waggling and pelvic thrusting and were comically erotic. The musicians played material similar to that for a dancing boy; quodlibets of tunes and song melodies that had been absorbed into the dance repertory, with liberal use of Logari dance tunes. Musicians claimed to have little regard for this kind of music but in the appropriate context they enjoyed playing, laughing at the antics of the dancers, and shouting comments and encouragements. Each dancer performed for only a few minutes before retiring. The guests did not volunteer to dance and were usually dragged to their feet by their young hosts. Very occasionally a real dancing boy might be hired, wearing makeup, women's clothes, and ankle bells.

Sometimes a comedian told jokes, sang songs, and performed comic dancing. These comedy routines stemmed from an old tradition, and earlier this century groups of comedians, perhaps Gharibzadeh who also performed *seil*, came to entertain the guests. Sometimes a comic dancer provided the entertainment, and performed various tumbling acts besides the usual comic–erotic dance routines. These entertainers were unpaid amateurs, known as *maskharebāz*, 'comedian', or as *jeikar*, 'joker' (an English loan word). Sometimes amateur singers from amongst the guests were asked to sit with the musicians and perform to their accompaniment. Several well known Herati singers, such as Kholu Shauqi, started their professional careers in this way. Occasionally a singer known to be lacking in ability was forced to sing with the band, to the delight of the audience and musicians, who played many wrong notes to increase the hilarity.

Then came the central ritual of the evening, the *takht-e dāmād*, 'the bridegroom's throne'. One or two rows of chairs were set out for the important guests and several trays of objects necessary for the ritual were laid before them. The musicians performed two wedding songs: first '*Heinā ba kārā*', followed by another, such as '*Olang olang*' or '*Dar majles-e heinā-ye to*'. The groom was led in by his father, or a senior member of the *qaum*, and they took their places in the middle of the front row of chairs. Then the groom's father performed a series of ritual actions. He took a new skin hat filled with *noqol* (richly sugared almonds) from the tray, a gift from the bride's family, and placed it on the groom's head, the *noqol* cascading over him. More *noqol* was thrown over him. A *malang*, or one of the cooks, carried a dish of burning *esfand* (aromatic rue) before him, and then round the assembly (to ward off the evil eye). A garland of artificial flowers was placed around the groom's neck and a lump of henna was bound to the little finger of his right hand. Then the tray of henna was carried amongst the guests for those who wanted to dye their fingers likewise. A tray of *noqol* was also distributed, a handful to each guest. The mullah said a prayer and photographs were taken by a professional photographer. The bridegroom was taken by his father to the women's party, where he joined his bride and engaged in further rituals.

At the end of the *takht-e dāmād* there was often more dancing and comedy routines. The course of this part of the event was at the discretion of the guests; the musicians maintained that they were simply the servants of the people. When the dancing came to an end the musicians performed a final *chashni* of songs, usually more *ghazal*s, and in the case of Amir Mohammad, very often a *rāg*. The mode favoured for the final items was *Āsā*, which was said to 'taste particularly sweet late at night'. This mode also had a special connection with spiritual poetry, and typically the programme drew to an end with several *naʿt*s, religious or mystical *ghazal*s. In this way the *majles* closed on a serious note, with thoughts of Islam, of God, and His Prophet.

The musicians were contracted to play until a certain time and when the last song was concluded the *rubāb* and *dutār* players laid down their instruments, the singer closed the bellows of the harmonium, and the tabla player placed the quilted covers over his drumheads. The remaining guests would often entreat the musicians to play for longer but they would normally refuse. They were served tea and brought a tray of *noqol* and sweet biscuits, on top of which lay a sealed envelope with the balance of their payment. The leader of the group pocketed the envelope without opening it, and the musicians divided the sweetmeats between them. Then they tied up their instruments in their covers, and asked for permission to leave.

The reception for women at the *ʿarusi*

While the men held their reception, a separate *majles* for women took place in an adjoining courtyard. Music was provided by a band of women *sāzandeh* from the Kucheh Golpasandha, singing and playing harmonium, tabla, and *dāireh*. It is worth giving some consideration to the role of women musicians, for they provide several revealing contrasts with the men.

The women's *majles* was much longer, and continued until the afternoon of the following day. The women's courtyard was carpeted, decorated, and illuminated as described for the men but less lavishly. A gaily decorated bandstand might be provided for the women musi-

Plate 9 Golpasand women musicians at a women's wedding party, with *dāireh*, harmonium, and tabla, 1977

cians, but more usually they sat and played on the carpeted floor. The women's reception was less formal and less structured than that of the men, partly because there were so many young children present. As they had to play for so much longer than their male counterparts, one of their concerns was to conserve their energy. This was one reason why it was necessary to have several musicians singing, and some flexibility as to who played what instruments. Another consideration was that women musicians took their babies and young children with them on engagements.

Like the men, women made a distinction between music for listening and music for dancing, but whereas at the *majles* for men the two aspects were clearly demarcated, amongst the women they were mixed together. In the early part of the *majles* music for listening was provided, until dancing was initiated by the hostesses. Singing and dancing were then interspersed and sporadic according to the ability and energy of the guests. The women did not start their performance of music with an instrumental piece and they did not hold the idea that the same mode should be maintained for a number of items; they were quite happy to change frequently from one mode to another. Most of their performance was in *Bairami*, *Jog*, *Pāri*, and *Kesturi*, and their repertory consisted entirely of popular and Herati songs. They did not introduce each song with a *fard* as the men did.

One of the main forms of entertainment at the women's reception was dancing, performed mostly by the girls and younger women amongst the groom's kin. It was up to them to organise the dancing and make the party exciting. The bride sat quietly in another room; her kin were not expected to take a prominent part in the festivities. As with the men, nobody wanted to put themselves forward and the girls and women usually had to be dragged to their feet to dance. Some of the dances performed at such receptions were the *Atani*, a group dance similar to that of the men and danced to the same music; solo dances like *Turisti*, *Logari*, *Shishkebābi*; *Shelangi* for two girls, *Seh Chakegi* for four girls, and *Kāghazbādbāzi* for little girls. Some of the dances were traditional, like the *Atani*, others were subject to fashion. Younger musicians might also dance if offered a tip, and they might perform a song-and-dance act, miming as they sang, and dancing during the *naghmeh* sections between verses.

Singing and dancing occupied the first part of the *majles* for women, starting from about six o'clock in the evening. The guests sat in groups drinking tea and smoking water pipes and watched the music and dancing. They ate the same meal as the men, with three women to a dish of rice and meat. The *takht-e dāmād* at the men's reception, and the solo dancing and other comic entertainments, were watched by many of the women from the rooftops. The groom was brought to join the women after the *takht-e dāmād*, sometimes not until the reception for men had come to an end. He then took part in another *takht* ceremony in which he and his bride sat together on a throne (cushions, a sofa, or chairs). In front of them were placed plates of cakes and sweets, a mirror, and a Koran. This ritual was called the *āyneh masraf*, 'using the mirror'. The mirror was placed before the couple and a white cloth was held over their heads so that they could gaze at their own image together. The bride and groom fed each other sweets and cake and read from the Koran in turn. During the *āyneh masraf* the musicians played wedding songs such as '*Bādā bādā*', '*Heinā ba kārā*', *Olang olang*', and '*Āhesteh buro*', while the guests clapped after each ritual. The bride and groom then retired to a private bedchamber. The musicians carried on playing for another hour or so, before the guests settled down for the night.

The following day was called *takht jam' koni*, the 'gathering up of the bridal throne'. After breakfast the music and dancing started again at nine or ten o'clock, and often more guests arrived. The musicians played intermittently throughout the morning. At lunchtime another similar meal of meat and rice was served. Afterwards, the music and dancing continued until about four o'clock, when the bride's dowry was displayed (*jahiz newā*). This consisted of a complete set of household goods, as well as clothes and gifts for the bride and groom, all provided by the bride's father. The bride and groom sat on a throne and each item of the dowry was held up individually and announced by one of the women musicians. This concluded the reception and the guests began to leave. The musicians were paid with an envelope of money placed on top of a dish of *noqol*, and material for one set of clothes (*dast rakht*) from the bride's dowry was given to them.

Ramazān concerts

Although *Ramazān*, the month of fasting, involved hardship, since it required abstinence from all food and drink during the hours of daylight, it was also a period of festivity by night. I was able to observe five consecutive *Ramazān*s in Herat (1973–7). In 1973 *Ramazān* started on 28 September, in 1977 it began on 15 August. During the day many shops were closed and people rested or slept for much of the time. In the evenings the shops stayed open and the streets were crowded. People went to bed late and rose early for a large meal before daybreak. Groups of boys toured the residential areas by night singing *Ramazāni* songs, and in mosques the Koran was read to assembled congregations. In some villages *sornā* and *dohol* music was played at night, and in the city the civic brass band performed this role. The idea of having concerts during the evenings of *Ramazān* may have come from such nocturnal music.

The recent practice of evening concerts probably originated in Kabul long before it became popular in Herat. Amir Jan told me that he had started the fashion for *Ramazān* concerts in Herat some years earlier, playing in a café in the new city. The Golpasandha had followed his example in later years. Amir Mohammad played his first season of *Ramazān* concerts in Herat in 1971 with a band of Golpasandha. By 1972 Amir Mohammad had established his own band in Herat and for the next four years they were a regular feature of *Ramazān*.

The kind of venue played by Amir Mohammad and other *sāzandeh* groups was a café (*kāfeh*), a large dining room in a modern building. For the concerts the tables were removed and a bandstand constructed and lavishly decorated with carpets, wall hangings, religious pictures, and a portrait of the current ruler (Mohammad Daud), all illuminated with coloured electric lights. As *Ramazān* moved progressively into the summer it became possible to hold outdoor concerts for audiences of up to 1,000. Admission for such concerts was usually twenty *afghāni*s, the same as entrance to the theatre. At the other end of the scale, a teahouse might engage a *dutār* band to play in the evenings, or a *dutār* and *zirbaghali* duo to play with amateurs amongst the customers, when no entrance fee was charged.

The structure of Amir Mohammad's *Ramazān* concert was similar to his performance at a wedding party, but rather shorter, lasting three to four rather than five to six hours. He began his first, long, *chashni* with a *naghmeh-ye kashāl*, followed by several *ghazal*s, then a programme of popular songs and *ghazal*s and sometimes a *rāg*. Then there was an interval of about half-an-hour. In the *Ramazān* concert no music was played for dancing, though Logari *naghmeh*s were played with certain songs. After the interval Rahim and Gada had solo spots with tabla accompaniment. Rahim played a *naghmeh-ye kashāl*, a *naghmeh-ye klāsik*, or his version of '*Chahārbeiti Siāhmu wa Jalali*', with '*Āmineh*' as a *pāzarb* (refrain) and '*Aushāri*' as a *reng* (dance piece). Gada played a *naghmeh-ye kashāl* or *naghmeh Uzbeki*. After the solo spots, which lasted about half an hour, Amir Mohammad moved to the *Āsā* mode, in which he sang the last few items, serious *ghazal*s of a religious or mystical kind.

The *Ramazān* concerts provided Amir Mohammad and his band with the opportunity to perform more in the musical genres they valued – *ghazal*s and *rāg*s – and they did not have to play for dancing. The band was sometimes augmented with *delrubā*, *sormandel*, and *tānpurā*, giving the band a more 'classical' appearance and sound. The audience had paid to be there and the music was the central point of interest. Individuals bought post-cards from vendors and sent written requests to the singer, a useful indication of what the public wanted to hear that night. Amir Mohammad worked hard to establish and maintain a good rapport with his audience. From his place on the bandstand he greeted patrons as they arrived, with a salute, or a bow (his hand on his heart), or by toasting them with his tea glass, all smiles and conviviality. He drank endless glasses of tea, calling for his pot to be replenished whenever it was empty, and smoked cigarettes incessantly.

In 1974 Ustad Rahim Bakhsh's band was engaged for the month and in 1975 Haji Hamahang played in Herat. In 1976 both Kabuli *ustād*s with their groups played the *Ramazān* season. Their concerts provided an ideal situation to observe the Kabuli *ustādi* style. They provided an interesting contrast. Rahim Bakhsh, who was made an official *ustād* by the Afghan Government in about 1975, was said to perform very much in the manner of Ustad Qasem, his teacher. His programme was heavily weighted towards art music. He sang mostly *ghazal*s, with a good deal of slow and fast *khyāl*. He always played two *naghmehā-ye kashāl*

Plate 10 Golpasand band at a *Ramazān* concert in 1974. Left to right: unknown *delrubā* player (Kabuli?); Ghulam Haidar (face hidden), *dutār*; Qader, *sormandel*; Ghani Landai, *rubāb*; Ali Ahmad, vocal and harmonium; Karim Khushnawaz, tabla; Ghulam Mohammad, *rubāb*

Plate 11 Amir Mohammad and his band play at a *Ramazān* concert in 1973. Left to right: Gada Mohammad, *dutār*; Amir Mohammad, vocal and harmonium; hidden behind him an elderly *delrubā* player from Kabul; Rahim, *rubāb*; Amir Mohammad's father-in-law, *tānpurā*; Latif (son of Ustad Nabi Gol), tabla

in his concerts, in *Yemen* at the start, and in *Kumāj* after the interval. Besides *rubāb* and tabla he had *delrubā* and *tānpurā* in his band, and one year a *sārangi* player.

Haji Hamahang had a similar line-up of musicians but his programme was less orientated towards Hindustani music: he sang *ghazal*s and popular songs in a *ghazal*-like style. His performance was characterised by the use of long strings of interpolated *fard*s, many seemingly extemporised, commenting on the situation around him. Some of this apparent spontaneity was staged; the *fard*s sung when a member of the audience presented him with a bouquet of flowers or when someone was moved to dance on an adjacent rooftop were repeated when the same things happened at subsequent concerts, as were the *fard*s he sang when the caged birds hanging above the bandstand started to sing. Unlike Rahim Bakhsh, Hamahang was reluctant to sing *khyāl* at his *Ramazān* concerts in Herat.

The economics of the *Ramazān* concert could involve large sums of money. In 1975 Hamahang was contracted to play for the month in Herat for 90,000 *afghāni*s, with accommodation (a single room) found and 500 *afghāni*s per day living expenses for the musicians. Hamahang would have taken about 45,000 of this, a considerable sum for a month's work. For the first week the courtyard where they played was full, selling about 900 tickets per concert at 20 *afghāni*s each, and the organisers of the concerts clearly made a large profit. Amir Mohammad played for 20,000 *afghāni*s for the month; he took 10,000, Gada and Rahim received 3,000 each and the tabla player (from Kabul) was paid 4,000 *afghāni*s. Amir Mohammad paid the *tānpurā*, *sormandel*, and *delrubā* players (relatives like his son and father-in-law) out of his own share.

The theatre

During my fieldwork in Herat the only theatre operating was the Herat Nanderi, owned and run by the local office of the Ministry for Information and Culture. From 1968 to 1973 a second theatre was in existence, the Behzad Nanderi, discussed by Sakata (1983:86). This closed down after Mohammad Daud came to power, when there was a ban on privately owned newspapers, magazines and places of entertainment throughout Afghanistan. The Herat Nanderi expressed government policy towards the performing arts and was of some importance as an indicator of trends.

The proscenium theatre was originally introduced into Afghanistan in the 1920s and was probably inspired by the example of theatre in Turkey, the source of many modern ideas at that time. The director of the Literary Circle of Herat in the late 1930s was an advocate of the theatre 'as an educational and socially beneficial force' (Gregorian 1969:357). The Herat Nanderi probably dated from the late 1940s. For some years it apparently enjoyed a good reputation amongst the progressive educated classes of the city. In those days the cast was all male, with female roles played by young men and boys. Then, as part of a government policy directed towards improving the status of women in the performing arts, women were introduced as actresses, singers, and dancers. The result of this policy was to lower the standing of the theatre, for the only women who could be recruited to perform before audiences of men were courtesans, who used the theatre to advertise themselves, as well as to earn surprisingly large salaries. It is noteworthy that the theatre, run by a government agency, featured the type of solo dance by a dancing girl that was banned by the police from being performed in a private house for an audience of men.

The plays that I saw at the Nanderi were melodramatic and comic. Sometimes the evening's dramatic entertainment consisted simply of a series of comic acts. Comedy was a well established Herati tradition in the folk drama (Baghban 1977). The more serious plays often contained strongly patriotic and nationalistic sentiments and frequently involved the denouncement of corrupt officials. The theatre also cultivated a rather self-conscious projection of Herati culture and there was a higher proportion of Herati songs in the theatre than in other performance situations. This tendency to cultivate Herati culture was well demonstrated by Karim Dutari's *dutār* orchestra, which played at the theatre for several months in the winter of 1975-6, and consisted of eight male and one female *dutār* players. Soraya, an actress and singer, had taken the unusual step of learning to play the *dutār* a little in order to play in the orchestra. Karim conceived of the orchestra as distinctly Herati in character, playing *mahali* music, and originally he wanted the musicians to be dressed in archaic Herati costume made from a coarse canvas.

The Herat Nanderi was located in the new city. It consisted of a stage at one end of a hall which could accommodate an audience of about 250 sitting on wooden chairs. A small area was reserved for women and in 1975 a gallery was built at the back of the auditorium for family groups. There was an orchestra pit at the foot of the stage, consisting of a low mud wall separating the musicians from the audience. An evening's performance at the Nanderi fell into two parts: first the *drām*, 'the play', and then the *konsart*, the 'concert', featuring a number of singers and some solo dancing. The musicians in the orchestra pit provided both incidental music for the play and the accompaniment for the concert.

The personnel of the theatre consisted of several kinds of performer, in addition to the administrative and production staff.

1. *The actors*. Nearly all also held menial jobs in government offices. They were Heratis, and some had worked in the theatre for many years. There were sometimes one or two fully professional actors, such as Olfat Herawi, who formerly ran his own theatre (the Behzad Nanderi) and was officially honoured by the government (Sakata 1983:86). Members of the production staff also played leading roles.
2. *The actress-singer-dancers*. Some women were both principal actresses and singers, others were singers who appeared in the plays in walk-on roles. Only one or two of the women also performed solo dancing. The theatre usually employed about five women at any one time, on various kinds of contract. Some of them were from outside Herat – from Kabul, Kandahar, and Jalalabad. Changes of women personnel occurred frequently.
3. *Male singers*. In 1977 the theatre employed Ghulam Dastegir as a singer of Herati songs. Like the actors, he worked in a government office by day. Bolbol Herawi, 'The Herat Nightingale', was also employed as a singer and performer of bird and animal imitations. His career as a performer was largely based on a few such routines. Nawak and Ghulam Nebi Zendeh Del were two other Herati singers who had an informal arrangement with the theatre whereby they could appear when they wished.
4. *The pit musicians*. The theatre band was the typical urban ensemble, with harmonium, *rubāb*, *dutār*, and tabla, and sometimes *tanbur* and *duzangeh*. Playing in the theatre was viewed by musicians with some disdain, for they had to play popular and dance music. They thought little of the women's musical skills, complained that they often sang out of tune, and that they took a long time to rehearse new songs (for which the musicians received no extra pay). Although the theatre provided regular employment, the pay was low. In winter, when the audience might be very small, the musicians received less and on nights when the performance was cancelled, nothing. In 1974 Ghulam Salwar told me his band received 350 *afghāni*s per night. As leader, he took 110 *afghāni*s and paid the others in the band 60 *afghāni*s each.

At that time there were only three women working in the theatre. One, Shemshad, a famous singer from Kabul, received *1,000 afghānis per night*, another received 250 *afghānis* per night, the third, who was young and considered to be learning the business, received 2,500 *afghānis* per month, a little more than a male musician. Ghulam Salwar, a singer and harmonium player, had run the theatre band since about 1963, and before that worked as a tabla player there. The musicians he employed were usually amateurs turned professional like himself. There were frequent changes in personnel and for a period in 1975 Salwar was replaced by a band of Golpasandha: Ghulam Mohammad, harmonium; Ghani Landai, *rubāb*; Haidar, *dutār*; and Jalil, tabla. With the exception of Jalil all had formerly played in the pit band of the Behzad Nanderi (for a photograph of that group see Sakata 1983:87). In 1976 Salwar was back in the theatre in his new partnership with Karim Khushnawaz.

Country fairs (*melehs*)

The word *meleh* referred to an expedition to the countryside for the purpose of recreation. Heratis who had studied English at school often used the word 'picnic' as a translation for *meleh*. This word was suitable for a small *meleh*, but here we are concerned with a much larger affair, for which the term 'country fair' is more appropriate. These *melehs* were a springtime phenomenon, centred around New Year's Day, which falls on 21 March in Afghanistan and Iran. They started each Friday as soon as the weather was judged warm enough, generally about the middle of February. Extra *melehs* were held on New Year's Day (*Now Ruz*) and on the Wednesday (*Chahārshambeh Awal*) and Thursday (*Panjshambeh Awal*) after New Year's Day, and then on every Friday up to the fortieth day of the New Year. Some *melehs* were held in the vicinity of shrines, and there are several reasons for deducing that the *meleh* was closely allied to the phenomenon of the ʽ*urs* in Pakistan and India, a pilgrimage to a shrine on the anniversary of the saint's death (literally his 'marriage').

The archetypal *meleh* in Afghanistan took place at Mazar-e Sharif in Afghan Turkestan, at the putative tomb of Ali (N.H. Dupree 1967:49–56). Thousands of pilgrims journeyed to Mazar at the time of New Year to take part in the raising of the standard on New Year's Day. The *Meleh-ye Gol-e Sorkh*, the 'Tulip Festival', continued for forty days, and was the occasion for much music making. The Herat *melehs* also continued over a period of forty days and *madā* mendicants (Slobin 1976:59) came from Mazar specifically for the *meleh* season. The music of the Herat *melehs* had certain connections with the music of Afghan Turkestan and the repertory of *meleh* songs often contained textual references to Mazar's Tulip Festival.

There were five main sites for holding *melehs* near the city of Herat: Takht-e Safar, Abu Walid, Shahzadeh Yaqub, Imam Shishnur, and Pul-e Malan (see map 2). These were the *melehs* that city dwellers went to, though they formed only part of the crowd at most *melehs*. *Melehs* occurred at other places in the Herat valley on some of the days mentioned but not on the same scale. At two sites, Abu Walid and Imam Shishnur, the tomb of a saint lay adjacent to the *meleh* site and visiting the shrine was an integral part of going to the *meleh*. Takht-e Safar was a terraced pleasure garden only a mile from Ansari's tomb at Gazer Gah. The *meleh* at Shahzadeh Yaqub was held some distance from the shrine to the saint of that name. At Pul-e Malan, an ancient bridge over the Hari river, there was a tomb in the locality but it is not clear if that was why the *meleh* was held there.

The timetable of *melehs* was approximately the same every year, varying in detail only in terms of which day of the week New Year fell upon. The *melehs* of 1977 are shown in table 8.

Country fairs (*meleh*s)

Table 8 *The* meleh*s of 1977, showing number of groups playing*

	Day	Location	Groups
	Fri 11 Feb	Takht-e Safar	1
	Fri 18 Feb	Takht-e Safar	2
	Fri 25 Feb	Takht-e Safar	2
	Fri 4 Mar	Takht-e Safar	3
	Fri 11 Mar	Takht-e Safar	3
	Fri 18 Mar	Takht-e Safar	3
Now Ruz	Mon 21 Mar	Takht-e Safar	2
		Abu Walid	2
		Shahzadeh Yaqub	3
Chahārshambeh Awal	Wed 23 Mar	Abu Walid	4
		Shahzadeh Yaqub	3
Panjshambeh Awal	Thurs 24 Mar	Shahzadeh Yaqub	7
	Fri 25 Mar	Shahzadeh Yaqub	7
	Fri 1 Apr	Imam Shishnur	4
	Fri 8 Apr	Imam Shishnur	3
	Fri 15 Apr	Pul-e Malan	2
	Fri 22 Apr	Pul-e Malan	4
	Fri 29 Apr	Pul-e Malan	2

Many activities went on at a *meleh*. Teahouse proprietors from the city took their paraphernalia to the *meleh* site and set up their teahouses there. At its simplest the teahouse consisted of a small carpeted area with a samovar nearby, where patrons sat and drank tea. Some teahouse owners also brought tents and awnings to provide shade for their patrons, and a few hired bands, and charged a higher price for tea. At the biggest *meleh*s there were half a dozen groups playing in such teahouses. Shopkeepers set up stalls selling a range of foods: nuts, sweets, biscuits, and fruit. Butchers set up shop, bringing carcasses of beef and mutton to supply the kebab restaurants. There were ice-cream sellers, *jelabi* makers (a type of Indian coiled sweet), and water sellers. Many other goods were on sale, especially items like hand mirrors, razor blades, perfumes, and trinkets. There were sellers of hand-made wooden toys such as rattles, drums, lorries, and cradles. These items were made and sold by Gharibzadeh. A notable feature of the *meleh*s were the hand powered roundabouts and Ferris wheels, also operated by Gharibzadeh.

Music making at the *meleh*s

The musicians at the *meleh*s were mainly amateurs turned professional who formed *dutār* bands. Such ensembles played almost exclusively popular music, with special emphasis on the Mazari repertory. Certain lower ranking members of the professional musician social group, who usually played in *dutār* bands, such as Ahmad, Kholek Sauz, and Amir, were much in evidence at the *meleh*s. Their bands were highly unstable in their personnel (in contrast to the bands run by the *sāzandeh*) and varied from *meleh* to *meleh*.

The *meleh* constituted a second-rate venue for the *sāzandeh*; the hours were long and the economic return low. Amir Mohammad's band never played at *meleh*s in Herat. In the 1974 *meleh*s Gada Mohammad played regularly in a *dutār* band but in 1977 he did not play at all; Amir Mohammad had told him not to, saying it was not good for his reputation as a musician.

Plate 12   Outdoor teahouse at a Takht-e Safar *meleh*, 1974. The tent in the background has a *dutār* band inside (see plate 13)

I never found Amir Jan or Ali Ahmad playing at a *meleh*. Only the younger *sāzandeh* musicians such as Hakim and Azin worked in such venues: it was considered good experience, they made some money, and it did not diminish their standing. In 1977, when detailed research on the *meleh*s was carried out, the only high ranking *sāzandeh* musician found at the *meleh*s was Karim Khushnawaz, who played at three of the biggest fairs (at Shahzadeh Yaqub) with his partner Ghulam Salwar. Mohammad Ali, Amir Jan's *delrubā*-playing son-in-law from Kabul, also appeared regularly at the *meleh*s of that season, with two boys he was training and promoting, who sang and played harmonium and tabla.

When *sāzandeh* musicians played at a *meleh* they did not perform wedding or *Ramazān* concert material, but played the same kind of popular music as a *dutār* band. Typically, the latter played all day, from about half past nine in the morning to half past five in the afternoon, with frequent breaks for refreshment. They sat up on a small bandstand inside the tent or enclosed area. They performed in *chashni*s, sets of songs in the same mode played without a break, lasting generally for forty-five minutes to an hour. The usual modes were *Bairami*, *Jog*, *Pāri*, and *Kesturi*, less frequently *Talang* (*Zaoul*) and possibly *Āsā*. The *chashni* often started with a short instrumental piece, but the *dutār* bands did not usually play a *naghmeh-ye kashāl* but a popular instrumental piece such as a *naghmeh-ye radiu*. Each new song was prefaced with a *fard*. Since they had to perform for so long it was usual for the several singers in the group to take turns to sing a *chashni*, and it was common for *shauqi* singers, or other musicians visiting the *meleh*, to sit in with the bands.

Country fairs (*meleh*s)

Plate 13 Bacheh Haji, vocal and *dutār*; Amin Bacheh Matari, vocal and *zirbaghali*; Hakim Khushnawaz, vocal and harmonium; Gada Mohammad, *dutār*; inside the tent shown in plate 12, seated on a bandstand made of wooden beds

Plate 14 Jalil Golpasand, vocal and harmonium; Bismillah, tabla; Ghani Landai, *rubāb*; Seid Gol, *dutār*; Ghulam Haidar, *dutār*; at a *meleh* in 1974

Jeshan

The annual independence celebration, *Jeshan*, provided a week of festivity in Herat that had some of the quality of a *meleh*. Each guild amongst the city's shop keepers and artisans erected a *kamp* ('camp'), a large booth in the park opposite the Governor's Offices in the new city. The open booths were constructed from timber frameworks covered with brightly coloured bolts of fabric and painted boards. The area inside was carpeted and laid out with chairs and low tables. To the side of the main row of *kamp*s were other rows of teahouses, kebab restaurants, and stalls selling fruit and other edible goods. *Jeshan* was celebrated in many ways, with military parades, sports events in the stadium, special performances in the theatre to invited audiences of officials and local grandees (who would never venture there in normal circumstances), high school galas in the cinema, with a speech by the Governor's wife (dressed in the uniform of a girl guide leader), theatrical sketches, music, and even fashion shows. In the evenings the guild members, with their wives, children, and other relatives, went to their camps, to meet and talk, drink tea, and visit other camps.

Jeshan in Herat was a time for various kinds of music making, but was not the major event in the musical diary that it seems to have been in some parts of Afghanistan (Sakata 1983:24–7). In contrast to the *meleh*s the teahouses did not hire bands; during the day and night groups of Chelu musicians, singing with *sārang*, *dāireh*, and *tāl*, were in evidence, as were *sornā* and *dohol* players, the town brass band, and the military band from the Herat barracks. The guilds hired *sāzandeh* groups and *dutār* bands to entertain their members and guests in the evenings. No detailed study of music was undertaken in this context but particular patriotic and nationalistic songs were sung at that time, especially songs in support of the Republic of Mohammad Daud. *Jeshan* was cancelled in 1973, the year Daud came to power, presumably to avoid the dangers of hostile crowds gathering, but resumed in 1974, with the date changed by a few weeks and officially designated in honour of the founding of the Republic.

Private parties

The performance contexts discussed so far were public. The wedding party, though closed to outsiders, was in a sense a public musical event, for the public address system guaranteed that the performance of the musicians was broadcast to all in the locality. But there were other more private performance events, which were held discreetly, even in secret.

Bacheh bāzi

Dancing boys and their dance performances were subjects that had to be discussed with some delicacy in Herat. The dancing boy usually performed at a small private party, to the music of *dutār* or *rubāb* accompanied by *zirbaghali* or tabla, or a small ensemble such as a *dutār* band. His face was made up, he was dressed in women's clothes, wore ankle bells, and his performance was flirtatious rather than erotic. In the popular stereotype of Herat the dancing boy was a *kuni*, a catamite. When people in Herat condemned music for exciting sexual thoughts and appetites, they were usually thinking of such performances.

The terminology relating to this activity is of some interest. The word *bacheh* in its usual sense simply meant 'boy'. In a narrower sense, and where the context made the meaning clear, *bacheh* referred to a good-looking teenage boy, a *bacheh maqbul*, a 'handsome boy', or a *bacheh birish*, 'a boy with no beard', and within this meaning of *bacheh* an even narrower sense referred to the dancing boy, the *bacheh bāzigar*. Well known dancing boys had names like Ramazan Bacheh or Ahmad Bachehgak. The word *bāzi* meant 'play', sometimes with a slightly mischievous connotation. The stick dance was *chub bāzi*, quail fighting was *karak bāzi*, *kāghazbād bāzi* was 'kite flying', and so on. The word *bāzi* also meant 'dance', with the verb form *bāzi kardan*. The term *bacheh bāzi* referred to the total activity of dancing boy performance; it referred both to the social event, where a group of men joined together for the purpose of staging and enjoying a performance of dancing, and to the dancing itself. The dancing boy enthusiast, who enjoyed spectating the dance of the dancing boy, was known as a *bacheh bāz*, a 'boy player'. The same term could be used for the man who enjoyed 'unnatural acts' with a catamite, and *bacheh bāzi* could also refer to such acts. This polysemy points to the conceptual link between this kind of dance and sex. A more neutral term for dance was *raqs*. To indicate the solo style of dancing boys one used terms such as *raqs-e bāzi*, or *raqs-e khānegi*, 'room dance', in contrast to *raqs-e maidān*, 'dance of the open space', such as the *Atan*.

Slobin (1976:116–21) makes some interesting comments on the dancing boy in Afghan Turkestan, where the tradition seems to have been particularly strong, and my own observations more or less agree with his. It is perhaps significant that the kinds of dance tune most favoured in Herat for such dancing were *Uzbeki* and *Logari* dance pieces, the first associated with Afghan Turkestan, the second with the Logar Valley, another important region for such dancing. *Bacheh bāzi* was prohibited by the authorities in Herat and such parties were sometimes raided by the police, the musicians and dancer arrested and fined or sent to prison. For this reason *bacheh bāzi* was usually held in secret. But police interference was not inevitable; to have a dancing boy at a wedding party would not result in trouble, and in the theatre it was just this kind of performance that was featured by women dancers, although in the opinion of some people *dokhtar bāzi*, 'girl play', was even more reprehensible than *bacheh bāzi*. One reason for the heavy-handedness of the authorities was that disputes and fights sometimes broke out at *bacheh bāzi* parties, when rivals might vie with each other for the attentions of the boy by giving him bank notes while dancing, perhaps having him pick the money off the floor or from the donor's hand with his teeth. Occasionally a man was stabbed to death at such parties.

While popular belief had it that all dancing boys were, in effect, homosexual prostitutes, I am simply unable to confirm or deny this. It was certainly not the case that the dancing session finished up as a sex orgy, nor should it be thought that all men with a keen interest in dancing boys were homosexually inclined; some were 'dancing boy fanciers' just as they might be pigeon fanciers or dog fanciers. *Bāzi* was a *shauq*, a spectacle, something to follow, to discuss, to compare performers and performances.

There were two modes of recruitment for dancing boys. There were a few Gharibzadeh families for whom being a dancing boy was a family profession. And some boys were recruited through family circumstance; the boy's father may have died or deserted his family and if there were no male kin to protect the widow or wife and her children the boy might be vulnerable to what most Heratis certainly saw as corruption. The career of a dancing boy was necessarily short, from about the age of twelve to seventeen or eighteen, when he could no longer be said to be a *bacheh birish*, a 'boy without a beard'. Many dancing boys became musicians after their career as dancers. Some looked for a suitable boy to teach to dance and then to take out for *bāzi*. Such a man might have a succession of boys under his tutelage. Each dancing boy had his *mordegau*, his 'keeper' or 'protector' (the same word also meant 'pimp') who looked after his business affairs, trained him in dancing, and usually played for him.

The dancing boy session usually took place in a small room in a private house at night. The event itself could be spoken of as a *mehmāni* or a *shau nishini* (see below). An evening's performance was organised into a series of *chashni*s, each twenty to thirty minutes long, with all the items in a *chashni* in the same melodic mode. The dancing was episodic, with sets of routines constituting the basic units of performance, each lasting for several minutes. In between units of performance the dancer retired to a corner of the room, then flounced once again into the middle of the dance area for the next routine. Some routines consisted of a pattern of dance movements repeated over and over, with the constant stamping of the feet in alternation, percussing the ankle bells. Others were more mime-like and communicated an idea or emotion, even 'told a story'. Some typical routines were:

> Kneeling before a guest and gazing deeply into his eyes
> Use of Indian hand dance gestures
> Eye movements combined with other body movements
> Shaking a shoulder to oscillate a padded breast
> Holding onto one end of a long silk scarf and executing circles underneath it
> Dropping slowly backwards onto the floor and lying with legs folded back at the knees in a submissive posture
> Dancing with one arm up and the other down, hands moving to look like a huge mouth opening and closing.

Some of these routines may well have been inspired by dancing in the Hindi films regularly shown at the cinema in Herat. The dancing was controlled in performance by the *mordegau*, who would call to the boy or signal in some other way what the next routine should be. Some dancing boys also sang in their performance.

The music played for dancing consisted of sequences of tunes of many kinds. Some were well known *naghmehā-ye bāzi*, *Uzbeki*, and *Logari* dance tunes, some were popular song tunes, some were traditional Herati dance tunes such as '*Aushāri*', some were *naghmeh*s from old popular songs. There did not seem to be any fixed relationship between specific dance routines and specific tunes; the *dutār* or *rubāb* player performed what seemed to him to be appropriate music at the time, but from hearing a recording of the music one would not know what the dance routine would have been. An exception to this might be when the *mordegau* was himself a *dutār* or *rubāb* player and had trained his boy to perform particular routines to particular tunes.

Mehmāni, shau nishini, meleh bāgh, and *shauq*

Heratis had a strong predilection for entertaining their friends in their houses, for dinner parties, for guest evenings, and for other kinds of small private gathering. Several types of social event may be defined at the outset.

> *Mehmāni*: when a number of guests were invited to a house for a meal, usually in the evening, when music might be played afterwards.

Plate 15 A dancing boy demonstrates a pose, 1974

Shau nishini: literally, a 'night sitting', when a number of guests were invited to a house in the evening after they had eaten, to drink tea, to talk, and perhaps to be entertained with music, often played by the guests themselves.

Meleh bāgh: literally, a 'garden party', but the word *meleh* here referred to a 'picnic'; a family or group of friends went to spend the day outside in a private garden or orchard, or in some well-known beauty spot, cooking food, sometimes also playing music.

Shauq: referred primarily to a group of *shauqi*s playing together, giving a performance to a small audience of friends, with the implication that 'a good time was had by all'. When musicians played together at a *mehmāni*, *shau nishini*, or *meleh bāgh* and the music went well one could say that a *shauq* was in progress. When weavers stopped work and played their *dutār*s in their workshop they, too, were holding a *shauq*. Although the implication was strong that the *shauq* was the activity of *shauqi* musicians, one could also use the term about *sāzandeh* when they were playing for their own private entertainment.

The practice of holding *mehmāni*s and *shau nishini*s depended upon certain spatial arrangements. Most houses had a guest room (*mehmān khāneh*) located close to the front door of the house, so that guests could enter without going into the parts of the house and courtyard normally occupied by the women. The guest room was usually the best appointed room in the house. When a man decided to give a lavish *mehmāni* he might send out written invitations, otherwise he sent one of the boys as a messenger. When guests arrived they were greeted by the hosts and escorted to the guest room. They had to be seated according to seniority but the guests themselves might not want to be ranked in this way and while everyone was shown initially to the 'high position' (*bālā*) they might soon move to sit somewhere else, vacating the high place for the next arrival to occupy. The guests were served glasses of tea and they talked amongst themselves. The host and his male kin were busy waiting on them and serving a meal of rice and meat, guests and hosts ate together sitting round a large tablecloth or plastic sheet spread in the centre of the room. After the meal the atmosphere became more relaxed. The men sat about, drinking tea, smoking, and chatting. Music might be provided by one or more *shauqi*s amongst them, or sometimes one or two *sāzandeh* musicians might be invited along, to be treated as guests, but also paid to play with the *shauqi*s present. A tabla player was often invited in this manner, for the tabla was an instrument that few *shauqi*s played. Or the host might hire a complete *sāzandeh* band, who might or might not eat with the guests, depending on the closeness of their friendship. Amongst the poorer classes *dutār* and *zirbaghali* players or a *dutār* band might be asked along. The *shau nishini* was in many respects like the *mehmāni* but less formal and without the serving of a meal. Guests arrived later in the evening and sat drinking tea and talking and perhaps enjoying music till deep into the night.

Sometimes Amir Jan held *mehmāni*s at his own house to entertain his patrons, friends, and amateur students, inviting them to come and have dinner and then to listen to music played by Amir Jan and his sons (example 1 was recorded at such a gathering). Amir Jan's guest room was a large upstairs room with a window overlooking the old city, a pleasantly breezy spot in the hot summer months. Round the walls hung framed photographs which his guests liked to take down and examine. The photographs illustrated his illustrious career and his contact with the famous musicians of Kabul. There was a photograph of Amir Jan singing and playing the harmonium at a wedding party which was dated 1311 (1933) when he was aged about eighteen. There were photographs of him playing with various groups over the years; one with Rahim Khushkhan as an old man sitting in with his band, another with Karim Dutari playing an early version of the fourteen stringed *dutār*. There were two photographs of Ustad Sarahang, one in which he was wearing a row of medals awarded for his excellence in music, another of Sarahang at a garden party in Herat. When guests came for dinner parties the talk was all about music. They looked at the photographs and asked about them, and Amir Jan reminisced and told anecdotes about music and musicians in Kabul and in India, describing his own visits to Kabul and his meetings with the *ustād*s, all the time creating and reinforcing the impression that he was a part of the Kabuli *ustād* scene.

Little further need be said about picnics held in the gardens and orchards; many Heratis had access to such places, which they either owned or which belonged to their relatives in the villages. There were also various beauty spots in the Herat valley, such as Takht-e Safar, Pul-e Pashtun, Shaydai, and Mir Daud. At each of these was a government owned pavilion which was available for hire and for sleeping in. One of the most famous beauty spots in the

Private parties

Plate 16 Safar, a weaver and amateur three-stringed *dutār* player, dances at a *meleh bāgh* held in an orchard near the city, 1974

Herat valley was Cheshmeh Obeh, about sixty miles up the river, in a wooded valley in the foothills, where there were hot mineral springs, a bath house, a number of buildings which could accommodate large numbers of people, and some smaller private rooms for families. During the summer some of the bigger guilds in Herat would organise visits to Cheshmeh Obeh, when busloads of their members would travel there to spend several days having a *meleh* and where music making was a frequent form of entertainment. Up to 200 men might go together on such occasions. The guild might hire a group of *sāzandeh* or a *dutār* band to go with them, or they might have some *shauqi*s amongst the guild membership. On a visit to Cheshmeh Obeh in 1975 I found a party of sixty employees of the Wool Company staying there, plus a party of six motor mechanics from the city, and a number of family groups. In the afternoon the mechanics staged some amateur theatricals, a comic enactment of a wedding, with the principal comedian playing the bride. Two of the mechanics played *rubāb* and *zirbaghali* and provided 'wedding music' and later played the *Atan* for the men to dance. Later in the evening they put on another play, a long comic sketch, which must have required a good deal of rehearsal, with music from an impromptu band of *rubāb*, harmonium, and *zirbaghali*. After that the musicians played till late into the night in one of the pavilions, to an audience of young men seated around the walls.

9 Music in the Herati value system

The place of music within Islam has been the subject of theological debate by Muslim authors for many centuries. Although the Koran does not make any explicit statements about music, a number of *suras* ('Koranic verses') have been variously interpreted as sanctioning or condemning music. Farmer (1929), Roy Choudhury (1957), and Robson (1938) provide useful summaries of the debate. Both Slobin (1976:25–7) and Sakata (1983:35–8) give some consideration to ideas about the lawfulness of music in Afghanistan, but their discussions refer mainly to the literary controversy rather than to ideas expressed by their informants.

The condemnation of music

There was a commonly held belief amongst Heratis of all classes that music was wrong from the religious point of view. Music might be described as *bad*, 'bad', or *bad kār*, 'bad work', as *qalat*, 'wrong', or as *harām*, 'forbidden'. It was often said that *'musiqi gonāh dāre'*, 'music incurs sin'. A *gonāh* was believed to be a sin or fault noted by the angels who sat on a person's shoulders writing down their good and bad actions, to be weighed on the scales at Doomsday, deciding on his or her fate. When asked *why* music was wrong, many people simply stated that the mullahs said it was sinful. But with more probing it was possible to discover a number of specific reasons for regarding music with disfavour.

Firstly, a very pragmatic reason often given was that performing or listening to music might lead people to neglect to say their prayers at the proper time. Music was recognised as too engrossing, an opinion which admitted the attraction of music and an inclination on the part of human beings to become absorbed in it.

Secondly, musicians were thought to risk becoming over-involved in music in ways that would compromise their wider duties as good Muslims in the world of work and economic affairs. Amateur musicians who became professional were judged to have allowed their love of music to get the better of them, and sometimes to have sacrificed good educational or work opportunities for pleasure. Related to this was the idea that playing and listening to music were spiritually unprofitable activities which contravened Mohammad's teaching that human beings should engage only in activities that brought spiritual benefits, like 'working, praying, and reading Islamic books'.

Thirdly, there was a strong conceptual link between music and other actions that were more explicitly proscribed by Islam, such as lascivious dancing, illicit sexual intercourse, and imbibing 'wine'. The conceptual connection of music with dancing boys was especially strong; such performers were beyond the pale, for not only did they dress in women's clothing and perform provocative dances, they were also said to be catamites.

Fourthly, there was an underlying idea that music was *kār-e sheitān*, 'the work of Satan'. The music profession was sometimes called a *kesb-e sheitāni*, 'a Satanic profession'. The *sornā* was apparently known as 'the penis of Satan' in the villages (Baghban 1977:84), and the upper bridge on the *dutār* was termed *sheitān kharak*, 'the Satan bridge'. According to one story, the *dutār* originally had no upper bridge, the strings were lashed to the neck, as on the *dambura*. Satan dived into the sea and came up with a sea-shell which he fashioned into an upper bridge for the *dutār*. Part of the *Jat* stereotype related to the belief that the Gharibzadeh had received their teaching from Satan, and had made pacts with him in which they committed serious crimes such as incest (*ibid.*).

Most of the ideas expressed by the Heratis can be found in the long-standing debate on the lawfulness of music. Many people had heard mullahs make such statements, and music was apparently sometimes mentioned in sermons as something which good Muslims should avoid. While I had the opportunity to question a few mullahs about the lawfulness of music it was perhaps a little difficult for me to find out what they really thought because I was a respected foreign guest in their city, known to be carrying out research on music. They might have spoken rather differently to an uneducated artisan with a *shauq* for music, or to a hereditary professional musician.

Writing answers to questions touching on Islamic law was one of the services provided by mullahs and the Khatib of Karukh, an important mullah in a provincial town forty miles from the city, and a graduate of the Theological College in Herat, once wrote for me the following paper (in Persian) on music.

> The bitter effects and the ominous fruits of music from the point of view of hygiene and psychology.

Scientists divide the human nervous system into two parts: the central nervous system and the vegetative nervous system. The vegetative system is divided into two parts, the sympathetic and parasympathetic.

Since these two kinds of nerves in the body have opposite effects to each other, therefore as long as external stimulation does not occur, they act opposite to each other and maintain the balance of the body, but whenever one of them loses its balance the order of the realm of the body will be disturbed.

Amongst the external stimuli which upset the balance between sympathetic and parasympathetic nerves is musical vibration. Music, with its exhilarating tunes or its sorrowful melodies, and particularly if it is accompanied by the grotesque vibrations of symphonic [*sinfonik*] music, will definitely upset the necessary balance, and in turn upset the sensitive basis of animal life, which includes absorption, excretion, perspiration and palpitation, and finally brings the person close to troubles and illnesses.

The tunes of exhilarating music, for example, gradually drive man towards psychological disturbances such as excessive wakefulness, sudden excitements, improper laughter and ridiculous and delirious talk. Persistence in this habit could cause mania, which is a sort of insanity.

The magazine *Dimanche* published in Paris wrote: 'Although during the past century scientists have noticed the bad effects of music on man's nerves, they were ignorant of its significance until a few years ago when Dr. Wolf Adler, professor at Columbia University, proved that, "The best and the most exhilarating melodies have the most ominous effects on man's nervous system."'

The most dangerous effects of music are:
    I Generating a weakness of the nerves.
    II Weakness in will and abnormal attention.
    III Stagnation of the mind; music is said to be the cover of the mind.
    IV Cause of high blood pressure.

Regarding the above mentioned harmful effects which nowadays man has realised, Islam, fourteen centuries ago, prohibited music.

This remarkable document is couched not in terms of the theological debate, but in terms of health and hygiene; Western scientific 'proof' that music upsets the balance of human physiological systems is used to vindicate the fact that Islam prohibited music long ago. That the argument is couched in modern Western physiological terms may have been for my benefit as a foreigner, but it is also an example of the tendency to claim that the discoveries of modern science were anticipated long ago by Islam. The argument is a modern version of the theory of the four humours, or of 'hot' and 'cold' elements, according to both of which sickness of the body (and mind) is related to an imbalance between the humours or elements.

Another such paper was solicited from Sheikh Ibrahim Munir, an Iraqi mullah who was teaching Arabic at the Theological College for a year. The paper is too long to reproduce here but makes the following points:

1. Several *hadith* ('Traditions of The Prophet') may be cited to show that Mohammad sanctioned performances of music on a number of occasions.
2. Intentionality and the uses to which music is put are of crucial importance. When music is well intentioned, either for worshipping God, or simply for recreation, it is not unlawful.
3. When music is used in a wrong may, and its performance occurs in mixed parties of men and women, or is associated with unlawful sexual intercourse, or with drinking alcohol, it is unlawful.

Although Sheikh Ibrahim was an outsider, who did not speak Persian, he was a legitimate informant, who played an active role in the religious life of the city during his year of residence, often leading prayers at the Friday Mosque and sometimes preaching the Friday sermon there. He was highly respected as an expert on Islamic law (*Hanifi* school) by the mullahs of Herat. The presence at the Theological College of mullahs from Arab countries, such as Iraq or Saudi Arabia, served as a source of information about a form of Islam that was operating in more modern types of Muslim society, and such mullahs were often critical of what they saw in Herat. Sheikh Ibrahim might be compared with other outsiders who operated in the social arena of Herat, such as Ustad Nabi Gol, or even Amir Mohammad. His paper on the lawfulness of music gave the Iraqi view, more tolerant than that of most mullahs in Herat. Yet there was evidence to show that at least some Herati mullahs agreed with him. Sheikh Ibrahim's paper was read to Abdul Wahab Saljuki, Herat's great ʿālem ('theological scholar'), who signed it after appending:

When music possesses the above conditions it is lawful, there is no fault in listening to music or playing music. Its teaching is also lawful.

Another point that emerged from discussions with mullahs was that music was more readily sanctioned in the context of joyous occasions, especially at festivities held to celebrate birth, circumcision, and marriage. In such contexts the good intentions behind the music were explicit. Two *hadith*s sometimes cited in Herat to support this idea can also be found in Roy Choudhury (1957).

On the day of *Buʿath*, ʿĀyisha was enjoying a song of some Ansār girls in the presence of the Prophet who was lying on his bed. Abū Bakr on entering the room rebuked them for playing the instruments of Shaitān in the house of the Prophet. The Prophet remonstrated the protest; He said, 'Don't disturb them' . . . 'Give her up, oh Abū Bakr. This is the day of ʿId.' After this the Prophet took rest. But ʿĀyisha winked her eyes and they departed. (*Ibid.*: 67–8)

Once an Abyssinian musician appeared in presence of the Prophet on the occasion of ʿId. The Prophet asked ʿĀyisha if she liked to enjoy music. On Āyisha giving assent, the Abyssinian was called in. The place of performance was the Prophet's own house. The mosque of the Prophet was adjacent to his house. The courtyard of the house of the Prophet and that of his mosque was the same. In fact, the performance took place in a sacred place – *hareem*. The Abyssinian acrobat sang and danced and ʿĀyisha enjoyed it for a pretty length of time. (*Ibid.*: 69)

The permissibility of music on these occasions tends to suggest that attitudes against music were simply the expression of an orthodox puritanism which was lifted in situations where it was deemed appropriate for people to enjoy themselves. Even then, mullahs did not necessarily approve of what went on. Abdul Wahab Saljuki had, according to his son, a proven record as an opponent of music. As a child he had once attacked women musicians at a women's wedding party by throwing the rotting head of a dead cat at them, and on another occasion in the 1950s he had beaten and evicted a band of Golpasand women who had been invited to play at a relative's circumcision party. At the wedding party where music was played the mullah might leave after he had performed his ritual function at the *takht-e dāmād*, or he might stay on and suffer in silence, not wishing to give offence to his hosts.

The condemnation of musicians

Many musicians, amateur and professional, told me about prejudice and critical remarks they had encountered as a result of their proclivity for music. This was one of the matters raised in a series of recorded interviews with a sample of *dutār* players in 1974, some of them amateurs, some amateurs turned professional. Their experience clearly varied a good deal, depending in part on the age and status of the musician: there had been more prejudice in the past, which was remembered by older musicians, and professionals were more likely to be the target of criticism.

Karim Dutari had a good deal to say about the criticism of musicians. His most telling remarks were as follows:

In the past mullahs have told me many times that it is wrong to play music, asking me not to play music, saying I was like a *Jat*. Once in Kabul I went to Pul-e Kheshti mosque to pray, dressed in a suit. The mullah told me, 'You are just a *Jat* dressed up in a suit. It's bad, it's sinful, you shouldn't do that. You call yourself an artist [*honarmand*], but an artist is someone who does beautiful calligraphy, or is a writer, someone who creates something. You, you are just a *Jat* dressed up in a suit, you sit behind your microphone singing and playing, and you say you're an artist!'

In this case the mullah was not fooled by the musician's apparent respectability, dressed in the clothes of the educated middle class; he invoked all the negative connotations of the term *Jat* in his condemnation of music. *Jat*, as we have already indicated (chapter 7), was the term every musician dreaded to hear applied to himself.

Ismail, the seventeen year old son of a wealthy Shiah Sayed family, highly educated and intending to study philosophy at university, was an amateur *dutār* and *chahārtār* player. He made the following comments:

No one in this world can avoid music, even those who say it is wrong enjoy music really. Perhaps even Mohammad enjoyed music, and the mullah sitting on the *manbar* [pulpit of a mosque] who says that music is not good cannot really avoid or ignore music. He likes music but because he is a [religious] fanatic he is frightened by music, but he still likes it. He's frightened because religion is very strong against music. . .

If music is wrong why are the mullahs singing the prayers in the mosques? Or singing [*rowzeh*] during *Muharram* in Iran? And when they read the Koran they sing it in a special mode [*sor*]. Most of the modes which they use when they sing the Koran are the same as the modes of the *dastgāhā* in Iran. . .

My family is more liberal than some in my *qaum*. When my father was alive I used to play *ney* [meaning here a fipple flute] and he liked that very much. He died by the time I started to play the *dutār*. My older brother encouraged me, and my mother and sisters know a little about music, they have a feeling for it and they enjoy it. But other relations, not such close ones, when they heard I was playing the *dutār* they said it was bad [especially for their reputation as Sayed]. They said nothing to me directly, they were whispering behind my back. No mullahs have told me not to play, they would have liked to but they didn't dare because they often visit our house and my family gives them money and other things [such as food and clothing] and they know I would be very unhappy with them and would tell them many things about music and religion. I don't believe that according to Islam people who play music will go to hell. If they live according to society's law they won't have any trouble.

I was told that Ismail had recently smashed his *dutār* at home in a fit of anger after his family had told him not to play during *Muharram*.

Some of these *dutār* players accepted that music was mildly sinful, unless it was played for a dancing boy or dancing girl at a dancing party, when it became a rather more serious matter. Although many of these *dutār* players reported criticisms by their families and by local mullahs they were ready to disregard these comments and did not give up music. They claimed that music was their *shauq* and said that if it was sinful God would forgive them, there were many other far worse sins in this world, this was nothing. Amateur musicians did not like to be seen with their instruments in the streets. If they were going to play somewhere they preferred to send a young relative with their instrument, or to travel by taxi. If instruments were carried they were hidden under coats or shawls if possible. The amateur did not want to be publicly identified as a musician. I once had occasion to walk through the old city with Amir Jan and his band carrying their instruments. A crowd of boys followed us, teasing the musicians and shouting out, 'Ding-a-ling! Ding-a-ling-a-ling!' It was a humiliating experience and one I presume they were quite used to.

Although the statements above were all made by *dutār* players they were representative of musicians in general. For example, in an interview with Amir Jan, at which his son Rahim added certain comments, the following statements were made:

Amir Jan: In the past we had many difficulties with mullahs, they were always telling us it [playing music] was forbidden. They said it's an unclean profession, it's bad, it's sinful. Now not many say that. The mullahs told us it was sinful.
Interviewer: What do you think?
Amir Jan: God knows about it, we don't know. There are worse sins in the world than this, this is nothing. God will forgive us for what we are doing. And with music we can sing for God, and for Mohammad, we can do that too. The mullahs were saying, 'You should not forget about God.' That's why they were telling us not to play music.
Rahim: We never forget God, we are religious, we believe in God and we pray. But this is our 'Satanic profession', what else can we do [to make a living]?
Interviewer: What do you say to the mullahs?
Amir Jan: I say, 'Go ahead and say what you want!'
Rahim: We were under a lot of pressure, there were a lot of comments from mullahs and from other people in the past. But we didn't give up our profession.

The condemnation of musicians

Amir Jan: If someone stopped me from playing music by force I would become ill. We are accustomed to it, we must listen to music and play music or we'll become ill.

Reasons for the change in attitudes towards music

Musicians and others were in agreement that at the time when I worked in Herat the negative attitudes towards music were much weaker than they had been ten or twenty years earlier. Some argued that the lawfulness of music had ceased to be an issue.

Who is going to think about such things today, who cares about such things now? They were doing so in the past but nobody thinks music is sinful now. (Mama Ghani)

Several reasons were offered to account for this change.

Firstly, there was the general increase in the popularity of music, expressed in statements such as:

Music and playing music have become more popular in recent years. Previously people did not know anything about music; now they have found a *shauq* for music. (Gada Mohammad)

Music had become more a part of everyday life, most obviously through radio broadcasting, the theatres of Herat, and the cinema with its Indian films. There were *Ramazān* concerts and more private parties for music than there had been in the past.

Secondly, there was increased contact with the outside world. The visits of Afghans abroad had shown that music was part of everyday life in most countries. This went along with pointing out that the times had changed and that Afghanistan had become more modern.

Thirdly, there was the example of amateur musicians who performed regularly on the radio.

People heard that Dr Zahir's son, Ahmad Zahir, was singing and playing on the radio. Many people in Kabul and in the provinces started playing and singing, saying, 'It's not bad if he's done it,' so they followed his example. (Karim Dutari)

It is clear in these and other accounts that radio broadcasting from Kabul was crucial: it can be seen as the single most important direct factor in changing general attitudes about music. It familiarised people with the everyday experience of music, and displayed a model of respectable musician status. The radio was a prestigious modern mass medium whose technology and style of presentation lent music a new kind of acceptability. Karim Dutari, in describing aspects of his career at the radio station, explained that some of his relatives were very religious. When he was playing *dutār* as a boy they said, 'It's his *shauq*' and they did not try to stop him. When he first worked at Radio Afghanistan he played under the name of Abdul Karim (not Mohammad Karim, his real name). When his relatives came to learn that it was him they said, 'Well, the radio's a good place, he can play there.'

The explanations given by Heratis for the decrease in prejudice against musicians really described changes in general social attitudes which were shaped by exhortation and example from secular authority. These attitudes were independent of mullahs, and not determined by the religious establishment. In an increasingly secular society the mullahs might have remained strongly opposed to music and have simply been ignored. People were quite ready to disregard what they perceived as orthodoxy, on the subject of music anyway. But in fact some mullahs had also changed their ideas.

Abdul Wahed, Abdul Wahab Saljuki's son, provided many examples of how mullahs had adapted to changing conditions. He described how he sometimes discovered his elderly father, who had been such a stern opponent of music in the past (see above), waiting to hear the news when music was playing on the radio. He would teasingly ask his father why was he listening to music? He replied that though he heard the music he was not listening to it for enjoyment. Abdul Wahed said that when he had foreign visitors he had often brought a *tanbur* player who lived nearby to play. His father knew they were playing music in his house and he never complained. He had changed his ideas about this and about other things.

Ustad Saluddin Saljuki called carpenters to make chairs for the teachers at the first school opened in Herat. Rashid's father and my father and other ʿ*ulemā* [theological scholars] came to the opening *majles*. They refused to sit on the chairs provided, carpets had to be brought for them. They said, 'The chair is for *kāfir*s, [unbelievers], if we sit on these chairs we will look like *kāfir*s. A very bad idea!' Now the mullahs at the Theological College sit on chairs ... The mullahs used to say that shaving the beard was *harām* [unlawful] in the time of Mohammad, now they say it is *halāl* [lawful]. The mullahs said, 'We must not impose the Islamic laws very harshly, we must make them a little free because the times have changed. If we don't do this it will be to our loss.' I believe this, too. (Abdul Wahed)

The mullahs used to turn their heads away when I walked by. Now they even say Salaam. (Amir Jan)

The positive values of music

In contrast to the various ideas about the negative aspects of music was another set of notions about music's positive values. One of the commonest metaphors was of music as *qazā-ye ruh*, 'the food of the soul'. Human beings were said to have a spiritual appetite for music, just as the body had a physical appetite for food. A variation of this metaphor was to say that music refreshed (*tāzeh*) the soul. Slobin (1976:24–5), in his discussion of the *shauq* for music, identifies this belief when he states that music is seen by Afghans as an activity that enlivens life. In Herat it was often said that '*musiqi del-e ādam zendeh mikone*'. *Del* could be glossed as 'heart', though the physical heart was usually called *qalb*. The *del* was the seat of feeling, the emotional centre, the place of consciousness. 'Music enlivens one's emotional heart' – music dispels boredom, relieves depression, and gives one vitality. Amir Jan once remarked to me that a man who plays music never grows old; his vitality remained undiminished. On another occasion he said he would like to journey to India where he would seek out Ram Narayan, the *sārangi* player and one of his favourite musicians. Sitting with Ram Narayan and hearing him play would ensure that his spirit remained young. No wonder that Amir Jan believed he would fall ill if prevented from hearing or playing music, for according to his own belief music gave him his vitality.

The same idea is expressed in Sufism.

Music is food for the spirit. When the spirit obtains its food, it attains its proper station and turns aside from the subordination of the body; then appears in the listener a commotion and a movement.
(Abul Qasim al Baghwi, cited in Roy Choudhury 1957:99)
Music is the food of the spirit, and when the spirit receives its food it turns aside from the government of the body. (Al-Kalabadhi, cited in Robson 1938:8)
The Sufi names music *Giza-i Ruh*, the food of the soul, and uses it as a source of spiritual perfection; for music fans the fire of the heart, and the flame arising from it illuminates the soul. (Khan 1962:59)

In Herat music was said to make one happy (*khush*), to give pleasure (*tahsir*), to give a good taste (*khub mazeh*), to be appealing (*delchasp*, 'clutching the *del*'). When listening to music one was borne away (*lezat bordan*). Music could be melancholic (*ghamgin*), sometimes described as *trājid* 'tragic' (an English loan word). I found Persian *dastgāh* music sometimes described in these terms, usually as an explanation of why the speaker did not like it. One of the most interesting statements I heard about music came from Ismail, the amateur *dutār* player:

> Music is a kind of language, telling something, but not directly. Through music people can tell about their feelings, their happiness, their sadness, their problems, the different things which happen inside them. Music is able to reflect these feelings.

Another metaphor applied to music was that of water. Music that was played well and gave pleasure was called *tar*, 'wet', while the opposite condition was *khushk*, 'dry'. A common compliment on listening to an especially appealing piece of music was *audār*, 'juicy' (literally, 'having water'). The sound of running water was one that Heratis generally found highly pleasurable. When heard on a tape recorder it evoked almost ecstatic memories of days spent out in the countryside, in a garden or some local beauty spot with a fine view, preferably in spring. The love of being in fertile surroundings was as well developed in Afghanistan as in Iran, while the garden was enshrined in Persian literature and miniature painting as a foretaste of paradise. A shaded garden provided the most exquisite surroundings for the performance of music. Music was seen as a part of nature, and as an element in the opposition between garden and desert, fertility and barrenness. It was a symbol of growth, of the conditions necessary for human life itself.

Heratis commonly held that music was attractive to animals as well as man, and that it fed their souls too. In Herati musical folklore the musician, usually a *dutār* player, sat in a garden or some beauty spot and played so well that the nightingales approached and eventually came to perch on the tuning pegs of the instrument. I also heard this story told about a *chahārtār* player and about a *sornā* player (when the birds perched on the bell of his instrument). When such tales were related others present would assert that they had seen the same thing, though I never witnessed it myself. I also heard of snakes attracted by the playing of the *dutār*, an image that could have a connection with the Indian snake charmer, a figure of Indian life certainly known in Afghanistan. I heard it argued that since birds and animals evidently liked music they must have 'a place in their *del* for music', and so it was natural that human beings should also.

Heratis had a great love of songbirds of all kinds. Even the cry of the caged partridge (*kauk*), or the unvarying 'mi-mi' of the quail (*karak*) were enjoyed as birdsong. Of all the birds known to the Heratis the nightingale was the most highly praised. It was the bird of *hazār dastān*, 'a thousand stories', it sang *rad bā rad*, 'turn by turn', varying its song (cf. Nettl 1983:208). It was recognised by Heratis that songbirds were stimulated to sing by hearing music, and sometimes caged birds were brought to performances. The resulting symphony, the sounds of music with the sounds of birdsong added to it, constituted the acme of Herati musical aesthetic enjoyment. It was truly *gol o bolbol*, 'roses and nightingales'; the flowers in the garden of music evoking the song of the nightingales.

Music and Sufism

Ideas held by Heratis about the positive values of music were also found in Sufi ideology, although they were not necessarily directly borrowed. Sufism was the crystallisation of ideas that had wide social currency and which were manifest in various aspects of popular religion (such as the cult of saints). One link between music and the mystical systems of thought that constitute Sufism was provided by musicians in Kabul, where many *sāzandeh* were adherents of the *Chishti* Sufi Order.

The *Chishtiya* are one of the most popular and influential mystic orders in India, established there by the twelfth-century Sufi Saint, Khwaja Muin al-Din Chishti. The order takes its name from the village of Chisht, in Western Afghanistan, 100 miles up the Hari river from the city of Herat. Khwaja Muin al-Din came originally from Isfahan, and finally settled at Ajmer in Rajasthan, where his tomb is the most important Muslim shrine in India and a great centre for pilgrimage at the time of the annual commemoration of the Saint's death (*'urs*). Currie (1978) gives a most useful account.

Most Sufi orders use for their ritual a type of *zikr*, 'recollection', which calls for the collective recitation of certain esoteric Names of God in a manner that involves 'the co-ordination of musical rhythms, breath control, and physical exercises to excite ecstacy' (Trimmingham 1971:104). The performance as a whole is undoubtedly musical, though not in itself definable as music. In Herat the *Qādiriya* and *Naqshbandiya* orders were dominant. The *Chishtiya* are notable for the more explicit use of music in the ritual of the *samā'*, the 'spiritual concert', which in India and Pakistan is the occasion for the performance of *qawwāli*, devotional or mystical poetry sung to the accompaniment of harmonium and tabla, a musical genre which is sometimes classified as a 'light' form of Hindustani art music (see Qureshi 1986).

There were several *Chishti khānaqāh*s in Kabul. One of them, off the Shor Bazar in the old city, was only ten minutes' walk from the Kucheh Kharabat, and musicians from the Kharabat often played there at the spiritual concerts held every Thursday night. The music played was in the Afghan urban style, with religious poetry sung to the accompaniment of harmonium, *rubāb*, tabla, *tanbur*, and two unusual instruments, the stone clappers called *qairaq* (see Slobin 1976:277-8) and the jingling tongs called *chimta* in India (Deva 1977:22). Various other instruments were also sometimes played there. During the evening's music a succession of singers took their turn, performing for about thirty minutes each, with frequent changes of personnel for the instruments. Both amateur and professional musicians played in the *khānaqāh*. They performed *na'ts* (religious *ghazal*s), *rāg*s, and religious songs in the popular music style, sometimes using currently popular song tunes. Some of the *na'ts* performed by Amir Mohammad at wedding parties in Herat were from the repertory of the Shor Bazar *khānaqāh*. It was there that the *sāzandeh* of Kabul could reconcile the apparently conflicting domains of music and religion, carrying out their accustomed musical activities, playing and singing in the Afghan style, in a context that explicitly endowed music with an elevated spiritual meaning. In certain respects the spiritual concert was similar to music played by musicians at one of their own rituals, such as a *gorbandi*.

Many of the *sāzandeh* of the Kucheh Kharabat were adherents of the *Chishti* order, though it is not known to what extent they were actually initiates of the order and received spiritual teaching. Given the general decline in the activities of the Sufi orders of Afghanistan in the last 200 years (Utas 1980) it is probable that few musicians had received formal initiation. No such *Chishti khānaqāh* existed in Herat, though visiting *Chishti*s would sometimes play at the tombs of Ansari and Jami, outside the city, and music was sometimes played at other shrines. The *meleh*s of Herat exemplified the same connection between music and saints. The Herati *sāzandeh* were not familiar with the details of *Chishti* ideology, only with its general tenor.

Music and Sufism

Most had visited the *khānaqāh* in the Shor Bazar and knew a little about Ajmer as a centre for pilgrimage. Only Karim Dutari amongst the professional musicians of Herat considered himself to be a *Chishti*, and had often attended the *khānaqāh* during his years in Kabul. On one occasion Karim and I visited a *Qādiri khānaqāh* near Herat on a Thursday evening. Karim joined in the circle of *zakirin* for the ritual, and afterwards, when tea was served in the *khānaqāh*, asked the permission of the *Pir* to play his *rubāb*, which he had brought along at my insistence. The *Pir* gave his consent and Karim played 'Sheikh Ahmad-e Jām', a Sufi song from Iranian Khorasan that was well known in Herat. The *Pir* praised the performance. The Khushnawazha were Shiahs and did not involve themselves directly in what they saw as a variety of Sunni religious observance, while the Golpasandha were more forthright in their enthusiasm for 'Khwaja Sahib Ajmeri' (Muin al-Din Chishti). Amir Mohammad was obviously more familiar with the details of *Chishti* ideas and practices in Kabul, as he had grown up in the Kucheh Kharabat. For the Herati *sāzandeh* it was perhaps enough to know that amongst the *ustād*s of Kabul an ideology existed which gave music, especially Hindustani music, an exalted place within a Muslim framework of belief.

10 Interpreting musical change in Herat

In the 1970s the city of Herat supported a rich musical life. Bands of male hereditary musicians and their amateur associates played genres which fulfilled the criteria of a 'traditional art music' proposed by Powers (1979:10–12): firstly, the music was purveyed by specialists who required teaching and indoctrination into this speciality by their seniors; secondly, the musical genres in question conformed to a musico-theoretical norm; thirdly, these genres were culturally grounded, connected with, and supportive of, cultural performances to which they were ancillary, yet also conceived of as an independent domain; fourthly, the music was patronised by individuals and groups, belonging to the elite, who professed connoisseurship. These specialist purveyors of art music also performed popular and dance music, and they played mostly at wedding festivities held by the wealthier classes of the city. The *'arusi*, the wedding party, was the occasion for an elaborate concert of music, the several stages of which gave a structure to the social event, and included special music for the central ritual of the 'bridegroom's throne'. In this sense musicians had a role as ritual specialists.

The situation that I observed in the 1970s, however, was of relatively recent provenance. Urban music in Herat had undergone some remarkable changes in the course of fifty years, from the 1920s to the 1970s, under the influence of musical developments in Kabul. These changes can be summarised as follows:

1. The harmonium, *rubāb*, and fourteen stringed *dutār* replaced the *chahārtār* and *santur* as the predominant instruments of urban music making.
2. Different tonal, modal, and rhythmic systems, that is, different principles of musical organisation, became predominant. These principles were systematised according to a modified form of Hindustani music theory.
3. New musical forms were adopted, notably the Kabuli *ghazal*, the *naghmeh-ye kashāl*, and the forms for popular and dance music.
4. There was an increase in the frequency of music making, at wedding festivities, concerts, in the theatres, and at small private parties.
5. There was a decrease in the condemnation of music and musicians by orthodox mullahs, and by the public at large.
6. There was the emergence of the high ranking hereditary professional musician, the *ustād*, or 'master-musician', a category that had certainly existed in previous epochs (e.g. at the Timurid court of Herat) but which had fallen into abeyance in the nineteenth century.

The analytical notion of *musical change* is highly problematic (Blacking 1979). Difficulties arise because a range of types of transformation has been described as such. But there can be no doubt that what took place in Herat over this period was a 'genuine' instance of musical change according to Blacking's criteria; it was a change *of the system*, and not simply an innovation within the system. It involved the discarding of one system adopted from outside (Iran) and its replacement with another, adopted from somewhere else (Kabul). Certainly the Heratis had made some changes to the new system they adopted, mixing in certain intervals and modes that derived from the system of Persian music they had previously followed. They continued to have an interest in Persian music: in Persian popular music, which they adapted for performance in the new Kabuli style, and in the *ghazal* as a song text. What is the significance of these changes in music and music making? Ethnomusicological theory would lead one to expect that they did not occur as isolated phenomena, but were part of a more general process of social and cultural change.

Modernism and modernisation

A study of the history of Afghanistan in this period reveals certain patterns of social, political, and economic change which would seem to intersect with the changes in music making manifested in Herat. They can be understood as facets of the twin processes of modernism and modernisation. It is expedient to consider these under three headings: the emergence of Afghan nationalism, the decreasing power of the religious establishment, and the introduction of modern technology.

Afghan nationalism and national identity

Music is a potent symbol of ethnic identity; like language, it is one of those aspects of culture which can, when the need to assert 'ethnic identity' arises, most readily serve this purpose. It may serve as an area of shared experience which helps to delineate the boundaries of a social group or nation. Its effectiveness in this respect may be twofold; not only does it act as a ready means for the identification of different ethnic groups, but it has potent emotional connotations and can express ethnic identity in a particularly powerful manner.

'A principal theme in the political history of Afghanistan has been the effort to create a unified nation-state' (Poullada 1973). The 'nation-state' is an ethnocentric Western concept but may still be usefully applied in this case, for that was the model that Afghan rulers presumably sought to emulate. Two factors hindered this development in the nineteenth century. Firstly, conflicts within and between the dominant Pashtun tribes prevented the emergence of Afghanistan as a state. Secondly, the number of different ethnic groups inhabiting the territory, with different languages and to some extent different cultures, has hindered the development of people into a single nation. Afghanistan did not begin to emerge as a 'nation-state' until the 1880s, under Amir Abdur Rahman. By building a powerful regular army which could confront the tribes, Abdur Rahman was able to bring the whole of the country under the control of Kabul.

In the 1930s a nationalist trend became clearly discernible. Gregorian (1969) gives a fascinating account of the arguments put forward by nationalist writers of the time. They recognised that one of Afghanistan's problems was its ethnic diversity, and the nationalists were preoccupied with establishing a common history, religious background, and ethnic origin for all the peoples of Afghanistan, claiming that they were descended from the same Aryan stock. The Pashto language was given great importance in this nationalist ideology, and it was only in this period that Pashto became an official language of the country along with Dari (Afghan Persian). It was argued that Afghanistan needed the development of a modern national culture.

Many urged that Afghanistan's folklore and traditional music be collected, and called for the development of a new literature reflecting both the nation's historical legacy and its present social realities, needs and aspirations. Poets and writers were exhorted to see themselves as vehicles of social change and their role as the awakening of the Afghan people.

(*Ibid*.: 349)

If it was the intention of the government to instil in the people a new spirit of nationalism as citizens of Afghanistan and to think of themselves as Afghans irrespective of ethnic origin, then the creation of new genres of urban music – Afghan art music and popular music – in Kabul may have served an important role in this process. We do not know to what extent the creation of a national music based on the musical style of the dominant ethnic group, the Pashtuns, with poetic texts in Dari, was the result of a deliberate policy to foster nationalism, although that result was achieved. Perhaps the adoption of Kabuli art music in Herat in the late 1930s, and of Kabuli popular music in the 1940s and 1950s, expressed a new feeling amongst Heratis of belonging to Afghanistan and of being Afghans. For Heratis to be seen and heard to subscribe to the dominant culture can be seen as a political statement, an act of allegiance. Certain essential symbols may be expressed in the instruments used for urban music in Herat. If the *rubāb*, with its strong Pashtun associations, represented the 'Afghan-ness' of the music, the *dutār*, the Heratis' own instrument, represented the 'voice' of Herat in the urban ensemble, the role of Herat as an integral part of Afghanistan. This absorbtion of Herati traditions into the Kabuli style is also revealed by the distinct social identity of *dutār* players within *sāzandeh* groups.

The power of the religious establishment

By power here I refer to the ability of the religious establishment to influence central political decisions in Kabul, and to exert control over peoples' lives at the local level through the mullahs. The power of the religious establishment has varied during the period in question, and since we may assume that orthodox Islam in Afghanistan was opposed to music as an unprofitable and even sinful activity, we may look for a correlation between this and the openness and frequency of public music making. The banning of music in Iran under Ayatullah Khomeini provides a modern example of the Islamic proscription of music backed by the power of the state.

Although Abdur Rahman took certain strong measures against the clergy in the 1880s, nationalising all religious endowments and instituting qualifying examinations for mullahs, he also formulated policies that resulted in an increase in their power. He used the mullahs to exacerbate a *jihād* (holy war) movement against the British and they gave, for the first time, religious sanction to the monarchy. In the 1920s the government initiated many social reforms that were opposed by the mullahs, who were unable to influence policy at the centre. The 1920s was a time of musical release from puritanical restraint, both in Kabul and Herat, though with different musical results (in Kabul this period saw the blossoming of Kabuli art music, while in Herat there was a vogue for Persian music). With the fall of Amanullah in 1929 and the return to a more traditional way of life, the clergy enjoyed a greater say in the running of the country, and music was once again subject to puritanical restraint.

Social reform proceeded slowly and cautiously over the next twenty years, but in the 1950s there was a period of rapid modernisation under the Prime Minister, Mohammad Daud (later

Modernism and modernisation

the first President of the Republic of Afghanistan). Once again this was a time of conflict between the government and the clergy, with the latter in a weak position, and a period of musical release, during which Radio Afghanistan assumed its role as the centre of musical patronage. As Heratis looked back from the 1970s they saw a great change in the status of music making, which they understood as a product of the process of modernisation. Mullahs might still say that music was sinful, but mullahs could now be said to be wrong by those they criticised. More significantly, the general attitude of the people had changed.

What we have seen so far is a simple quantitative relationship between the role of the clergy and the amount of musical activity, but there was also a more intimate qualitative relationship between social and musical factors. Mullahs did in fact differentiate between different kinds of music in terms of the amount of sin they incurred, and this depended in part upon the intentions of the performers and the purpose of the music. The Iranian music of Herat in the 1920s was at least a serious, grave, and melancholic style, with texts drawn from the great tradition of Persian poetry, but since then there had been a change towards exactly those elements that mullahs condemned. The music became faster, rhythmically more exciting; it was altogether more like dance music. Song texts became more overtly romantic.

The eclipse of the mullahs as agents of social control in Herat since about 1950 was the result of political processes, following the gradual assertion of power by the central government and the development of modern institutions. To this extent the musical change can be seen as the passive result of a political process, but there is also the possibility that music played a more active role. Through operating a policy of popularising music, the government must have been aware that it was placing itself in conflict with the traditional values of the mullahs. When the government set up loud-speaker systems in many towns and cities, including Herat, to relay radio broadcasts, and the streets were filled with the sounds of music, it was perhaps hard to maintain the attitude that music was sinful. Here we may have an interesting case of music not as 'the mirror of society', as popular metaphor puts it, but as a dynamic force that can be used to change society. Music, itself a symbol of modernism, and itself modernised, was a powerful stimulus with which to 'awaken the people'.

Music as an aspect of modern technology

The modern European world came to Afghanistan from India, in the nineteenth century. India, under British rule, was the closest site of modernised prototypes for Afghans to emulate and from which to obtain technical assistance. A further factor was the Afghans' natural affiliation with predominantly Sunni Hindustan, and avoidance of contacts with Shiah Iran. While British experts were brought to Kabul by Abdur Rahman (mainly to expand the royal workshops, which provided equipment and supplies for the Afghan army), other technical expertise was provided by Indian Muslims, especially in the field of education. The Muslim culture of North India was undoubtedly one that the people of Afghanistan were likely to 'resonate' with, and historically there has been comparatively free interchange between the two regions. In the context of the general trend it is understandable that music should have been adopted from India, the source of many new ideas at that time. The *ustād*s, brought originally to Kabul from India in the 1860s, can be regarded as foreign experts who carried out a 'technical overhaul' of Afghan music in the process of creating a new national music. This was itself a way of modernising the music, and, from the perspective of modernism, of improving it.

Amongst their contributions, the *ustād*s introduced the '*ilm-e musiqi*, the 'science of music', a set of theoretical constructs about the tonal system, scale types, melodic modes, and principles of rhythmic organisation which underlay the music they played. This knowledge provided a terminology that allowed these abstract concepts to be discussed, while note names and tabla *bol*s (syllables) could serve as oral or written notation. The Herati musicians accepted that this knowledge derived from Indian music theory, and indeed took considerable pride in this fact. The science of music in itself was a kind of technological knowledge. A further technical innovation was the adoption of the harmonium, an instrument which worked acoustically in a totally new way (being a free reed aerophone) and which was constructed like a machine, with its levers, springs, and stops.

Contrasts with Mashhad

These underlying trends would seem to have encouraged firstly, the development of a national music, based on the music of the politically dominant ethnic group in Afghanistan, the Pashtuns, secondly, the wider patronage of music, which encouraged the recruitment of musicians, and thirdly the increased technical complexity of music and the adoption of abstract theoretical concepts. The manifestation of these changes in Herat is further illuminated by a comparison with its 'twin city' of Mashhad, in Iranian Khurasan, made possible by research carried out by Stephen Blum in Mashhad in 1969 (Blum 1972). Mashhad is the closest city to Herat and developed as its commercial rival from the sixteenth century onwards. There has been a great deal of interchange between the two since that time.

Blum was primarily concerned with recitation and unaccompanied singing practised by specialists such as the *naqqāl* and the *darvish*. The preponderance of such performers in Mashhad, usually in teahouses, in the bazaars, or in public parks, was linked to Mashhad's role as an important centre of Shiah pilgrimage (to the tomb of Imam Reza). Somewhat similar specialists in verbal art were also found in Herat, though evidently far fewer than in Mashhad, but were not really the object of my research. Another kind of performer discussed in some detail by Blum was the *motreb*, and the subspeciality of *luti*, transvestite male dancer. The *motreb*s of Mashhad would seem to correspond to the barber-musicians and barber-actors (*ustā*s) of Herat. They operated in groups, in which the *sornā* and *dohol* were prominent, and they played other instruments such as the *gheichak*. As well as singing and dancing, their performances involved short plays, puppetry, acrobatics, wrestling, and other kinds of entertainment. In essence, as Blum notes, they were comic entertainers.

The musicians of Mashhad who appear to have been most nearly equivalent to the urban male *sāzandeh* of Herat were those who made up the various *orkestrāhā* (orchestras) that played at middle class wedding festivities for men, and for women (when the musicians were usually hidden behind a curtain). Such orchestras consisted of a singer (male or female) with, for example, violin, flute, accordion, *dāireh*, and *dombak*, or, to give another example from Blum, violin, clarinet, accordion, *dāireh*, and *jaz* (trap drum set). The *orkestrā-ye irāni* at Radio Mashhad consisted of two violins, *tār*, flute, clarinet, *santur*, and *dombak*. Like the Herati *sāzandeh*, these musicians were acquainted with an art music system, in this case the *dastgāh* system, and they played some *dastgāh* material. Nettl and Foltin (1972:45) recorded performances of the *darāmad* of *Chahārgāh* from a number of musicians in Mashhad who were evidently of this kind. They also performed Iranian film and popular songs, Indian film songs, and some Western dance music such as tango, waltz, and 'jerk'. Like the Herati *sāzandeh*, their repertory extended from serious art music to modern dance music. These orchestras were run by agencies (*bongāh*) usually located in the shops of instrument makers and sellers; some of the musicians also ran small schools of music. Printed music books, with modified Western staff notation, formed an important medium for learning and teaching. Blum gives little information about the recruitment of these musicians, but comments, very revealingly, that they had 'an aura of middle-class respectability, and the musicians in these ensembles enjoyed a considerably greater social status than did the carriers of the *motreb*, *luti* and *jāhel* traditions' (1972:190). They stressed their amateur origins to dissociate themselves from *motreb*i, the activities of the *motreb*s (*ibid.*: 265).

Blum's data are important for this study for several reasons. It would appear, for example, that Herat in the 1920s was not unlike Mashhad in the 1960s, with an urban art music loosely based on the Iranian *dastgāh* system, performed by practitioners who were mainly amateur by origin, and who clung to their amateur status to dissociate themselves from low ranking hereditary professional musicians. In both regions there were other types of performer who were much more rooted in traditional Khurasani music, a connection shown in the use of the two stringed *dutār* and the *sornā* and *dohol*. An important difference was that whereas Iranian Khurasan had minorities of Turks, Kurds, and Baluchis, with their own musical traditions that existed in parallel with those of the Persian speaking population, in Herat the main ethnic minority was Pashtun. At the time of Blum's and my fieldwork, Herat and Mashhad showed divergences that expressed the differential impact of musical activity in even more remote centres, Tehran and Kabul. Mashhad emulated conditions in Tehran where, since the early part of the twentieth century, music had been dominated by figures who were amateur by origin, where Western staff notation had been adopted, and a Western-style conservatoire teaching Persian art music had been set up. Kabul provided a quite different model of musician status, that of the high ranking hereditary professional, exemplified by the court musician, who advocated a traditional form for the oral transmission of musical knowledge.

The high ranking hereditary musician

When Herati musicians adopted Kabuli art music in the 1930s they also took on the system of social organisation prevalent in the musicians' quarter in Kabul amongst a group of male hereditary musicians who performed Hindustani art music and were familiar with Hindustani music theory. The Kabuli musicians placed considerable emphasis on ranking amongst themselves, and attached great importance to the master–student relationship, formalised by the tying of a string around the wrist of the pupil at a meeting of musicians. This relationship served for the transmission of musical knowledge, gave the individual a charter to perform, and legitimised stylistic differences.

The organisation of musicians in Kabul appears to be similar to that of Muslim musicians in North India, particularly Delhi, described by Neuman (1980). This similarity is hardly surprising; presumably the Indian court musicians established this system in the Kucheh Kharabat in the late nineteenth century. It would, however, be a mistake to make too much of the apparent similarities. Not enough is known about the situation in Kabul to say how closely Neuman's analysis, with its separation into soloist and accompanist roles, and associated social structures (*ibid.*: chapter 4), fits the data. Kabul constituted a single court but it did not develop into the seat of a *gharānā*, an individual stylistic school of Hindustani music. It became much more than a *gharānā*, for out of the mixing of Indian and Afghan elements an Afghan national music was created.

A distinctive feature of the musicians of Kabul was the segmentation between the descendants of Indian court musicians and the barber-musicians, with the former initially training the latter. This did not necessarily result in the barber-musicians serving as accompanists to the *ustād*s. Soloists and accompanists could be recruited from the same families. For example, Ustad Rahim Bakhsh, the singer and harmonium player, had two brothers, Akin Bakhsh and Azin Bakhsh, who played *rubāb* and tabla respectively. Ustad Hashem, Afghanistan's greatest tabla player from the 1960s on, was a descendant of Indian court musicians, and was also acclaimed as a *khyāl* singer and player of the sitar, *sarod*, and *rubāb*. Amir Mohammad, a barber-musician, sang *ghazal*s and *klāsik* accompanied by Fazl Ahmad, an *ustād* descendant, on tabla. Ustad Mohammad Omar, the *rubāb* player, of barber-musician descent, was as highly respected as the greatest vocalist *ustād*s. Through their contact with the *ustād*s Afghan barber-musicians could be elevated to the same rank.

In Herat the situation was a replica of the Kabuli model, with certain local idiosyncracies. The number of *sāzandeh* musicians was very small. Only two of them, Amir Jan and his brother Karim, knew enough about Hindustani music to be recognised as competent practitioners by the Kabuli *sāzandeh*. The cleavage between *ustād*s and barber-musicians was reproduced and represented by the Khushnawaz and Golpasand families. The *dutār* players and other amateurs turned professional recruited into *sāzandeh* bands in Herat mirrored the important role of amateurs turned professional in Kabul. The *sāzandeh* invoked a high ranking social identity that was intimately bound up with the prestigious art music they aspired to perform. The difference between this new status and the pre-existing status for hereditary musicians is most obvious when we compare men *sāzandeh* of the city with players of the *sornā* and *dohol*, who embodied the attributes of low rank, high ritual importance, and licence to deviate identified in Merriam's classic discussion of musician status (Merriam 1964:chapter 7). In contrast, the *ustād-e musiqi*, the 'master of music', was an artist (*honarmand*) equivalent to a writer, poet, calligrapher, or miniature painter, capable of producing an art product that could be as uplifting as those of the other arts, and even used for religious purposes (as in Chishti ritual).

This analysis throws new light on the significance of the ʿ*ilm-e musiqi* (the 'science of music'), quite apart from its role in the domain of musical cognition. The knowledge of this science was an important part of *honarmand* status and high rank. It rendered respectable both music and musicians: the very possibility of speech discourse about the structural elements of music changed the status of music in an Islamic society which regarded it with some suspicion. Respected areas of knowledge in Herat, as in other parts of the Muslim world, were referred to as ʿ*ilm*, 'science'. The characteristic of an ʿ*ilm* was precisely that degree of classification and codification that demanded a special set of concepts and terminology, and was the domain of specialist practitioners. Gada Mohammad told me there were three ʿ*ilm*s: the science of the Holy Koran, technical science, and the science of music. Amir Jan spoke to me of their being fourteen ʿ*ilm*s recognised by the mullahs, one of them being music. When I asked him how that could be, given the bad name of music from the mullahs' point of view, he replied, with a twinkle in his eye, that perhaps they called it an ʿ*ilm-e sheitān*, 'a science of Satan'.

Playing the *ustād*

In one sense, it could be argued, the Herati *sāzandeh* were 'playing at being *ustāds*'. They emulated the musical and social role of the Indian court musician, but on just about every 'objective' criterion theirs was a simplified or diminished version of 'the real thing'. Their music theory was incomplete, their knowledge of *rāgs* and *tāls* limited in scope and inaccurate by Indian standards. Despite the importance they attached to the teacher–student relationship, most Herati *sāzandeh* developed their musical skills as a result of early exposure to music and familial encouragement to become performers, and not through formal instruction. They did not practise much. Their performance of Hindustani music (mainly in the form of *naghmeh-ye klāsik* on the *rubāb*) was simple and archaic. But these differences, evident to the analyst who has the opportunity to compare the situation in Herat with that in India, were of little concern to the Herati *sāzandeh*, who had little direct contact with Indian musical life. Shorn of their ideology and role playing as *ustāds*, the men *sāzandeh* might be compared to the women *sāzandeh* of Herat, who employed very little musical terminology and attached little importance to the teacher–student relationship. Girls became musicians through taking part in performances at wedding parties, and received no lessons. There can be no doubt that their programme of musical enculturation, in a family life orientated around musical performance, produced highly competent musicians.

But there is another sense in which one may be said to 'play the *ustād*', and this is shown by an analysis of Amir Jan's role in the adoption of *ustād* status in Herat. Amir Jan reached maturity at a time when many changes were taking place to make Herat a modern city, and when new professions were becoming available. The crucial formative experience in Amir Jan's life came at around the age of twenty or twenty-one when he became Ustad Nabi Gol's *shāgerd*. If Ustad Nabi Gol can be viewed as equivalent to a Sufi *pir*, then Amir Jan acted as though he were Ustad Nabi Gol's *khalifeh*, his local representative, empowered to organise local musicians on his behalf. This enabled Amir Jan to dominate the music scene in Herat for many years. This dominance was supported by his own musicality, further developed by the training he received from Nabi Gol, making him knowledgeable about Kabuli music and fluent in the use of oral notation (*sargam* system). His father had been an amateur turned professional and Amir Jan *could* have claimed the status of *shauqi* (cf. Mashhad). Instead, he stressed the fact that his father was a professional, and that he himself was a *hereditary* musician, maintaining a family profession. His *qaum* was not tainted with a reputation for easy morals and prostitution, and that made it possible to 'play the *ustād*' and be taken seriously by the people of Herat.

By stressing the values of the Kabuli *sāzandeh*, Amir Jan invoked a system of ranking amongst musicians in Herat in which, by definition (as the only student of a Kabuli *ustād*), he occupied the top position. By using other musicians to perform in bands of which he was leader, and by instructing them in some degree, he was able to make them all his students, and they had to acknowledge him as their master. He established the *sāzandeh* claim to be the only legitimate purveyors of music for payment. The denigration of amateurism, part of the Kabuli ideology, allowed him to ward off the competition from amateurs turned professional, the irony being that his father had been exactly that. In this way he outflanked the competition, and gained control of the music profession.

As he grew older and near the end of his singing career his position was challenged by Amir

Mohammad from Kabul, who succeeded in taking over the effective role of *ustād* in Herat, though Amir Jan retained that honorific status. Amir Mohammad came from the community from which Amir Jan had derived his knowledge, he was an insider, and could 'play the *ustād*' more effectively than Amir Jan. Furthermore, he was from a barber-musician family, not the descendant of Indian court musicians, and disturbed Amir Jan's hegemony over his rivals the Golpasandha. It was at this critical stage of his career that I knew Amir Jan.

Alas, there was no opportunity to see the drama between Amir Jan and Amir Mohammad played out. Herat was enveloped by war and in 1983 I learned that Amir Jan was dead, though whether as a result of the fighting was not revealed. His death marks the end of a particular chapter in the long history of music culture in the city of Herat.

Glossary 1

Musical instruments

Adequate information on the instruments mentioned in the text is available elsewhere, it is therefore unnecessary to provide anything more than very brief descriptions here. The reader is referred to other sources. For Iranian instruments I rely heavily on During (1984), though Caron and Safvate (1966) and Zonis (1973) also contain useful information. *The New Grove Dictionary of Musical Instruments*, ed. Sadie, lists most of the instruments mentioned here but I have not cited *Grove* when other sources are adequate.

armonia Small portable 'Indian' harmonium, a free reed aerophone, with bellows pumped by one hand, the digitals fingered with the other. See *Grove*, ed. Sadie 1984, vol. 2:131; Sakata 1983:203.

chahārtār Herati term for the Iranian *tār* (see below).

chimta Idiophone consisting of metal tongs with circular metal jingles attached. Used for religious music in Pakistan and India. See Deva 1977:22.

dāireh Frame drum, with jingles (iron rings) attached inside the frame. Played mainly by women. See Sakata 1980a, 1983:204; Slobin 1976:264-7.

dambura Fretless two stringed long-necked lute strongly associated with northern Afghanistan. See Slobin 1976:212-24; Sakata 1983:194-5.

delrubā An Indian bowed lute having the finger-board of the sitar, with wide curved frets arched over sympathetic strings. See *Grove*, ed. Sadie 1984, vol. 1:569.

dohol Double-headed frame drum beaten with a heavy stick on the upper head and a thin flexible stick on the lower one. Played with the *sornā* by barber-musicians. See Sakata 1980a, 1983:202.

doholak Twin-headed barrel or cylinder drum played with the hands. Typical of Pashtun music and closely related to similar drums in Pakistan and India. See *Grove*, ed. Sadie 1984, vol. 1:562-3.

dombak The single-headed goblet drum of Iran (also called *zarb*), usually of wood, with corrugations around the upper part of the shell. See During 1984:89-91.

dutār Long-necked plucked lute. At least three types are known in Herat, with two, three, or fourteen strings. Other types of *dutār* are found in Afghanistan, such as the *Uzbek* and *Turkmen dutār*s. See Baily 1976; Sakata 1978b, 1983:192-3; Slobin 1970:116-18.

duzangeh A pair of rattles, each with a wooden handle projecting into a wider cylinder of wood, to which are nailed a quantity of small bells. They are shaken or the handles are stamped on the ground. Intended to imitate the bells (*zang*) worn by dancing boys (or girls). Herati.

gheichak Term for three types of bowed lute: (1) *sarinda*, (2) *kemāncheh*, (3) spike-fiddle with large tin can as resonator found in northern Afghanistan. See Sakata 1979a, 1983:200; Slobin 1976:243-8.

kemāncheh   Iranian spike-fiddle of the *rabāb* family. See During 1984:75–81.

naqqārakhāneh   Archaic ensemble of drums, trumpets and oboes playing royal, ceremonial, civic or military music, usually from a tower or gateway. See *Grove*, ed. Sadie 1984, vol. 2:748–9.

ney   Rim blown oblique flute. See During 1984:67–73; Sakata 1979b, 1983:201; and Slobin 1976:251–6 for the closely related *tüidük*.

piānu   Occasional term for *armonia*. Western piano, an instrument found in the Kabul court by the late nineteenth century.

qairaq   Polished stone clappers. See Slobin 1976:277–8.

qānun   Plucked board zither, common today in Arab and Turkish music. See During 1984:94, *Grove*, ed. Sadie 1984, vol. 3:169–71.

rabāb   Family of spike-fiddles having a membraneous belly. See Farmer 1931:103–4; *Grove*, ed. Sadie 1984, vol. 3:177–83.

rubāb   Short-necked, double-chambered plucked lute. The Afghan *rubāb* is strongly associated with Pashtun music and is considered to be the 'national instrument' of Afghanistan. See Baily 1976; Sakata 1977, 1983:197.

santur   Dulcimer (hammered zither). An important Iranian instrument, also found in Kashmir, and formerly in Afghanistan. See During 1984:59–66; *Grove*, ed. Sadie 1984, vol. 3:291–2.

sārang   Term for (1) *sārangi*, (2) *sarinda*.

sārangi   Bowed lute with skin belly and many sympathetic strings, fretless, usually used to accompany vocal music in Pakistan and India. See *Grove*, ed. Sadie 1984, vol. 3:294–6.

sarinda   Double-chambered bowed lute, member of the *rubāb* family, the small lower chamber has a skin belly, the upper chamber is open. Strongly associated with Pashtun music in Afghanistan. See *Grove*, ed. Sadie 1984, vol. 3:297–8.

sarod   Plucked lute, and instrument of North Indian classical music, a modern development of the Afghan *rubāb*, with metal strings and a fretless metal finger-board. See *Grove*, ed. Sadie 1984, vol. 3:298–9.

sāz-e Kashmiri   Form of *rabāb* spike-fiddle found in Kashmir.

sehtār   Small, long-necked plucked lute of Iran. See During 1984:39–46. Also a type of long-necked lute found in Kashmir. See *Grove*, ed. Sadie 1984, vol. 3:353–4.

sekh   An idiophone consisting of a suspended rifle barrel struck with a metal beater. Herati.

sitar   Large, long-necked plucked lute of North Indian classical music. See *Grove*, ed. Sadie 1984, vol. 3:392–400.

sormandel   A board zither used as a drone instrument in Afghanistan, Pakistan, and India. See *Grove*, ed. Sadie 1984, vol. 3:477.

sornā   Double reed aerophone of the oboe family. Played with the *dohol*. See Sakata 1980b, 1983:202.

surnay   Form of *sornā* in Kashmir.

tabla   Pair of small kettle drums, played with the hands. Very common in Pakistan and North India. See Sakata 1980a, 1983:203; *Grove*, ed. Sadie 1984, vol. 3:492–7.

tāl   Pair of small cymbals. See Sakata 1983:205; Slobin 1976:271–3.

tamburā Name for an archaic form of long-necked lute in India, presumed to be the ancestor of the sitar (see sitar in *Grove*, ed. Sadie). Closely related to the *sehtār* and to the older forms of *dutār*.

tanbur Large, long-necked plucked lute with sympathetic strings. Characteristically Afghan and especially common in Mazar-e Sharif and Shomali regions. See Sakata 1978a, 1983:196; Slobin 1976:235-40.

tānpurā Large long-necked lute used as a drone instrument in Pakistan and India. See *Grove*, ed. Sadie 1984, vol. 3:514-15.

tār Long-necked, double-chambered plucked lute of Iran and the Caucasas. See During 1984:47-58.

tulak A transverse or fipple flute of wood or metal. See Sakata 1983:202.

'ud The Arabian lute. See *Grove*, ed. Sadie 1984, vol. 3:687-93.

zirbaghali Single-headed goblet drum, usually of pottery. Widespread throughout Afghanistan. See Sakata 1980a, 1983:204; Slobin 1976:261-4.

Glossary 2

Musical and other terms

afghāni The unit of currency in Afghanistan. In 1976–7 one pound sterling = 130 *afghāni*s.
āhang A melody.
ālāp In Afghanistan, a brief textless vocal ornamentation usually sung in the context of a *ghazal*. In India refers to an introductory section in free rhythm, cf. *shakl* in Afghanistan.
āmad The descending scale of a melodic mode.
antara A vocal or instrumental composition, usually contrasted with *āstāi* and having a higher tessitura. In vocal music the *antara* corresponds to the verse. Derived from Hindi *antrā*.
'arusi The final stage in the marriage process. A lavish wedding party.
Āsā A melodic mode commonly used in Afghan urban music.
āstāi An instrumental or vocal composition, usually contrasted with *antara* and having a lower tessitura. In vocal music the *āstāi* corresponds to the refrain. Derived from Hindi *sthāyi*.
āstāi-ye tabla The later section of a *shakl* in which the tabla joins with the melodic instrument. Probably a vestigial form of *vilambit gat* (slow instrumental composition in Hindustani music).
Atan The national dance of Afghanistan. Several sub-types, such as *Atan-e Logari*, *Atan-e Rāsteh Qadimi*, and *Atan-e Wardaki*.
āvāz Iranian term for singing in free rhythm.
āwāz Voice; song; a song.
bacheh bāzi The performance of a dancing boy. Homosexual acts with boys.
Bairami The most common melodic mode of Afghan urban music. Corresponds to *Rāg Bhairvi*.
bāzigar A dancing boy.
Beiru A melodic mode corresponding to *Rāg Bhairav*.
beit A poetic couplet, consisting of two *misrā'*s; poetry.
bol Hindi = 'speak'. A mnemonic syllable used by tabla players.
bolbol Nightingale; a songbird.
chahārbeiti A poetic form consisting of four *beit*s (eight *misrā'*s). Often applied to the quatrain, which may be more properly called *dubeiti* (two *beit*s = four *misrā'*s).
chashni A set of songs or tunes played one after the other, ideally all in the same mode.
Chelu A small ethnic minority in Herat, white tent itinerants, strongly associated with prostitution.
cheshm sefid One who does not acknowledge the authority of his elders and betters. Brazen.
Chishti Sufi order established in India by Khwaja Muin al-Din Chishti. The *Chishtiya* (members of the *Chishti* order) are notable for the use of devotional music in their ritual.

Glossary 2

Chub Bāzi The stick dances performed in Herati villages to music of the *sornā* and *dohol*. Several sub-types, such as *Chub Bāzi Baluchi*, *Chub Bāzi Dālbāzhā*, and *Chub Bāzi Rāsteh*.

Dādreh A rhythmic cycle (*tāl*) of six time units (*matras*).

dasteh A group. *Dasteh sāz* = group of musicians.

dastgāh The name of the modal suite in Persian art music. Twelve *dastgāhā* (plural of *dastgāh*) are known, each consisting of a sequence of distinct melodic modes. Sometimes used to mean a single melodic mode in Herat (and so synonomous with *maqām* and *rāg*).

dhrupad An austere and ancient form of Hindustani vocal music.

Diwāt The sixth degree of the scale, which can take *komal* or *tiwra* forms (*Da* and *De*). From Hindi *Dhaivat*.

Dom The musician 'caste' in Pashtun/Pukhtun society.

Duni Section of the Kabuli *ghazal* form, an instrumental rendering of the *āstāi* melody to which the refrain is sung.

dutāri A *dutār* player.

'*Eid* A Muslim festival. Two '*Eid*s occur in the year, one at the end of *Ramazān* ('*Eid-e Ramazān*), the other at the climax of the annual pilgrimage to Mecca ('*Eid-e Ghurbān*, the '*Eid* of the Sacrifice).

fard An interpolated couplet of poetry, usually sung in free rhythm.

Fārsi The Persian language.

fātehkhāni A stage in the marriage process, literally 'reading prayers'.

filmi Pertaining to the movies; film music; popular songs inspired by film music.

Gandār The third degree of the scale, which can take *komal* or *tiwra* forms (*Ga* and *Ge*). From Hindi *Gāndhār*.

gat An instrumental composition in Hindustani art music.

Gedeh A rhythmic cycle (*tāl*) of four or eight time units (*matras*).

gharānā A courtly stylistic school in Hindustani vocal or instrumental art music; the members of such a school, usually kinsmen.

Gharibzadeh Ethnic minority in the Herat area following a number of low ranking professions, notably barber, also musician, actor, blacksmith, turner, horse dealer, sieve and drum maker.

ghazal A poetic form in Persian, Pashto, Urdu, and other languages. A musical form for the singing of such poetry.

gor The first beat of a rhythmic cycle (*tāl*); the point of resolution of a rhythmic cadence.

gorbandi The ceremony in which a master musician (*ustād*) accepts a student (*shāgerd*) by tying a band of seven coloured threads around the student's wrist.

gusheh An individual melodic mode in Persian music. The basic unit from which the *dastgāh* is constructed.

Hindi Pertaining to India.

Hindustan North India, including Pakistan.

honarmand An artist.

'*ilm-e musiqi* The science of music. Music theory and terminology.

Irāni Pertaining to Iran.

Jat A derogatory term applied in Herat to the Gharibzadeh.

Jog A musical scale rather than a melodic mode, commonly used in Herati local music.

Kābuli From Kabul, the capital of Afghanistan.
Karj The tonal centre of a musical scale, usually the note *Sa*.
Kausieh A common melodic mode in Afghan urban music.
kesbi A professional musician.
Kesturi A common mode in Afghan urban music, and in Pashtun regional music.
khām Raw, unskilled, immature (cf. *pokhteh*).
khānaqāh A building where Sufis congregate to perform the ritual of the *zikr*; the guest house of a *pir*.
khāndan To sing; song; a song.
khyāl A genre of Hindustani vocal music; literally 'imagination'.
kiliwāli Of the village (Pashto); Pashtun regional music; Afghan popular music.
klāsik Classical (music); Hindustani vocal music.
komal The flattened form of a note (cf. *tiwra*).
Kumāj A melodic mode commonly used in Afghan urban music.
lā Thickness, layer. Often used synonomously with *lai*.
lai Rhythm, musical metre, tempo. *Bi lai* = without *lai*, in free rhythm.
Logari A style of music from the Logar Valley, a Pashto speaking area in south-east Afghanistan. Characterised by the use of short, instrumental dance tunes.
Madam The fourth degree of the scale, which can take *komal* or *tiwra* forms (*Ma* and *Me*). From Hindi *Madhyam*.
mahali Local, rural, rustic. Regional music, folk music. In the context of this study, traditional Herati music.
majles A reception. The wedding party, especially with musical entertainment.
malang A religious mendicant.
maqām A melodic mode, a Middle Eastern mode (cf. *rāg*).
maqām-e Hindi A Hindustani melodic mode (i.e. a *rāg*).
maqām-e Pārsi A Persian melodic mode.
matla' The first couplet (*beit*) in a *ghazal*.
matra The basic unit in the organisation of rhythmic cycles (*tāl*s). A rhythmic beat. From Hindi *mātrā*.
Mazāri From Mazar-e Sharif in northern Afghanistan; music from this region.
mehmāni A dinner party, usually in the evening in a private house, with lavish food.
meleh A country fair, held during *Now Ruz*. *Moloh bāgh* = a picnic in a private garden. *Meleh-ye Gol-e Sorkh* = the spring fair held at Mazar-e Sharif starting on New Year's Day (21 March) and continuing over a period of forty days.
misrā' A line of poetry, half of a couplet or *beit*.
Mogholi A rhythmic cycle (*tāl*) consisting of seven time units (*matra*s).
Muharram A month in the Muslim lunar calendar respected by Shiahs as a period of mourning (which actually extends to the end of the succeeding month of *Safar*).
musiqi Music. A musical instrument.
naghmeh An instrumental composition. In the popular song form it constitutes the independent instrumental section. *N. bāzi* = a dance tune; *n. chahārtuk* = a four part instrumental composition, *n. kashāl* = an extended instrumental piece, *n. klāsik* = a classical instrumental piece, etc.
na't Religious song, properly a *ghazal*, often about Mohammad.

Nikot The seventh degree of the scale, which can take *komal* or *tiwra* forms (*Na* and *Ni*). From Hindi *Nishad*.

not Musical notation, usually the *sargam* system.

Now Ruz New Year in the Persian solar calender (21 March).

orkestrā An orchestra, ensemble, small group of musicians.

paliteh An improvised melodic section played over a rhythmic cycle in the context of a *naghmeh-ye klāsik* or a *naghmeh-ye kashāl*. Derived from Hindi *palta*.

Pancham The fifth degree of the scale (Pe). From Hindi *Pancham*.

pardeh A note; a fret on a lute, a finger hole on the *sornā*, a digital on the harmonium. *Pardeh Irāni* = a tonal system with Persian intervals; *Pardeh Hindi* = a tonal system with Indian intervals.

Pāri A common mode in Afghan urban music, and in Pashtun regional music.

Parsi An Iranian. A Herati Shiah.

Pilu A common melodic mode in Afghan urban music.

pir The hereditary leader of the local chapter of a Sufi brotherhood.

pokhteh Cooked, skilled, matured, well crafted (cf. *khām*).

qaum Groups of varying size constituted by bonds of kinship.

radif The repertory of Iranian art music, consisting of the twelve *dastgāh*s.

raft The ascending scale of a melodic mode.

rāg A melodic mode; a Hindustani melodic mode. A musical form of Hindustani vocal (*khyāl*) or instrumental (*ālāp* and *gat*) music.

Ramazān The month of fast in the lunar calendar.

Rekap The second degree of the scale, which can take *komal* or *tiwra* forms (*Ra* and *Re*). From Hindi *Rishabh*.

reng A dance tune.

rubābi A *rubāb* player.

rubā'i A type of quatrain in poetry.

Safar The lunar month of mourning which follows *Muharram*.

sam The first beat of a rhythmic cycle (*tāl*) in Hindustani music (cf. *gor*).

samwādi A functionally important note, see *wādi*. Derived from Hindi *samvādi*.

sargam The system of note names used in North India, Pakistan, and Afghanistan. A type of improvised passage in the performance of *khyāl* when the note names are sung over a rhythmic cycle.

sāz Music; musical instrument. The *sornā*.

sāzandeh A hereditary professional musician. In the context of this study usually an urban male hereditary musician.

seh A cadential pattern in which a melodic and/or rhythmic pattern is repeated three times, the last beat of the third repetition falling on the *gor* beat.

seil The Herati folk drama, performed out of doors, at night, usually in a village, by Gharibzadeh actors, consisting of a series of short comic plays, with music provided by *sornā* and *dohol*.

shāgerd A student; an apprentice.

shakl An introductory section played or sung in free rhythm (cf. *ālāp* in Hindustani music). An extempore exegesis of the melodic characteristics of a mode. *Shakl-e sāz* = the collective playing of *shakl* phrases by the various members of a band at the start of a performance.

shau nishini An evening gathering of friends in someone's house for the purpose of recreation.
shauq A hobby or other recreational pursuit, especially music; a gathering of *shauqis* for the purposes of playing music for their own enjoyment.
shauqi An enthusiast. An amateur musician.
shirinikhori A stage in the marriage process, literally 'eating sweets'.
sim-e bajgi The upper drone string on the *rubāb*.
simkāri A technique used by *rubāb* players in which the upper drone string is struck in alternation with the main melody strings.
sor A note; a musical scale; the tuning of a musical instrument. *Sor kardan* = to tune an instrument; *bi sor* = out of tune.
tablegi A tabla player.
takht-e sāz A bandstand.
tāl Rhythm. A rhythmic cycle such as *Dādreh*, *Gedeh*, and *Mogholi*.
tekieh A building where Shiahs commemorate the matyrdom of their saints, especially during *Muharram*.
Tintāl A rhythmic cycle (*tāl*) of sixteen time units (*matras*), very common in Hindustani music.
tiwra The sharpened form of a note. From Hindi *tivr*.
ustād A master in some field of knowledge or the arts. A master musician. A teacher.
Uzbeki Pertaining to the Uzbek peoples of northern Afghanistan.
wādi A functionally important note in a melodic mode. Derived from Hindi *vādi*. Cf. *samwādi*.
Yemen A common melodic mode in Afghan urban music.
zikr A form of Sufi ritual.
ziyārat The tomb of a saint.

Items on the cassette

SIDE 1

Example 1 *Ghazal 'Piram o ārezu-ye wasl-e jawānān dāram'* in *Rāg Kesturi*
Amir Jan (vocal and harmonium); Rahim (*rubāb*); Ghulam Nebi (fourteen stringed *dutār*); Naim (tabla).

Example 2 *Naghmeh-ye kashāl* in *Rāg Pilu*
Karim Dutari (fourteen stringed *dutār*); Karim Khushnawaz (tabla).

Example 3 *Naghmeh-ye kashāl* in *Rāg Kausieh*
Amir Mohammad (harmonium); Rahim (*rubāb*); Gada Mohammad (fourteen stringed *dutār*); Fazl Ahmad (tabla).

Example 4 *Khyāl* in *Rāg Bairami*
Amir Mohammad (vocal and harmonium); Rahim (*rubāb*); Gada Mohammad (fourteen stringed *dutār*); Fazl Ahmad (tabla).

Example 5 *Naghmeh-ye klāsik* in *Rāg Des*
Rahim (*rubāb*); Naim (tabla).

SIDE 2

Example 6 *Kabuli* song *'Kajaki'*
Ali Ahmad (vocal and harmonium); Amir (*rubāb*); Ghulam Haidar (fourteen stringed *dutār*); Jalil (tabla and vocal refrain).

Example 7 *'Chahārbeiti Shomāli'*
Amir Mohammad (vocal and harmonium); Rahim (*rubāb*); Gada Mohammad (fourteen stringed *dutār*); Fazl Ahmad (tabla).

Example 8 *Filmi* song *'Chal chal chal mere sāthi'*
Mahmud (vocal and harmonium); Amir Jan (*rubāb*); Ghulam Nebi (fourteen stringed *dutār*); Naim (tabla).

Example 9 *Irāni* song *'Fereshteh jān qashangi'*
Amir Mohammad (vocal and harmonium); Rahim (*rubāb*); Gada Mohammad (fourteen stringed *dutār*); Jalil (tabla).

Example 10 *Irāni* song *'Eh del belāi delbar'*
Anar (vocal and harmonium); Bibi Jan (tabla); Urak (*dāireh*).

Example 11 *Mazari* song *'Seil-e gol-e sorkh be Sekhi Jān-e'*
Amir (vocal and harmonium); Ahmad (fourteen stringed *dutār*); Kholek Sauz (fourteen stringed *dutār*); Bolbol Hairawi (*zirbaghali*); Ghulam (*duzangeh*).

Example 12 *'Naghmeh Uzbeki'*
Gada Mohammad (fourteen stringed *dutār*); Naim (tabla).

Example 13 *'Naghmehā-ye bāzi'*
Mahmud (vocal and harmonium); Amir Jan (*rubāb*); Ghulam Nebi (fourteen stringed *dutār*); Naim (tabla).

Items on the cassette

Example 14 Wedding song '*Heinā ba kārā*'
Mahmud (vocal and harmonium); Amir Jan (*rubāb*); Ghulam Nebi (fourteen stringed *dutār*); Naim (tabla).

Example 15 Wedding song '*Olang olang*'
Amir Jan (vocal and harmonium); Mahmud (vocal); Rahim (*rubāb*); Naim (tabla).

Example 16 Herati/Iranian song '*Hai Rebābeh*'
Ghulam Nebi Zendeh Del (vocal and *dāireh*); Gada Mohammad (fourteen stringed *dutār*).

Example 17 Herati song tune '*Mui Talāi*'
Rahim (*rubāb*); Naim (tabla).

Bibliography

Abu' l-Fazl. 1927. *The Āʿīn-i Akbarī*. Trans. H. Blochmann, 2nd edition, D.C. Phillott (ed.), Calcutta: The Asiatic Society of Bengal
Adamec, Ludwig W. 1973. *Historical and Political Who's Who of Afghanistan*. Graz: Akademische Druck-u. Verlagsanstalt
Ahmed, Nazir 1954. The Kitab-i-Nauras. *Islamic Culture*, 28:333-71
Baghban, Hafizullah 1977. The context and concept of humor in Magadi Theatre. Ph.D. thesis, University of Indiana
Baily, John 1976. Recent changes in the dutār of Herat. *Asian Music*, 8-1:29-64
　1977. Movement patterns in playing the Herati *dutār*. In John Blacking (ed.), *The Anthropology of the Body*. London: Academic Press, 275-330
　1979. Professional and amateur musicians in Afghanistan. *World of Music*, 21(2):46-64
　1980. A description of the naqqarakhana of Herat. *Asian Music*, 11(2):1-10
　1981a. A system of modes used in the urban music of Afghanistan. *Ethnomusicology*, 25(1):1-39
　1981b. Cross-cultural perspectives in popular music: the case of Afghanistan. In Richard Middleton and David Horn (eds.), *Popular Music 1*. Cambridge: Cambridge University Press, 105-22
　1985. Music structure and human movement. In Peter Howell, Ian Cross and Robert West (eds.), *Musical Structure and Cognition*. London: Academic Press, 237-58
　1986. Review of Lorraine Sakata: *Music in the Mind: the Concepts of Music and Musician in Afghanistan. Ethnomusicology*, 30(1):173-4
　1987. Principes d'improvisation rythmique dans le jeu du *rubāb* d'Afghanistan. In *L'Improvisation dans les musiques de tradition orale*. Ouvrage collectif, Editeur general: Bernard Lortat-Jacob, Société d'Etudes Linguistiques et Anthropologiques de France, Paris
Bartók, Bela, and Albert B. Lord 1951. *Serbo-Croation Folk Songs*. New York: Columbia University Press
Beliaev, V. M. 1960. *Abdurrakhman Dzhami: 'Traktat o muzyke'*. Tashkent: Izd-vo ANUzSSR
Beveridge, Annette Susannah 1922. *The Bābur-nāma in English*. Vol. 1. London: Luzac and Co.
Bhanu, Dharma 1955. Promotion of music by the Turko-Afghan rulers of India. *Islamic Culture*, 29:9-31
Blacking, John 1979. Some problems of theory and method in the study of musical change. *Yearbook of the International Folk Music Council*, 9:1-26
Blum, Robert Stephen 1972. Musics in contact: the cultivation of oral repertories in Meshed, Iran. Ph.D. thesis, University of Illinois. University Microfilms
Browne, Edward G. 1902. *A Literary History of Persia. Vol. 1: From the Earliest Times*. Cambridge: Cambridge University Press
　1928. *A Literary History of Persia. Vol. 3: The Tartar Dominion (1265-1502)*. Cambridge: Cambridge University Press
　1930. *A Literary History of Persia. Vol. 4: Modern Times (1500-1924)*. Cambridge: Cambridge University Press
Burnes, Sir Alexander 1842. *Cabool: Being a Personal Narrative of a Journey to and Residence in that City in the Years 1836, 7 and 8*. London: John Murray
Byron, Robert 1937. *The Road To Oxiana*. London: Jonathan Cape
Caron, Nelly, and Dariouche Safvate 1966. *Iran. Les Traditions Musicales*. Paris: Buchet/Chastel
Caws, P. 1974. Operational, representational and explanatory models. *American Anthropologist*, 76:1-10

Conolly, Arthur 1838. *Journey to the North of India, Overland From England, Through Russia, Persia, and Affghaunistaun.* Vol. 2. London: Richard Bentley

Currie, P. M. 1978. The shrine and cult of Muʿīn al-Dīn Chishtī of Ajmer. D.Phil. thesis, University of Oxford

Day, C. R. 1891. *The Music and Musical Instruments of Southern India and the Deccan.* Reprinted 1977, Delhi: B.R. Publishing

Deva, B. C. 1977. *Musical Instruments.* New Delhi: National Book Trust, India

Doubleday, Veronica 1982. Women and music in Herat. *Afghanistan Journal*, 9(1):3-12

1988. *Three Women of Herat.* London: Jonathan Cape

Dupree, Louis 1973. *Afghanistan.* Princeton: Princeton University Press

Dupree, Nancy Hatch 1967. *The Road to Balkh.* Afghan Tourist Organisation, Kabul

1975 *Kabul: City at the Crossroads.* NYC: The Afghanistan Council of the Asia Society, Special Paper

During, Jean 1984. *La Musique iranienne. Tradition et évolution.* Paris: Editions Recherche sur les Civilisations

Elphinstone, Mountstuart 1815. *An Account of the Kingdom of Caubul and its Dependencies in Persia, Tartary, and India.* Reprinted 1969 with notes by Alfred Janata, Graz: Akademische Druck-u. Verlagsanstalt

English, Paul 1973. The traditional city of Herat, Afghanistan. In L. Carl Brown (ed.), *From Madina to Metropolis: Heritage and Change in the Near Eastern City.* Princeton: The Darwin Press, 73-90

ERCON 1973. Hydrogeological investigation of the Hari Rud Basin. Phase 1 Report, unpublished

Farhat, Hormoz 1965. The *dastgāh* concept in Persian music. Ph.D. thesis, University of California, Los Angeles. University Microfilms

1980. The evolution of performance style and the contemporary *dastgāh* 'suite' in Persian music. Paper read at Society for Ethnomusicology Conference, Bloomington, Indiana

Farmer, Henry George 1929. *A History of Arabian Music.* Reprinted 1973, London: Luzac and Co.

1931. *Studies in Oriental Musical Instruments.* First Series, Glasgow: The Civic Press

1939. An outline history of music and musical theory. In Arthur Upham Pope and Phyllis Ackerman (eds.), *A Survey of Persian Art.* London: Oxford University Press, Vol. 6:2,783-804

Ferrier, J. P. 1857. *Caravan Journeys and Wanderings in Persia, Afghanistan, Turkistan and Beloochistan; With Historical Notices of the Countries Lying Between Russia and India.* London: John Murray

Fox Strangways, A. H. 1914. *The Music of Hindostan.* Oxford: The Clarendon Press

Gregorian, Vartan 1969. *The Emergence of Modern Afghanistan.* Stanford: Stanford University Press

Grönhaug, Reidar 1978. Scale as a variable in analysis: fields in social organization in Herat, northwest Afghanistan. In Fredrik Barth (ed.), *Scale and Social Organization.* Oslo: The Norwegian Research Council for Science and Humanities

Halim, A. 1945. Music and musicians of the court of Shah Jahan. *Islamic Culture*, 19:354-60

1956. History of the growth and development of North-Indian music during Sayyid-Lodi period. *Journal of the Asiatic Society of Pakistan*, 1:46-64

Hoerburger, Felix 1968. Supplementary jingling in the instrumental folk music of Afghanistan. *Journal of the International Folk Music Council*, 20:51-4

Jairazbhoy, Nazir A. 1971. *The Rāgs of North Indian Music. Their Structure and Evolution.* London: Faber and Faber

Kaumudi 1950. Mingling of Islamic and indigenous traditions in Indian music. *Indian Historical Quarterly*, 26:129-37

Kaye, Sir John William 1874. *A History Of the War In Afghanistan.* 3rd edition, Vol. 1. London: Allen

Khan, Hazrat Inayat 1962. *The Sufi Message of Hazrat Inayat Khan.* Vol. 2. London: Barrie and Rockliff

Kippen, James 1985. The traditional tabla drumming of Lucknow in its social and cultural context. Ph.D. thesis, Queen's University Belfast

Kunst, Jaap 1959. *Ethnomusicology.* The Hague: Martinus Nijhoff

Leyden, John, and William Erskine 1921. *Memoirs of Zehīr-ed-Dīn Muhammed Bābur, Emperor of Hindustan. Written by Himself, In the Chaghatāi Tūrki.* Annotated and revised by Sir Lucas King. Vol. 1. London: Oxford University Press

Madadi, Abdul Wahab n.d. The rise and fall of music in Afghanistan. *Pashtun Zhagh*

Malleson, George B. 1880. *Herat. The Granary and the Garden of Central Asia*. London: W.H. Allen and Co.
Merriam, Alan P. 1964. *The Anthropology of Music*. Evanston: Northwestern University Press
Nettl, Bruno 1972. Persian popular music in 1969. *Ethnomusicology*, 16(2):218-39
 1983. *The Study of Ethnomusicology: Twenty-nine Issues and Concepts*. Urbana: University of Illinois Press
Nettl, Bruno, and Bela Foltin 1972. *Daramad of Chahargah: A Study in the Performance Practice of Persian Music*. Detroit: Information Coordinators, Inc.
Neuman, Daniel M. 1980. *The Life of Music in North India: the Organization of an Artistic Tradition*. Detroit: Wayne State University Press
Niedermayer, Oskar von 1924. *Afghanistan*. Leipzig
Pacholczyk, Jozef 1978. Sufyana Kalam, the classical music of Kashmir. *Asian Music*, 10(1):1-16
Popley, Herbert A. 1921. *The Music of India*. London: Oxford University Press
Poullada, Leon B. 1973. *Reform and Rebellion in Afghanistan 1919-1929: King Amanulla's Failure to Modernise a Tribal Society*. Ithaca: Cornell University Press
Powers, Harold S. 1979. Classical music, cultural roots, and colonial rule; an Indic musicologist looks at the Muslim world. *Asian Music*, 12(1):5-39
Qureshi, Regula Burckhardt 1986. *Sufi Music of India and Pakistan: Sound, Context and Meaning in Qawwali*. Cambridge: Cambridge University Press
Rao, Aparna 1981. Qui sont les Jat d'Afghanistan? *Afghanistan Journal*, 8(2):55-64
Rizvi, S. N. Haidar 1941. Music in Muslim India. *Islamic Culture*, 15:331-40
Robson, James 1938. *Tracts on Listening to Music*. London: The Royal Asiatic Society
Roy Choudhury, M. L. 1957. Music in Islam. *Journal of the Asiatic Society, Letters*, 23(2):43-102
Sadie, Stanley (ed.) 1984. *The New Grove Dictionary of Musical Instruments*. 3 vols. London: Macmillan Press
Sakata, Hiromi Lorraine 1977. Afghan musical instruments: the rabab. *Afghanistan Journal*, 4(4):144-6
 1978a. Afghan musical instruments: the dambura. *Afghanistan Journal*, 5(2):70-3
 1978b. Afghan musical instruments: the dutar and tanbur. *Afghanistan Journal*, 5(4):150-2
 1979a. Afghan musical instruments: ghichak and saroz. *Afghanistan Journal*, 6(3):84-6
 1979b. Afghan musical instruments: the nai. *Afghanistan Journal*, 6(4):144-6
 1980a. Afghan musical instruments: drums. *Afghanistan Journal*, 7(1):30-2
 1980b. Afghan musical instruments: sorna and dohl. *Afghanistan Journal*, 7(3):93-6
 1983. *Music in the Mind: the Concepts of Music and Musician in Afghanistan*. Kent: Kent State University Press. With two accompanying cassettes
Signell, Karl L. 1977. *Makam: Modal Practice in Turkish Art Music*. Seattle: Asian Music Publications
Skillman, Teri 1986. The Bombay Hindi film song genre: a historical survey. *1986 Yearbook for Traditional Music*, 18:133-44
Slobin, Mark 1969. Instrumental music in northern Afghanistan. Ph.D. thesis, University of Michigan. University Microfilms
 1972. Review of Felix Hoerburger: *Volkmusik in Afghanistan, nebst einem Exkurs über Qorʿan-Rezitation und Thora-Kantillation in Kabul*. *Asian Music*, 4(1):72-4
 1974. Music in contemporary Afghan society. In Louis Dupree and Linette Albert (eds.), *Afghanistan in the 1970s*. New York: Praeger, 239-48
 1976. *Music in the Culture of Northern Afghanistan*. Viking Fund Publications in Anthropology No. 54, Tucson: University of Arizona Press
Solis, Theodore 1970. The Sarod; its Gat-Torā tradition with examples by Amir Khan and three of his students. M.A. thesis, University of Hawaii
Tagore, S. M. (ed.) 1965. *Hindu Music from Various Authors*. Reprint of 2nd edition 1903, Varanasi: Chowkhamba Sanskrit Series Office
Trimmingham, J. Spencer 1971. *The Sufi Orders in Islam*. Oxford: Clarendon Press
Tsuge, Gen'ichi 1970. Rhythmic aspects of the *Āvāz* in Persian music. *Ethnomusicology*, 14(2):205-27
Utas, Bo 1980. Notes on Afghan Sufi orders and khanaqahs. *Afghanistan Journal*, 7(2):60-7
Vámbéry, Arminius 1864. *Travels In Central Asia*. London: John Murray

Willard, N. A. 1834. A treatise upon the music of Hindustan, comprising a detail of the ancient theory and modern practice. In Tagore 1965
Wolfe, Nancy Hatch 1966. *Herat*. Kabul: The Afghan Tourist Organisation
Wright, Owen 1978. *The Modal System of Arab and Persian Music A.D. 1250–1300*. London: Oxford University Press
Wulff, Hans E. 1966. *The Traditional Crafts of Persia*. Cambridge: Massachusetts Institute of Technology
Zonis, Ella 1973. *Classical Persian Music: an Introduction*. Cambridge: Harvard University Press

Index

Note: very few references are made to plates or to the musical examples, except in the latter case to the singer or main instrumentalist. Further information about the examples is given on pages 173-4, and a list of plates is provided on page vii, though more information is provided in the individual plate captions. *n* = footnote

Abdur Rahman Khan, 5, 26, 27, 28, 157, 158, 159
Abu'l-Fazl, 15
Abu Walid, 5, 136, 137
Adamec, Ludwig, 29
Afghan 3, 9, 18
afghāni (currency), 104, 107, 109, 120, 132, 134, 135, 136, 168
Afghanistan, 3-5, 25-8, 30-1, 157-160
āhang, 38, 168
Ahmad Shah Durrani, 4, 24
Ahmad Zahir, 84, 85, 151
Ahmed, Nazir, 16
ālāp, 41, 62, 64, 76, 168
ālāp and *gat* (Hindustani instrumental music), 26, 77-9; see also *gat*
Ali Ahmad Delahang, 84-5, 105, 107-8, 114-16, 120, 122, 127, 138
āmad, 41-3, 49, 64, 168
Amanullah Khan, 19, 22, 26, 27, 30, 158
Amir, xi, 91-2, 105, 107, 108, 110, 116, 122, 123, 137
Amir Jan Khushnawaz, x, xi, xii, 1, 29, 34, 37, 39, 42, 44, 46, 47, 48, 50-4, 56-7, 61-7, 74, 76, 77, 83, 87, 94, 96-7, 99, 104, 105, 106, 108-10, 112-17, 119, 120, 122, 127, 132, 138, 144, 150, 152, 162-4
Amir Khusro Balkhi, 61, 110-11
Amir Mohammad from Kabul, xii, 58, 72-6, 85-6, 88-9, 105, 109, 114-19, 121, 122, 127, 129, 132, 134, 137, 148, 154-5, 162, 163-4
Anar, 89 90
Ansari, Khwaja Abdullah, 7, 10, 136, 154
antara, 61, 61n, 62, 64-74, 76, 79, 82, 84-92, 96, 98-9, 168
armonia, see harmonium
āstāi, 61, 61n, 62, 64-74, 76, 79, 82, 84-92, 96, 98-9, 168
āstāi-ye tabla, 68, 77, 127, 168
'Aushāri', 35, 93, 94, 128, 132, 142
āvāz, 19, 22, 24, 50, 79, 95, 168
āwāz, ix, 35, 168

Babur, 3, 12, 13, 14
Baghan, Hafizullah, 36, 102, 135, 147

Baily, John, ix, 18, 31, 33, 42, 46, 51, 68, 74, 81, 82, 101, 102, 165, 166
Bala Hisar, in Kabul, 27
barbers, 34, 102-3, 108, 115, 117, 169
barber-musicians, 21, 27, 30, 33, 34, 35, 102, 107, 108, 109, 115, 116, 117, 121, 160, 162, 164, 165, 169
Bartok, Bela and Albert Lord, 60
beit, 58, 59, 60, 61, 62, 64, 65, 66, 85, 99
Beliaev, V. M., 14
Beveridge, Annette Susannah, 12n
Bhanu, Dharma, 16, 111
bhog, 67
birdsong, 66, 100, 153
Blacking, John, xii, xiii, 156
Blum, Robert Stephen, 94, 160-1
bol, 19, 51, 52-4, 56-7, 160, 168
Browne, Edward G., 14, 16, 62
Burnes, Sir Alexander, 25
Byron, Robert, 3, 4, 29, 86

Caron, Nelly and Dariouche Safvate, 22, 165
Caws, Peter, 56
chahārbeita, 82
chahārbeiti, 35, 50, 85, 94, 95, 132, 168
  Chahārbeiti Shomāli, see Shomāli
chahārtār, 19, 20, 21, 22, 28, 36, 46, 51, 149, 153, 156, 165
  chahārtār players of the 1920s, 20-1
chashni, 72, 89, 92, 127, 128, 129, 132, 138, 142, 168
cheshm sefid, 121, 168
Chelu, 34, 115, 117, 124, 140, 168
chimta, 154, 165
circumcision, 84, 89, 102, 103, 121, 148, 149
Conolly, Arthur, 4
court music and musicians, 12-16, 17, 18, 19, 24-8, 30, 34, 37, 79, 111, 113, 115, 117, 156, 161, 162, 163
Currie, P. Mark, 154

dāireh, 19, 20, 33, 34, 35, 36, 58, 89, 98, 99, 110, 125, 129, 140, 160, 165
dambura, 32, 92, 147, 165

Index

dance
  Atan, 35, 128, 130, 141, 145, 168; see also '*Aushāri*'
  bacheh bāzi, 93, 117, 140-2, 168; see also *naghmeh-ye bāzi*
  Chub Bāzi, 35, 141, 169
  other dances, 128, 131
dastān, 82, 153
dastgāh, ix, 16, 19, 22, 23, 28, 40, 46, 48, 49, 74, 94, 150, 153, 160, 161, 169, 171
Day, C. R., 26
delrubā, 83, 103, 104, 107, 118, 132, 134, 138, 165
Deva, B. C., 154, 165
dhrupad, 24, 26, 67, 74, 169
Dick, Alastair, xii, 24, 60n
dohol, x, 18, 19, 21, 35, 93, 94, 102, 103, 115, 119, 124, 131, 140, 160, 161, 162, 165, 166, 169
doholak, 74, 82, 83, 93, 165
Dom, 18, 28, 169
dombak, 19, 160, 165
Doubleday, Veronica, x, xiii, 36, 89, 116
drone strings, 31, 32, 33, 44, 66, 68, 70, 79, 85, 172
duni, 61, 62, 65, 66, 79, 82, 91, 92, 169
Dupree, Louis, 3, 4, 5
Dupree, Nancy Hatch, 24, 136
During, Jean, xii, 19, 22, 165, 166, 167
dutār, x, 31-3, 147, 165, 167, 169
  two stringed *dutār*, 19, 31-2, 35, 44-6, 94, 97, 147, 161
  three stringed *dutār*, 31, 32, 46, 92
  fourteen stringed *dutār*, 31-3, 36, 38, 46, 49, 65-8, 70-1, 92, 119, 135, 156, 158
  dutār bands, 32, 33, 91-2, 107, 132, 137-8, 140, 144, 145
  dutār makers, 33, 119
  dutār players, x, 32-3, 55, 103-4, 107-10, 114, 118-20, 135, 137, 142, 149-50, 153, 162, 169
duzangeh, 91, 92, 135, 165

ʿ*Eid*, 124, 148, 149, 169
Elphinstone, Mountstuart, 17, 18
English, Paul, 6-9

falak, 85
fard, 62, 64, 65, 66, 87, 88, 89, 117, 127, 130, 134, 138, 169
Farhat, Hormoz, xii, 16, 22, 39, 41, 44, 45, 46, 47, 48, 49, 55
Farmer, Henry George, 14, 15, 16, 26, 146, 166
Ferrier, J. P., 4, 17-18
film, x, xi, 81, 83, 86, 92, 142, 151, 160, 161
filmi (musical genre), 38, 82, 86-8, 169
folk drama, 35, 94, 102, 135
forud, 16, 22, 23
Fox Strangways, 50

Gada Mohammad, xii, 58, 72, 85, 88, 92, 98, 105, 109, 110, 115, 117, 118, 119, 120, 132, 134, 137, 151, 162
ganda bandhan, 121; see also *gorbandi*
gat, 26, 55, 76, 77, 78, 79, 169
gharānā, 25, 162, 169
Gharibzadeh, 9, 33, 34, 35, 102, 110, 115, 128, 137, 141, 147, 169
ghazal, 19, 22, 24-8, 35, 49, 55, 57, 60-6, 72, 76, 77, 79, 80n, 81, 82, 83, 93, 94, 107, 109, 111, 113, 114, 122, 127-9, 132, 134, 154, 156, 157, 162, 168, 169, 170
Ghazni, 2, 3, 5, 26, 83
gheichak, 12, 13, 14, 19, 160, 165
Ghulam Haidar, 84, 105, 107, 120, 122, 136
Ghulam Mohammad Shabahang, 105, 107, 114, 136
Ghulam Nebi Zendeh Del, 94, 98-9, 110, 135
Ghulam Salwar, 105, 108, 110, 127, 135, 136, 138
Golpasand family (Golpasandha), x, xi, 34, 35, 58, 105, 107-8, 109, 110, 114, 115-16, 117, 119, 120, 121, 122, 129, 132, 136, 149, 155, 162, 164
gor, 51, 52, 65, 68, 75, 78, 86, 92, 121, 169, 171
gorbandi, 121-3, 154, 169
Gregorian, Vartan, 4, 5, 24, 30, 111, 134, 157-8
Grönhaug, Reidar, 6, 9
gusheh, 22, 23, 46, 49, 169

Haidar Pineh, 20, 21, 23, 28, 29
Halim, A., 16
Hamahang, Haji, 62, 96, 108, 111-12, 132, 134
Hanifi, 10, 148
harmonium, 20, 27, 28, 34, 36, 38, 41, 58, 71, 84, 120, 144, 156, 160, 165 (under *armonia*)
Hoerburger, Felix, 38
honarmand, 117, 149, 162, 169

Imam Shishnur, 5, 20, 136, 137
India, ix, 3, 4, 16, 17, 18, 19, 24, 25, 26, 27, 28, 29, 39, 40, 41, 42, 44, 55, 56, 74, 77, 78, 79, 81, 83, 86, 111, 113, 119, 121, 136, 144, 152, 153, 154, 159, 160, 161, 163, 165, 166, 167, 168, 169, 171
intervals, 38-40, 44-50, 99
Iran, ix, xi, 2-3, 6, 10, 14, 15, 16, 19, 20, 22, 23, 24, 26, 31, 39, 44, 48, 49, 55, 79, 81, 83, 88-90, 94, 98, 108, 136, 150, 155, 156, 158, 159, 160-1, 165, 166, 167, 169

Jairazbhoy, Nazir, xiv, 39, 40, 42, 50
Jalil Ahmad Golpasand, 84, 88, 105, 107-8, 109, 114, 115, 116, 117, 122, 136
Jami, Abdur Rahman, 7, 10, 14-15, 154
Jat, 6, 102, 103, 115, 147, 149, 169
Jeshan, 27, 104, 140

Kabul, 2, 3-5, 8, 10, 18, 20, 24, 30-1, 33, 34, 51, 79, 83, 85, 86, 102, 115, 132, 144, 149, 151, 154, 156-64

Index

Kābuli (musical genre), 83–5
Kabuli art music, *see* music
Kabuli musicians, 24–31, 33, 56, 81, 87, 88, 104–11, 124, 132, 134–6, 144, 151; see also *ustād*s, and Amir Mohammad, Hamahang, various Ustads
Kandahar, 2–4, 18, 23, 26, 82, 83, 135
Karim Dutari, xii, 20, 32–3, 40, 50, 57, 58, 70–1, 95, 105, 110, 115, 119–20, 122, 135, 144, 149, 151, 155
Karim Khushnawaz, 51–2, 54, 57, 70–1, 104–10, 114–15, 120, 122, 136, 138, 162
karnā, 18
Kaumudi, 16
Kaye, Sir John William, 4
kemāncheh, 14, 18, 19, 165, 166
Khan, Hazrat Inayat, 152
Kholu Shauqi, 46, 98, 110, 128
Khushnawazha, x, 20, 29, 35, 104–6, 108–9, 114–16, 163–4
khyāl, 26, 74–6, 79, 110–2, 132, 134
Kippen, James, xii, 113
Kunst, Jaap, 14

lai, 50–5
landay, 82, 85
Leyden, John and William Erskine, 12, 12*n*, 13
Logari (musical genre), 82, 92–4, 141–2; see also *nagmeh*

Madadi, Abdul Wahab, 24, 25, 31, 83, 110
Mahmud Khushnawaz, 87–8, 93–4, 95–6, 97, 104, 105, 116, 122
Malleson, George B., 4
maqām, 14–15, 16, 18, 22, 40, 49, 169, 170; *see also* mode
Mashal Ghori, Ustad, xii, 11, 26, 28
Mashhad, 2, 3, 15, 23, 46, 160–1, 163
master-student relationship, 112–15, 118, 121–3, 163
matra, 51–4
Mazar-e Sharif, 2, 32, 69, 91, 92, 136, 167, 170
Mazāri (musical genre), 91–2, 136
mehmāni, 62, 142, 144
meleh (spring fair), 91, 136–9, 140
  meleh bāgh, 143, 144
  Meleh-ye Gol-e Sorkh, 91, 136
Merriam, Alan P., 14, 103, 162
mode, 14–5, 18, 21–2, 40–50, 58 (see also *maqām*, *rāg*)
modernisation, modernism, 6, 8–9, 23, 30, 83–4, 94, 109, 134, 148, 151, 157–60, 160–1, 163
Moghuls, Moghul Empire, 3, 12, 15, 16, 18, 24
Muharram, 10, 116, 150, 170, 171
Muin al-Din Chishti, 154–5
mullahs, 146–52, 158–9
music
  art music: Hindustani, 24–6, 28, 44, 49, 74–80, 110–13, 162; Kabuli, ix, x, 26–9, 31, 33, 37, 46, 49, 60–80, 81, 103, 115, 122, 132, 154, 156, 158, 161; Kashmiri, 18; Persian, 16, 19–23, 24; Timurid, 3, 12–16
  popular music, 30–4, 36, 46, 61, 81–100, 122, 127, 132, 135, 137–8, 142, 156
  regional, 81–3, 94–100
  religious, 35, 49, 153–5
musicians, *see* barber-musicians, *chahārtār* players, court musicians, *dutār* players, Kabuli musicians, *sāzandeh*, *shauqi*, *ustād*s

naghmeh (instrumental piece or section)
  n. *bāzi*, 92–4, 142
  n. *chahārtuk*, 67
  n. *kashāl*, 66–74, 79–80, 127, 132
  n. *klāsik*, 76–80, 132
Naim Khushnawaz, 52–4, 62, 76, 87, 92–4, 99, 104–6, 108, 109, 116, 119, 121–3
naqqārahkāneh, 18, 94, 166
naʿt, x, 94, 129, 154, 170
Nettl, Bruno, 22, 88, 153, 160
Neuman, Daniel, 25, 28, 113, 161
New Year (*Now Ruz*), 32, 136–7, 170–1
ney, 13, 14, 150, 166
Niedermayer, Oskar von, 27
notation, 39, 56–8, 113, 160, 161
nowheh, 35

Pacholczyk, Jozef, 18
Pakistan, xi, 2, 26, 28, 79, 82, 83, 86, 111, 136, 154, 165, 166, 167, 169, 171
paliteh, 76–8
Pashtuns, 3–4, 9–10, 17–8, 24–6, 81–3, 157–8, 160
Peshawar, ix, 2, 4, 17, 18, 26, 82, 123
piānu, 27, 82, 166
pir, *see under* Sufism
poetry, 27, 60–6, 85, 99, 134
Popley, Herbert, 53
Poullada, Leon B., 157
Powers, Harold S., 156
practice (or lack of it), 113, 121, 163
Pul-e Malan, 5, 91, 136–7
purdah, 8, 115–16

qairaq, 154, 166
Qandahārbāni, 24
qānun, 13, 14, 16, 166
qaum, 9–10
qawwāli, 154
quodlibet, 93, 128, 142
Qureshi, Regula Burckhardt, 154

rabāb, 14, 166
Radio Kabul, Radio Afghanistan, xii, 30–3, 39, 81–3, 159

Index

raft, 41–3, 49, 64, 171
rāg, ix, 40–4, 115, 171; *see also* mode
Rahim Khushkhan, 20, 21, 29, 110, 144
Rahim Khushnawaz, 47, 48, 49, 62, 72, 75, 76, 77, 78, 85, 88, 96, 99–100, 104–6, 109, 115, 117, 118, 122, 132, 134, 150
Ramazān, 85, 125, 131-4
Rao, Aparna, 34, 102
reng, 22, 132, 171
Reshtia, S. Q, xii, 27, 30
Rhythmic cycles, 51–3, 57, 121
Rizvi, S. N. Haidar, 16
Robson, James, 146, 152
rowzeh, 35, 150
Roy Choudhury, M. L., 146, 148, 152
rubāb
    Afghan, 1, 19, 26, 30–1, 33, 34, 46–8, 60, 76–9, 99–100, 156, 158, 166
    family, 26
    fretting, 19, 38, 46–8, 99
rubāʿi, 62, 64, 65, 66

Sadie, Stanley, 165-7
Safar, 10, 116, 171
Safavids, 3, 10, 14, 15, 16
Sakata, Hiromi Lorraine, ix, xii, xiv, 25, 35, 36, 83, 85, 93, 94, 95, 96, 101, 102, 107, 134, 135, 136, 140, 146, 165–7
Saljuki family
    Abdul Wahed, xi, xii, 152
    Abdul Wahab, 148, 149
    Ustad Fekri, 11
sam, see *gor*
santur, 18, 19, 20, 21, 22, 156, 166
saptak, 39-40
sārang, 19, 21, 25, 140, 166
sārangi, 76, 83, 109, 134, 152, 166
sargam, in performance of *khyal*, 76; *see also* notation
sarinda, 14, 19, 34, 82, 83, 166
sarod, 26, 78, 162, 166
saz, ix, 35, 171
sāzandeh
    sornā and *dohol* players, 18, 27, 35–6, 102–3, 160, 162
    urban female hereditary, 33–5, 58–9, 83, 89–90, 95, 96, 108, 114–16, 125–6, 129–31, 134–6, 141, 148–9, 163
    urban male hereditary, ix, x, 20, 29, 34–5, 56, 58, 101–23, 124, 154–5, 160–4, 171
sāz-e Kashmiri, 18, 166
science of music (*ʿilm-e musiqi*), 14, 15, 36, 37–59, 113, 114, 118, 160, 162, 169
seh, 52, 68, 70, 76, 78, 171
sehtār, 18, 166
sekh, 19, 20, 22, 166
Shahzadeh Yaqub, 5, 136-7, 138

shakl, 1, 22, 41, 48–9, 57, 58, 64, 66, 68, 70, 74, 75, 76, 77, 78, 88, 92, 95, 97, 99, 168, 171
    shakl-e sāz, 71, 72, 127
Shashmaqām, 15
shauq
    hobby, enthusiasm, 141, 147, 150, 151, 152, 172
    music session, 143, 172
shauqi, 101–2, 114, 118–20, 172
sheitān, 146-7, 162
Sher Ali Kan, 25
Shomāli, 83, 85-6
'*Siāhmu wa Jalali*', 94-5
Signell, Karl L., xii, 13, 13n
sitar, 16, 27, 33, 78, 79, 81, 82, 111, 162, 165, 166, 167
Skillman, Teri, 86
Slobin, Mark, ix, xii, 14, 15, 24, 30, 31, 32, 35, 36, 81, 82, 85, 91, 93, 96, 101, 102, 126, 136, 141, 146, 152, 165–7
Solis, Theodore, 26
sor, 37–50, 55, 58, 150, 172
sormandel, 103, 132, 134, 166
sornā, x, 18, 19, 21, 35, 38, 40, 93, 94, 102, 115, 119, 124, 131, 140, 146–7, 153, 160–1, 165, 166
Sufism, x, xii, 3, 10, 16, 35, 94, 111, 112–13, 152, 153–5, 163, 168
    chilla, 113
    khānaqāh, 10, 154, 155, 170
    pir, 10, 112–3, 155, 163, 171
    samāʿ, 111, 154
Sufyāna Kalam, 18
Sultan Wardak, 61, 105, 107, 120
surbāhār, 79
surnay, 18, 166
sympathetic strings, 26, 32–3, 38, 58, 165, 166, 167

tabla, 19, 20–1, 25, 29, 33–4, 50–5, 57, 103, 111, 114, 120–3, 144, 162, 166, 168, 172
Tagore, S. M., 26
tāl
    cymbals, 19, 22, 34, 36, 166
    rhythm, *see* rhythmic cycles
tamburā, 15-16, 167
tanbur, 32, 33, 36, 38, 67, 69, 82, 92, 109, 135, 152, 154, 167
tānpurā, 103, 132, 134, 167
tappā, 82
tār, see *Chahārtār*
teahouse, cafe, 32, 91, 92, 107, 132, 137, 140, 160
Tehran, 19, 161
tekieh, 10, 115
theatre, 6, 83, 94, 104, 107, 108, 124, 127, 132, 134–6, 140, 141, 151, 156
Theological College, Herat, 147, 148, 152
tihāʿi, see *seh*
Timurids, 3, 10, 12–16, 156

Index

tonal systems, 38-40, 44-6, 99
tonal functions, 22, 41-2, 44-8, 55, 57
Trimmingham, J. Spencer, 154
Tsuge, Gen'ichi, 50
tulak, 19, 82, 167
Turkestan, 93, 96, 136, 141

ʿ*ud*, 12-14, 167
ʿ*urs*, 136, 154
Usman, Ghulam Faruq, 29, 44
USSR, xi, 2, 3, 55
*ustād*s of Kabul, 25-30, 110-13, 116-18, 132-3, 159-60, 161-4
Ustad Ghulam Husein, 27-8
Ustad Hashem, 162
Ustad Mohammad Husein (Ustad Sarahang), 28, 44, 75, 79, 111, 114, 115, 121, 144
Ustad Mohammad Omar, xii, 30-1, 33, 67, 77, 109, 118, 119, 162
Ustad Nabi Gol, 28, 29, 77, 104, 109, 112, 113, 115, 117, 148, 163
Ustad Qasem, 27-8, 30, 62, 67, 79, 117, 132
Ustad Rahim Bakhsh, 72, 132-3, 162
Ustad Sheida, 28
Utas, Bo, xii, 10, 112, 154
Uzbeki (musical genre), 69, 81, 83, 92, 93, 132, 141, 142, 172

Vámbéry, Arminius, 4

weddings, 22, 29, 104, 109, 117, 124, 125-31, 148, 156, 160
Willard, N. A., 26
Wolfe, Nancy Hatch (Dupree), 3
women, x, xiii, 8, 19, 35-6, 110, 125, 128, 129-31, 144, 148, 160, 165; see also *sāzandeh*
Wright, Owen, xii, 12, 13*n*
Wulff, Hans E., 8

Zahir Shah, 25
zirbaghali, 19, 20, 32, 33, 36, 91, 93, 108, 132, 140, 144, 145, 167
Zonis, Ella, 16, 22, 165
zurkhāneh, 19